Art as Sanctuary

RELIGIOUS CULTURES OF AFRICAN & AFRICAN DIASPORA PEOPLE

The book series examines the religious, cultural, and political expressions of African, African American, and African Caribbean traditions. Through transnational, cross-cultural, and multidisciplinary approaches to the study of religion, the series investigates the epistemic boundaries of continental and diasporic religious practices and thought and explores the diverse and distinct ways African-derived religions inform culture and politics. The series aims to establish a forum for imagining the centrality of Black religions in the formation of the "New World."

Art as Sanctuary

Conjuring an Africana Aesthetic

MICHAEL D. HARRIS

Edited and with an introduction by

Dianne M. Stewart and Theophus H. Smith

Foreword by Richard J. Powell

DUKE UNIVERSITY PRESS DURHAM & LONDON 2026

Printed in the United States of America on acid-free paper ∞
Project Editor: Lisa Lawley
Designed by Matthew Tauch
Typeset in Garamond Premier Pro IBM Plex Sans
by Westchester Publishing Services

Library of Congress Cataloging-in-Publication Data
Names: Harris, Michael D., 1948–2022, author. | Stewart, Dianne M., editor. | Smith, Theophus Harold, editor. | Powell, Richard J., [date] writer of foreword.
Title: Art as sanctuary : conjuring an Africana aesthetic / Michael D. Harris ; edited and with an introduction by Dianne M. Stewart and Theophus H. Smith ; foreword by Richard J. Powell.
Other titles: Religious cultures of African and African diaspora people.
Description: Durham : Duke University Press, 2026. | Series: Religious cultures of African and African diaspora people | Includes bibliographical references and index.
Identifiers: LCCN 2025021619 (print)
LCCN 2025021620 (ebook) |
ISBN 9781478017691 (paperback)
ISBN 9781478015062 (hardcover)
ISBN 9781478022305 (ebook)
Subjects: LCSH: African American arts. | African Americans—Music. | African diaspora in art. | Arts and society—United States.
Classification: LCC NX512.3.A35 H377 2026 (print) | LCC NX512.3.A35 (ebook) | DDC 700.89/96073—dc23/eng/20250625
LC record available at https://lccn.loc.gov/2025021619
LC ebook record available at https://lccn.loc.gov/2025021620

Cover art: Ben Jones, *Billie Holiday #1*, 1998. Mixed media, 15 × 10 in. From the collection of Sydne Tarry. Courtesy of the artist. Photo by Manuel Acevedo.

PUBLICATION OF THIS BOOK HAS BEEN SUPPORTED BY GRANTS FROM THE DEPARTMENT OF AFRICAN AMERICAN STUDIES ENRICHMENT FUND AT EMORY UNIVERSITY AND DR. CAROL ANDERSON, THE ROBERT W. WOODRUFF PROFESSOR OF AFRICAN AMERICAN STUDIES AT EMORY UNIVERSITY.

THIS BOOK IS DEDICATED TO SYLVIA ARDYN BOONE

Contents

Illustrations

Foreword

Richard J. Powell

On an initial perusal of Michael D. Harris's *Art as Sanctuary: Conjuring an Africana Aesthetic*, a reader might ask, "Can you find safety in a painting?" or "Can music provide one with a refuge from trouble or danger?" A deep dive into Professor Harris's book answers these questions in a variety of ways, with each of his responses shaped by the particular philosophical understandings that have been handed down to us by assorted thinkers and believers from the African diaspora. Harris also bolstered his replies to these questions via the lived experiences of the makers and audiences of art: people for whom the past is never disconnected from today or tomorrow, and for whom ancestorism has the remarkable capacity to safeguard and sustain when the world's negativities feel as if they are about to pounce on and overwhelm us.

Knowledgeable about selected West and Central African religions and their interpreters (in the latter category, the art historian Rowland Abiodun and the cultural theorist Fu-Kiau Bunseki), Michael Harris employs these philosophies to establish the ontological bases of black people's aesthetic orientations: sensibilities that acknowledge the God-given potentialities to profoundly effectuate (*ashé* among Yoruba peoples), or perspectives that are ever mindful of a person's spatial and genealogical position in the universe (termed *tendwa nzá* by Kikongo speakers). Harris augments these African philosophies with their parallel mindsets in the greater "Africana" cultural sphere: from the syncretized forms of Judeo-Christianity in Afro-Atlantic communities to the syncopated hymns and semitoned harmonies of the spirituals, gospel music, the blues, jazz, salsa, rhythm and blues, reggae, and hip-hop. One moves through *Art as Sanctuary* with the sense that black art and its practitioners reflect these aforementioned folkways and religious practices either knowingly or unconsciously and by doing so make profound connections with—and provide forms of asylum to—their audiences. "Often *it* spoke *to them* and *for them* and *with them*," Harris writes about expressivity in the arts (emphases mine), giving black art anthropomorphic configurations and competences that speak to its guardianship role. "And *it* loved *them*," he added, endowing the arts with human emotions that veer into filial, carnal, and spiritual domains.

In chapter 2 of *Art as Sanctuary*, titled "Etymologies and Black Love," Harris presents a comprehensive history of these cultural and artistic refuges, examples of metaphorical safe havens and creative therapeutics that, as experienced by socially and psychologically damaged people, "heal[ed] the fissures in the black consciousness" (p. 68). Many of these sanctuaries have a performative dimension, an "expressiveness coded in the improvisation of gospel music," Harris writes, "dancing emotional utterances as one was filled with the spirit, the sensuous hip rolls in slow dances, and octave jumps in saxophone solos" (p. 68). That such rapturous actions might be artistically conceived in ways that vault pictorial representationalism is suggested throughout *Art as Sanctuary*, as seen, for example, in abstract paintings by artists such as James Phillips and Adger Cowans. This emotional expressiveness was also noted by Harris in conceptual works of art like Fahamu Pecou's *Watch the Throne* (figure I.3), a mixed-media assemblage where a whimsically gold-leafed barber's chair—upholstered in an African textile—invoked an "interior black life," while also alluding to the gold stools of Asante royalty and the barbershop as a communal yet intimate safe space.

When Michael Harris writes about African Americans seeking refuge and retreating into their own cultural patterns and practices, where they can express themselves without external controls or judgments, one discerns not only a scholar's understanding of a community formulating its own social and artistic preserve: One also intuits from Harris's text an artist's insights and his firsthand sense of this soul-saving cultural experiment. Indeed, when Harris writes that this book is "written figuratively from within the sanctuary of the Africana diaspora experience *and that phenomenological way of being*" (my emphasis), it casts his visual analyses of works by pioneering black artists such as Romare Bearden and William H. Johnson in a fresh light (p. 5). Compositional breaks (or "jump spaces") in mixed-media collages and in paintings created with a collage sensibility have their equivalent in mid-twentieth-century jazz's notational modulations and percussive structures: aesthetic theories learned during Harris's years studying painting with artist Al Smith at Howard University and later elaborated on under art historian Robert Farris Thompson's tutelage at Yale University. These aural/visual intervals perform multiple roles in Harris's text: They characterize a black or African diaspora aesthetic, and they are schematic "retreats," or what Harris describes as "places to find, exchange, modify, and enhance African and, eventually, African American identity and culture" (p. 66).

At the outset of *Art as Sanctuary*, Michael Harris announces that this book is a continuation of a more-than-half-a-century-old discussion "about the creation of a vocabulary for talking about . . . a black aesthetic founded within those New World sanctuaries where we reimagined and reinvented ourselves" (p. 17). Referring to the historically significant Conference on the Functional Aspects of Black Art (CONFABA), held at Northwestern University in Evanston, Illinois, in the spring of 1970, Harris's "New World sanctuaries" were not simply geographic places like the Black Arts Movement cultural capital of nearby Chicago. Harris's cerebral, self-inventing abodes were CONFABA's flesh-and-blood attendees, African American luminaries like the art historians Sylvia Boone and Samella Lewis, the curators Edmund Barry Gaither and David C. Driskell, and the visual artists Margaret Burroughs, Elizabeth Catlett, Aaron Douglas, Jeff Donaldson, Lois Mailou Jones, and Charles White. These and the other CONFABA attendees were repositories of knowledge and, in addition to imparting valuable lessons and modeling lives of artistic edification and cultural celebration, embodied the philosophical tenet that, as outlined by Donaldson and highlighted by Harris, the "function of art is to liberate man in the spiritual sense of the word, [and] to provide more INTERNAL space."[1]

Michael Harris's articulation of this objective for *Art as Sanctuary* is the key to its greater mission: a text whose goal is the realization of the aesthetic nature, or higher self, of peoples of African descent; a liberatory perspicuity leading to a state (or "space") of inner peace, enlightenment, and transcendence beyond the material world. While students of art history, African and African American studies, and visual studies more broadly will find *Art as Sanctuary* quite useful, scholars of religion and religious cultures of African and African diaspora peoples will be especially interested in Harris's book. What *Art as Sanctuary* proposes is an entrée into an Africana spirituality and ethos, by way of the African diaspora's ever-present but rarely consulted "Rosetta stones," or the works of visual art, music, and literature that contain the designs, colors, and textual codes that, once elucidated, open the doors onto a sanctum sanctorum, or a metaphorical holy place.

Art's ability to create a spiritual refuge, or at least an atmosphere of heightened attention to a people's interior world, was not regarded as sanctuarial by Michael Harris alone. Think of the saxophonist Wayne

Shorter's composition "Sanctuary," most famously performed and included on jazz legend Miles Davis's 1969 record album *Bitches Brew*. The music historian Ted Gioia has described "sanctuary" as covering a range of emotions, "from pointillistic introspection to electronic brutalism before emerging as a smoky groove tune."[2] Perhaps the song's haunting character, first surfacing in a duet by trumpeter Miles Davis and keyboardist Chick Corea and culminating in several intermittent crescendos and counterstatements by Davis's full band, have an analogue in Harris's *Art as Sanctuary*: a text that takes readers through historical thickets and cultural groves and concludes with the ancestral benedictions and praises of "Bebop Ghosts and Freedom Songs." Harris's photograph in *Art as Sanctuary*'s conclusion of fellow AfriCOBRA members Jeff Donaldson, Murry DePillars, and James Phillips, like Miles Davis's spare repetitions of Wayne Shorter's imploring ballad, bring to the fore Harris's debt to ancestorism, where intimates and eventual forefathers form corporeal patterns whose creative contributions not only canopied and nourished a vast, barren landscape but anchored and harbored the scholar/artist Harris.

Posthumous publications have an elegiac aura surrounding them, and *Art as Sanctuary* is no exception. But Professor Michael D. Harris's death in 2022 and our feelings of loss and bereavement in no way subtract from *Art as Sanctuary*'s resounding paean to black spirituality and its indelible presence in the arts and cultures of peoples of African descent. Rather than dark, funereal draperies and silent tears, these pages are infused with triumphant voices, unconstrained laughter, and colorful flashes of Yoruba *adire*, Kongo pile weave, and Asante kente cloths. And moans too, sorrowful, full-throated intonations that in time and the brief span of a disremembered generation become a humming sound, an Aretha Franklin melisma accentuated by inferential vocalizations, rhythmic handclapping, and ecstatic amens. Instead of sitting passively on a mourner's front-facing church pew, we are enlisted in *Art as Sanctuary* to celebrate a people's passage out of slavery and other racialized indignities and, in Harris's phraseology, to conjure an aesthetic: not merely an intellection concerning the arts or beauty per se but a social philosophy of artistic invention, or erudition-in-action. Harris's call to invoke an alternative aesthetic may have manifested itself after his premature passing, but his message nevertheless rings loud and clear, and it wholly resonates at a time when, in a hyphenated, post-black-everything era, one shouldn't lose sight of the gift that black spirituality offers us all.

EDITORS' INTRODUCTION

Michael D. Harris

Cultural Theorist of Africana Identity, Art, and Spirituality

Dianne M. Stewart and Theophus H. Smith

Our late colleague Michael Harris (1948–2022) has gifted us with a masterwork of artistic display—and not only that. His mastery includes aesthetic discrimination and coherent theory. The display features carefully selected works of art and depiction that comprise the "autobiographical" journeys of "Africana" peoples from the continent to the diaspora. The theory maintains that the significance of these artworks is not reducible to the artists' "racialized" identity. Rather, the art substantiates the theory—a philosophical and aesthetic theory—that the universal is best discovered in and manifested through the particular. In this case Harris painstakingly shows how the universality of cultural creativity in human experience finds expression through the artists' particular identities. To substantiate that theory, sustained throughout the book, he enlists the terms *sanctuary* and *black interior*. As Africans were dispersed from their homelands, their "lived experience in the Americas had an exterior and an interior; a sanctuarial, protected space to counter the exterior racialized reality" (p. 4). In synchrony with the artists' existential journey, from home continent to other lands, Harris conveys the reader from one "sanctuarial interior" to another.

To chart that journey Harris adopts Elizabeth Alexander's concept from the title of her book *The Black Interior* (2004). In that interior space, he argues, "the kinds of expression emerging from it, rather than being trapped in the dynamics of race, more often reflect the complexities of culture" (p. 6). Here the reader remains in Harris's reliable hands through every milieu of cultural formation. From the slavery period to the present, he keeps outwitting our conventional tendency to collapse into merely race-based assessments. At the same time, reflecting "the complexities of culture," he vividly displays expressions and performances based on racialized experience: "My reading of culture extends beyond a parochial African American, or black, circumstance to include Old World African cultural syntax—syntax that might be foundational for linguistic, spiritual, or expressive responses to New World formations, experiences, and developments" (p. 6).

The sanctuaries of these protected spaces range from churches to dance halls, from political rallies to barbershops and beauty parlors, from burial grounds to family reunions. But the artworks themselves also constitute sanctuaries and interiors. In charting the way that black art variously conveys the interior sanctuaries of particular cultures, Harris eloquently depicts the experience and condition of being black as "the geologic pressures that formed black culture" (p. 18). But he insists that such pressures (and fissures) "are not the culture itself" (p. 18). Rather, he offers a universal definition of *culture* as "the matrix humans form to organize and codify their relationships to themselves, each other, nature, and the divine, and perhaps . . . ultimately a form of humanism" (p. 178). In arriving at that perspective, he refers to particular interlocutors who have engaged him in exploring culture as patterns of "human-centered expression and intention at the heart of such an aesthetic" (p. 178). Those conversation partners include Robert Farris Thompson (1932–2021).

Thompson is well known for the magisterial manner in which he advanced scholarly reception of a black Atlantic visual tradition, and its aesthetic significance, from West Africa to the diaspora. But equally influential for Harris was Paul Carter Harrison's pursuit of a phenomenological approach to aesthetic theory. Harrison (1936–2021), an African American playwright and theorist, skillfully applied to Africana aesthetics the phenomenology elaborated by the Austrian German philosopher Edmund Husserl (1859–1938). That approach enables data to disclose themselves as subjects in their own right while "bracketing" our prejudgments and projections as matters extrinsic to the data's fundamental manifestations.

> This book is written figuratively from within the sanctuary of the Africana diaspora experience and that phenomenological way of being. I use the term *Africana* to elude the racial implications and history of the term *black*, though the term denotes the real experience of being black in a racial context and the confinement of that term generated, in

> part, by the need for cultural sanctuary. This book has been conceived around both a literal and metaphorical use of *sanctuary* to describe places of safety in the black experience and the condition of psychological security as well as locales of spiritual expression, self-renewal, and cultural celebration. (p. 5)

In chapter 1, "The Moan: Calling Forth Culture," Harris provides a first case study in such a phenomenology of black aesthetics. Beginning with the pressure chamber of the slave ships during the notorious Middle Passage, he elaborates the experience of moaning as embodied expression that involved both form and function.

> Folk with dialects and languages unintelligible to one another understood the moan. It marked a misery they shared. . . . [Ed] Spriggs says:
>
> > They couldn't speak to each other. And they couldn't speak to the master. But what they had in common was the fact that they were in pain and they were fearful of what was going on. You put your own imagination to *that*. And they moaned. And they moaned. And that moan became syncopated. You had the boat moving. You had a whole different rhythm of life that kept that moan going.
> >
> > Then they got to shore, and living in the plantation setting, the moan became a hum. What they could remember, that song they had in them. And they still had the language problem. It's the moan. And their moan became a hum. (pp. 28–29)

So syncopated moaning gave birth to rhythmic humming, and group humming led eventually to musical expression. Admittedly it is difficult to document the transition from moaning together, to humming together, to singing together. "The moan in the slave ship hold and its link to verbal and musical expression on either side of the Atlantic is as difficult to document as it is to quantify that thing in black music" (p. 40). Nonetheless, we may extrapolate how the transition from group humming to shared singing, and later forms of communicative and coded expression, may have occurred in examples such as work songs and church singing. As enslaved Africans became plantation workers and domestic servants in the colonized Americas, "other cultural dynamics were in process at the same time as black cultural re-formations were evolving in black homogeneous spaces" (p. 48). Those "other cultural dynamics" include the arts, as Harris details in subsequent chapters. Here he is concerned to show how such "cultural re-formations were evolving" (p. 48) in concert with racialized identity: "As Enwezor claims . . . '[T]he remaking of African memories and reconciling them with the Euro-American experience of their new home . . . gives form to an entirely new self-understanding, one neither purely African nor wholly European or American . . . [as] the black subject negotiated the cultural boundaries between Africa, Europe, and America'" (p. 48).

To show the complex, hybrid, or creole nature of black racialized identity, Harris adopts a metaphor from Édouard Glissant. The rhizome metaphor unsubstantiates the claim that slavery entirely eviscerated or dispossessed enslaved persons of their African cultural heritage. Rather, that heritage persists, in Glissant's terms, as "an enmeshed root system, a network spreading either in the ground or in the air, with no predatory rootstock taking over permanently" (p. 48). Moreover, Glissant emphasizes, that similarity of black cultural identities to a rhizome consists in the remarkable phenomenon of rootedness without "a totalitarian root" (p. 48). Thus, chapter 1 concludes with a summary emphasis on the multivalent nature of "an Africana aesthetic," an emphasis that includes sanctuaries as havens for "insider experiences" resulting in complex versus monolithic cultural identities:

> Insider experiences in sanctuary settings, both secular and sacred, often affirmed new kinship bonds. Those experiences can be found through references, codes, signifiers, symbols, gestures, and all sorts of indicators in the music, language, performance practices, and visual expressivity of Africana cultures. This matrix of meaning and creative expression is the basis of an Africana aesthetic. (p. 49)

From the slavery period highlighted in chapter 1, Harris proceeds to display aesthetic formations through black musical expression in chapters 2 and 3. In chapter 2, "Etymologies and Black Love," he embeds an implicit phenomenology of art itself as an agent or actor, and people—the artists and their communities of reference—as its collaborators. More specifically, the arts manifest themselves as a lover performing care and consolation and providing resources for collaborative works of love. In that regard the chapter shows how music and visual expression constitute (a) the syntax of (b) diverse love languages. On the one hand, (a) the "etymologies" of songs, dance, and images are parsed and displayed. Citing Robert

Farris Thompson in that regard, Harris refers to "'organizing principles' of African musical performance in song and dance" as they "mingled with New World and European elements to create . . . a black Atlantic visual tradition" (p. 51). On the other hand, (b) love is the significance of that communicative relationship between the arts and the community they serve.

Here artistic genres and media provide sanctuaries of love and care in the face of oppression and trauma. As Harris notes in chapter 4, "perhaps the blues," for example, "can be thought of as . . . a transformative lexicon, born of shared misery and oppression, giving hope and catharsis" (p. 89). Later Harris exults in that transformative power as he joins Jim Perkinson in quoting Paul Gilroy's aesthetic tribute to "blues, jazz, gospel, reggae, soul, funk, and hip-hop . . . as complex re-creations of communal identities under duress of modern structures of oppression that *transfigure violence into beauty*" (p. 67). That beauty of the arts, and the love that creates and exults in such beauty, provides sanctuarial spaces in Harris's phenomenology. Attentive to the affective power of love conveyed through the arts, chapter 2 concludes with an appreciative expression of endearment: "Visual art relevant to these people often referenced their music, folkways, and religious practices. Often it [visual art] spoke to them and for them and with them. And it loved them" (p. 69).

Chapter 3 offers a case study of a particular sequence of continuities, "From *The Banjo Lesson* to *The Piano Lesson*: Reclaiming the Song." Here Harris expertly conveys the reader from Henry Ossawa Tanner's 1893 classic painting *The Banjo Lesson* to Romare Bearden's 1983 collage *The Piano Lesson* and then to August Wilson's 1987 play of the same name: "Tanner's important painting opened a new discourse in African American art and began the formation of a new artistic vocabulary of black visual representation. Ninety years later Romare Bearden was a master of that vocabulary, and he articulated a blues and jazz version of Tanner's *Banjo Lesson*" (p. 80). That genealogy culminates with August Wilson's Bearden-inspired *The Piano Lesson*, which was awarded the Pulitzer Prize in 1990. These periods of cultural formation, from the late nineteenth to the late twentieth century, likewise demonstrate Harris's concern to articulate aesthetics beyond focusing on racialized identity.

In chapter 4 he shows, for example, that by "defining the blues culturally . . . the racial stigmas, dogmas, and strictures that the postblack idea seeks to evade are relegated to a contextual significance instead of being a part of an essentialist identity" (p. 93). Then another one of Harris's interlocutors, Dwight Andrews, offers a comparably disruptive claim: "The roots of black music lie not only in the adaption and synthesis of various African musical practices but also in the African conceptualization of music as power" (p. 93). In conversation with Andrews, Harris argues, "When the black preacher rises to his singsong cadence in preaching, he is, in effect, singing the sermon and exploiting the metaphysical powers of sound as perceived within an African and, by extension, African American ontological and cosmological framework" (p. 93). These reorienting perspectives are consistent with the entire framework of Harris's book and the aesthetic discernment that he maintains throughout.

Chapter 4 further explores the cultural dynamics that undergird black aesthetics by highlighting Romare Bearden's avowed reference to African-derived spiritual elements such as conjuration. While exploring that connection, Harris cites Rachel Delue's claim of a "special relationship" between Bearden's collage series *Conjur Woman* and "the very medium of collage" (p. 112). Here we are invited to imagine how the arts participate in ritual and spiritual phenomena: "In moving to collage in the early 1960s, not only was Bearden evoking his own experiences and memories, but 'he understood the medium to have value beyond the artistic'" and "believed that as an object, a literal *thing*, a collage might do powerful, transformative work" (p. 112).

That synergy between African spiritual continuities and artistic creativity culminates in chapter 5, "Gospel, *Tongues*, and Bearing Witness," which begins with a narrative account of Oprah Winfrey's now-classic Legends Ball in May 2006:

> At the Sunday event wrapping up the three-day weekend, BeBe Winans started singing the gospel song "Changed." He then passed the microphone to Shirley Caesar, then to Dionne Warwick, and on to Yolanda Adams, Chaka Khan, and Gladys Knight while the choir on the stage sang the chorus. Oprah said, "Jesus came!" . . . It was unscripted, completely improvised, and those who knew what was happening gave amens, moaned, clapped, stood and shouted, and sang along. . . . Black religiosity, ecstatic expressiveness, came out into the light as the very famous and nearly famous alike rode the spirit of the moment. Later, newswoman Diane Sawyer said, "For the rest of my life that may be the most transcendently spiritual moment I've ever been part of." What Sawyer experienced was "going to church." Black church. (p. 114)

With that account Harris illustrates how elements of African heritage spirituality continue to be expressed in contemporary performance and production. Chapter 5 thus encapsulates the entire book by demonstrating that such elements remain a hallmark of cultural continuities from precolonial African creativity to the worldwide creativity of black people today. To substantiate that claim, chapter 6, "*Undone*: Bottle Trees, Charms, and Flashing Spirits," and chapter 7, "Talking in Tongues: Revisiting/Reflecting Kara Walker," describe those continuities with vivid displays of art and in compelling formulations of theory. In these two co-resonant chapters, Harris analyzes alluring and haunting depictions within the visual artworks and installations of Renée Stout, Alison Saar, and Kara Walker. These artists unapologetically explore black female embodiment under captivity and/or black female autonomy and empowerment within the sanctuaries of Africana spiritual cultures.

In chapter 6 Harris examines spiritual themes that bridge African and African diasporic sacred worlds in the works of Stout and Saar. He astutely identifies cosmological, somatic, and sensorial dimensions of an Africana aesthetic inspired by the physiological, corporeal, and sociocultural experiences of black women in the United States and the wider diaspora. Through art pieces that lead viewers into the seclusion of black women's "sanctuarial spaces," including those on and within the body (coiffed hair, the womb, the eyes, etc.), Harris explains how Stout and Saar creatively incorporate Yoruba and Kongo visual and symbolic vocabularies. Both artists deploy these and other African spiritual and aesthetic technologies to evoke themes pertaining to the life cycle, kinship, the natural world, the crossroads, and invisible powers.

Situating their works within a broader African aesthetic repertoire, Harris also engages feminist rejections of androcentric traditions in their installations:

> Several African American female artists . . . have created images and sculptures that . . . resist the masculinist tradition of the reclining nude and subvert its assumption of the consumption of the female body by the male gaze of the viewer. Saar and Stout both used signifiers of spiritual and cultural systems and practices in their works to turn potentially sensuous nudity into a ritual form resisting the colonizing male gaze. Ritual nakedness is symbolic of the removal of secrets and agendas, and examples abound in African art, including the male and female Ogboni or Oshugbo figures in Yoruba art representing the secret society of ruling elders. (p. 139)

Stout's and Saar's "body works," as Harris describes them, are simultaneously teeming with lucid and opaque messages, amplified by depictions of Africana material religion, such as bottle trees, Kongo *minkisi* figures (sing. *nkisi*), African-styled masks, and other elements. Their artistic innovations compel viewers to consider the historical horizon of black female captivity and resistance while inviting them to ponder dimensions of black female interiority within that violent and traumatic horizon.

Many motifs from chapter 6 bleed into and undergo intensification in chapter 7's discussion of similar themes. Harris devotes this chapter to a nuanced analysis of the artistic work and installations of Kara Walker. Here, however, he argues that Walker's visual and film projects can be interpreted as a provocative and rageful resistance to racist structures and histories through perspectives from outside the black interior. She consciously indicts intersecting networks and architects of racist-sexist violence in her own life and other black women's lives, depicting horrifying scenes and tropes of black female subjugation, trauma, and powerlessness. Thus, Harris maintains that "Walker expresses the rage of the black experience and the psychic injuries seldom visualized but commonly present among sensitive people. Her audience is not primarily a black one, but like so many before her, she seems to be speaking to power from a public space. . . . In a shamanic sense, she visually takes us on a journey through chaos, disfigurement, and discord toward a re-membering of her/our fragmented (dismembered) psyche. Her journey through the deluge and racial apocalypse is also our journey to wholeness and healing and potential transformation" (p. 170). By expressing the rage stemming from black women's and the wider black community's experiences, Walker makes public her own and her viewers' private pain and challenges them to take uneasy journeys of re-membering what has been dismembered and denied in America's racial and sexual nightmare.[1] Harris resolutely and deftly includes Walker's art in this study as a counterexample to the book's prevailing theme. He demonstrates how her collections, located outside the sanctuarial spaces of the Africana experience, interrogate the continuing existence of those spaces.

From one time frame to the next, from the slavery period to the present, we see how the diverse creativity of black people can be "interpreted through the cultural syntax of African cultural foundations and their rootedness in a spiritualized or inflected reality" (p. 177). Harris's conclusion, "Bebop Ghosts and Freedom Songs," reiterates that "black as an identity has been ground into the epistemological frame for so long that it has naturalized a racialized reality (and ontology) that is a fundamental assumption" (p. 187). Accordingly, he does not deny that "racialized identity" persists and will persist in lived experience as well as artistic creativity. Nonetheless his more nuanced claim is twofold. On the one hand, he allows that creative works and performances are "not separable from racialized experiences and structures" (pp. 187–88). On the other, he insists and demonstrates that universal human forms of culture and racialized identity formations "are linked but not equally exchangeable" (p. 188). With that resolution Harris concludes, "Africana cultural expression in today's world often finds sanctuarial spaces within which to grow and evolve," with "verbal expression" and "human voicings" often animating and linking "old spiritual etymologies to contemporary creative practices" (pp. 188–89). Readers of *Sanctuary* are thereby invited to experience Africana cultural aesthetics in its interior continuity that spans the ancient and the present, the invisible and the visible, in ways both culturally recursive and creatively innovating.

INTRODUCTION

Sanctuary and the Black Interior

> My mouth shall be the mouth of those calamities that have no mouth, my voice the freedom of those who break down in the solitary confinement of despair.
>
> AIMÉ CÉSAIRE, *NOTEBOOK OF A RETURN TO THE NATIVE LAND* (1939)

> If black racial identity speaks to all things done to people of recent African ancestry, black cultural identity was created in response to them. The division is not neat; the two are linked, and it is incredibly hard to be a full participant in the world of cultural identity without experiencing the trauma of racial identity.
>
> TA-NEHISI COATES, "MY PRESIDENT WAS BLACK" (2017)

Race is a persistent signifier so deeply ingrained within the everyday of America that it quietly inhabits almost all concepts and definitions relating to people of African descent, coloring them in a way that traps both black and white identities within a process that renews the condition of race. What do I mean? The identities of black or white exist only within a racialized context. Each notion requires a tacit acknowledgment of the other to have any meaning. Race is not a biological or genealogical reality, but it is a social reality. Toni Morrison asks, "What is race (other than genetic imagination) and why does it matter?"[1]

The experience of race has been one fraught with danger and violence on many levels. African Americans historically and culturally have sought safe spaces, private spaces to be, express, or invent themselves. These sanctuaries, or safe havens, might imply ritual spaces where affirmations of spirit and culture could take place and often were actual sanctuarial spaces—churches or religious gatherings—or safe communal or familial spaces like barbershops, family reunions, dance halls and roadhouses, and the like.

In this volume I argue that art by African American artists, still defined in practice racially, and often generated by the artist's racialized experience, offers additional richness if we explore cultural elements and signifiers embedded consciously or unconsciously in the artist's work. Often these signifiers reference practices or aspects that are found in their lived experiences within the communal commonality of sanctuarial safe havens. Symbolic or codified references, like the concept of conjuring, which we find appearing periodically in the work of Romare Bearden, and more recently that of Renée Stout, evoke kindred identification from those who share the intimate understanding of the language of these spaces and their practices.

The *experience* of race is real and can be ubiquitous for African-descended people in the Americas, and it has varying levels of prominence in the lives of African Americans, Cubans, Brazilians, and others in the African diaspora. However, the richness of cultural practices to be found in the lives of people when they turn inward can be discovered within creative expression and within the cultural syntax of their lives. In the hostile, often racialized or differentiated environments that emerged from slavery, people created sanctuarial spaces, places of respite from oppressive and demeaning experiences. This is what Elizabeth Alexander has called the *black interior*. That interiority includes symbolic, gestural, implicit and explicit references to or excavations from this sanctuarial place. Whether it be the sacred with churches or ring shouts or prayer meetings, or African-derived rituals and ceremonies, or the secular with dance halls, family reunions, house parties, barbershops and beauty parlors, sanctuarial spaces can be excavated from artistic expression to reveal this richness, and might offer a more appropriate logic for the discussion of African American art.

For example, Kerry James Marshall's 1993 painting *De Style* (figure I.1) roots itself in a barbershop with a linoleum floor and offers details that evoke familiar elements from that cultural space. Notice the shifting details of black hair and personal style; the black-and-white shoes of the main figure; the tall natural hairstyle of the woman on the left edge of the work; the partial photograph on the wall of a boxer, presumed to be Muhammad Ali; a bowling trophy to the right; and the large bling ring worn by a partially seen male on the far left of the work. All of these elements set a conglomeration of familiar tropes and signs. For many African American males, the barbershop is a safe space with its own rituals and cultural cues.

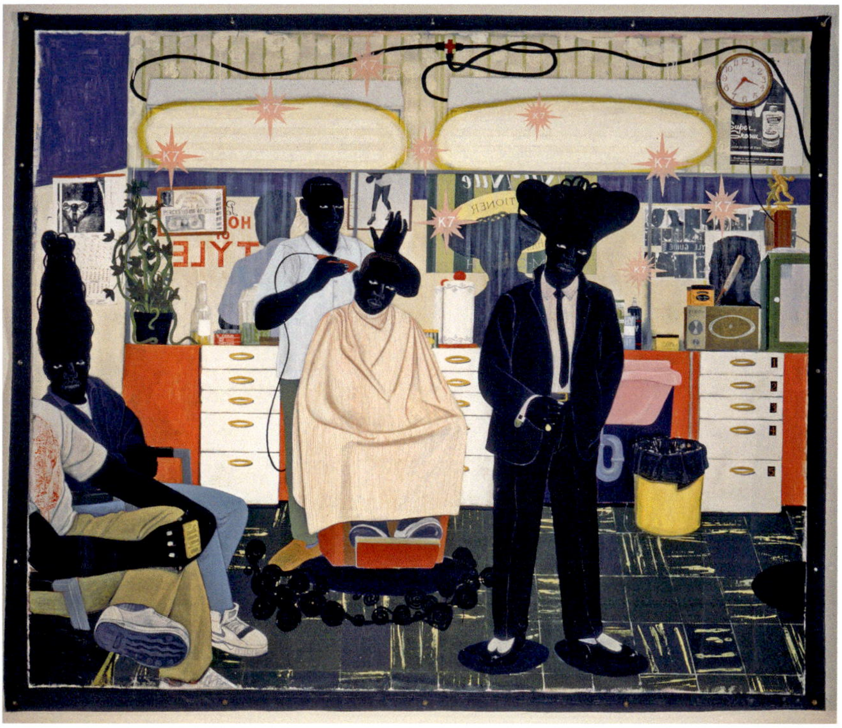

I.1 Kerry James Marshall, *De Style*, 1993. Acrylic and collage on canvas, 8 ft., 8 in. × 10 ft., 2 in. Los Angeles County Museum of Art. © Kerry James Marshall. Courtesy of the artist and Jack Shainman Gallery, New York.

Beverly Robinson has written that many African cultures had ritual practices solidifying a person's sense of self and belonging. These practices were the basis of a person's sense of cultural self, not their pigmentation. Reconfigured ritualized spaces and practices resisted the dehumanization of enslavement and the subsequent forms and practices of race. Robinson writes, "These rituals, sacred and secular, would include knowing the names of your gods, your ancestors, and yourself, and knowing your community and clan affiliation. . . . You would understand your place in a culture where oral traditions prevailed over written ones. An awareness of communal traditions—language (including gestures), tales, games, humor, music, dance, religion, riddles, food, and other forms of folklore—was part of the human knowledge carried by the men and women transported across the Atlantic."[2]

Artists want to make art that excels in whatever artistic and cultural context they live within. They must master what passes for excellence in their frame while adding, particularly in contemporary times, their own unique voice, virtuosity, insight, and freedom to be. This volume seeks to be a part of a conversation about looking at art by Africana artists in the African diaspora in ways unbound by the assumptions and conventions of race. It is possible that race and racism are linked, self-renewing phenomena reincarnated daily by acknowledging them; speaking them back into existence by making them the assumptions that are to be opposed.

Ta-Nehisi Coates, in writing about President Barack Obama, describes the situation in this way: "Historically, in black autobiography, to be remanded into the black race has meant exposure to a myriad of traumas, often commencing in childhood. Frederick Douglass is separated from his grandmother. The enslaved Harriet Ann Jacobs must constantly cope with the threat of rape before she escapes. . . . Black culture often serves as the balm for such traumas, or even the means to resist them."[3] However, the title of an online article by Jennifer Baker suggests that "Art Must Engage with Black Vitality, Not Just Black Pain." Baker argues, "While the violence isn't new, the medium has evolved. It's available on a loop, on screens of varying sizes, in texts of all kinds."[4] In the Americas the vitality is contextualized by the pain, but black existence is more than trauma.

Consider also that this discussion, though built around many works of art and visual culture, is not object based. It is more formed on the idea of art as a verb, as doing something, and with its meaning involving more than its objecthood, genesis, or provenance.

Robert Farris Thompson says, "Theories make sense of collisions of culture, ancient to modern. But the lived experiences of African and African American artists provide sources for understanding too." That lived experience in the Americas had an exterior and an interior; a sanctuarial, protected space to counter the exterior racialized reality. Thompson goes on to say, "Their lived experiences are equal to any ideology, anytime. Lived experiences stem from the people, choice memories of improvisation, choice memories of moral decision. They radiate common sense."[5] One interpretation of this aesthetic approach can be defined as phenomenology. As playwright and scholar Paul Carter Harrison describes this: "These are not necessarily conscious decisions. This is really, in your cultural experience, how you perceive relationships (unless it has been tutored out of you). It's not *doing* aesthetics; aesthetics emerge from your perception of reality."[6] So the response to differing experiences is interpreted through the cultural syntax of African cultural foundations and their rootedness in a spiritualized or inflected reality, whether consciously or not.

This book is written figuratively from within the sanctuary of the Africana diaspora experience and that phenomenological way of being. I use the term *Africana* to elude the racial implications and history of the term *black*, though the term denotes the real experience of being black in a racial context and the confinement of that term generated, in part, by the need for cultural sanctuary. This book has been conceived around both a literal and metaphorical use of *sanctuary* to describe places of safety in the black experience and the condition of psychological security as well as locales of spiritual expression, self-renewal, and cultural celebration.

Coates described his assessment of a sanctuarial space in *Between the World and Me*:

> But I would watch how black people moved, how in these clubs they danced as though their bodies could do anything, and their bodies seemed as free as Malcolm's voice. On the outside black people controlled nothing, least of all the fate of their bodies, which could be commandeered by the police; which could be erased by the guns, which were so profligate; which could be raped, beaten, jailed. But in the clubs, under the influence of two-for-one rum and Cokes, under the spell of low lights, in thrall of hip-hop music, I felt them to be in total control of every step, every nod, every pivot.[7]

It could be that the foundation for this writing was a childhood trip that seemed, without my knowing, to use the *Green Book* (a guide developed in 1936 for black travelers to help them negotiate the racialized topography of the United States safely) as we drove from Cleveland to Kinston, North Carolina, to see an uncle and, for the first time, encountered real segregation, and then to St. Augustine, Florida, and on to the Sir John Hotel in Miami, where black folk could stay, and then to sit embarrassed on an orange crate in a restaurant kitchen in Macon, Georgia, during the return journey.[8] Unlike the subtle racism and residential segregation of Cleveland, it was during this journey that I saw segregated bathrooms and water fountains—both usually in vastly different conditions—and we spent time at the designated black beach or were denied food at certain stops because of our color. We always were watchful and guarded.

Though racial antagonism and conflict born of slavery is the context for the seeming ubiquitous need for sanctuary among people of African descent in the Americas, we cannot overlook settings where humor and music and food were shared. This is Elizabeth Alexander's black interior. And the kinds of expression emerging from it, rather than being trapped in the dynamics of race, more often reflect the complexities of culture. Alexander defines these interior spaces as "black life and creativity behind the public face of stereotype and limited imagination. The black interior is a metaphysical space beyond the black public everyday toward power and wild imagination that black people ourselves know we possess but need to be reminded of." She suggests that tapping into this black imaginary "helps us envision what we are not meant to envision: complex black selves, real and enactable black power, rampant and unfetishized black beauty."[9]

African American art still lingers near racialization in art historical investigations and art museum categorical designations, and work by African American artists often is contextualized as American or contemporary art in ways that can miss important factors for reading intention, perspective, and even biography in the work. My reading of culture extends beyond a parochial African American, or black, circumstance to include Old World African cultural syntax—syntax that might be foundational for linguistic, spiritual, or expressive responses to New World formations, experiences, and developments. Notions of the postblack or postracial seem, in this sense, to be markers on a continuum of terms and interpretations more than overwhelming realities.

A cultural/experiential reading of artwork, either categorically or interpretatively, can open up layers of meaning and might complicate and enrich some of the ways work is examined. As Romare Bearden expressly told art scholar Mary Schmidt Campbell about his work, "I seek connections, so that my paintings can't be only what they appear to represent."[10] African and African American life is filled with spiritual intonations, symbolic gestures, stylized expressive forms, verbal shifts and semantic play, social and communal awareness, and music. Often this is embedded, implied, or alluded to in the art. So much of this effects transformation, spiritual evocation, and temporal and spatial transcendence in the lives of people. As Thompson writes, "Spirit does not date. Spirit needs no visa."[11]

Dianne Stewart has written about how African people used their spiritual foundations and "the preservation of their heritage." She says African practitioners in Jamaica "were actively engaged in the processes of transmitting to posterity a culture and spiritual outlook that imbued human existence with meaning and gave purpose to a people's collective consciousness. In spite of exile, enslavement, and the psychosocial disorientation they cause, oppressed Blacks in contemporary Jamaica are still able to 'journey' to Africa for empowering and sustaining resources to resist annihilation."[12]

Stewart argues that resistance to dehumanization manifested in African-derived religious systems in the Americas that were developed "systems of thought, ritual, and social ethics."[13] This conflicted with self-serving European misconceptions that African scholar and theologian Engelbert Mveng attributed to the creation of "anthropological poverty." "It consists in despoiling human beings not only of what they have, but of everything that constitutes their being and essence—their identity, history, ethnic roots, language, culture, faith, creativity, dignity, pride, ambitions, right to speak."[14]

The conflict between African cultural ways of being and the forces of erasure explained by Mveng is a crucial aspect of W. E. B. Du Bois's idea of double consciousness as the shifting conflict black people have with being American.[15] Has the tension between those two yet unmerged identities taken a new placidity in the twenty-first century? The election of Barack Obama as president seemed to offer evidence of a changing racial dynamic, but the vitriolic, disrespectful, and often overt racist responses to him by many white people seem to reflect clearly that antagonism, while diminished from earlier eras, persists. Calls for President Obama to provide his birth certificate resurrect the slave codes and subsequent black codes of the nineteenth century and the power dynamic of white people being able to demand that black people show their papers to prove that they fit into the social spaces organized to maintain white supremacy and power. To return to Coates: "Whiteness in America is a different symbol—a badge of advantage. In a country of professed meritocratic competition, this badge has long ensured an unerring privilege, represented in a 220-year monopoly on the highest office in the land."[16]

The codes of racial definition and control are examples of what Michel Foucault posits in a discussion of panopticism. This is a system of constant surveillance that Foucault, in *Discipline and Punish*, describes as measures to be taken against a plague of leprosy in the seventeenth century when houses were closed off and a system of constant inspection and registration were put in place; a process of quarantine and purification began to operate. Around this time blackness was defined similarly by Europeans as either fundamentally dangerous or as a diseased condition threatening the social order.[17] Defining blackness as an abnormality allowed an image against which techniques and institutions were organized to measure and supervise abnormality, whether the plague or the social abnormality of the black Other. As Foucault theorized:

> Inspection functions ceaselessly. The gaze is alert everywhere: "A considerable body of militia, commanded by good officers and men of substance", guards at the gates, at the town hall and in every quarter to ensure the prompt obedience of the people and the most absolute authority of the magistrates, "as also to observe all disorder, theft and extortion". . . .
>
> This surveillance is based on a system of permanent registration.[18]

The acceptance of this disempowered abnormality ever under scrutiny can be an insidious underlying assumption in efforts to theorize escapes from the racialized category of blackness. Martha Schwendener wrote during a January 2016 review of several exhibitions at the Studio Museum in Harlem that Romare Bearden "looked to Picasso, who he felt honored and validated African art rather than merely using it for his own artistic ends."[19] Given Picasso's denials for many years about having been influenced by African art, I wonder how this artist could *validate* the art of all the varied cultures, or even the art recovered from colonial enterprise in the Francophone areas of Africa feeding Paris in the late nineteenth and early twentieth century, by his borrowings. Must the panoptic white gaze be approving before art and culture of the African diaspora is to be valid? Could it be that the inadequacy of the peripheral vision of that gaze is the abnormality? Toni Morrison argues:

> How hard they work to define the slave as inhuman, savage, when in fact the definition of the inhuman describes overwhelmingly the punisher. . . .
>
> The necessity of rendering the slave a foreign species appears to be a desperate attempt to confirm one's own self as normal.[20]

Consider figure I.2 as an example of the approving white gaze and black assimilation as "a desperate attempt to confirm one's own self as normal." Historically, black people in the United States have used codes and cues in public spaces when white people were present to suggest a cultural and experiential solidarity. Media scholar Christine Acham calls this a "dual address" awareness of two audiences and the production of a

I.2 M. Darly, *A Mungo Macaroni*, 1772. Hand-colored etching, approx. 7 × 5 in. (plate mark); approx. 10¾ × 5½ in. (sheet). Lewis Walpole Library, Yale University, Folio 72 771 D37 v.4 plate 14. *Macaroni* became a term to mean a person of any rank who exceeds the ordinary bounds of fashion, usually distinguishable by his tight-fitting clothes, oversized sword, delicate shoes, and large wig. They often were mocked for excessive, "effeminate" concern with outward appearance. The subject of this one is Julius Soubise (ca. 1754–98), a freed Afro-Caribbean who became a well-known fop at the time. Courtesy of Lewis Walpole Library, Yale University, New Haven, CT.

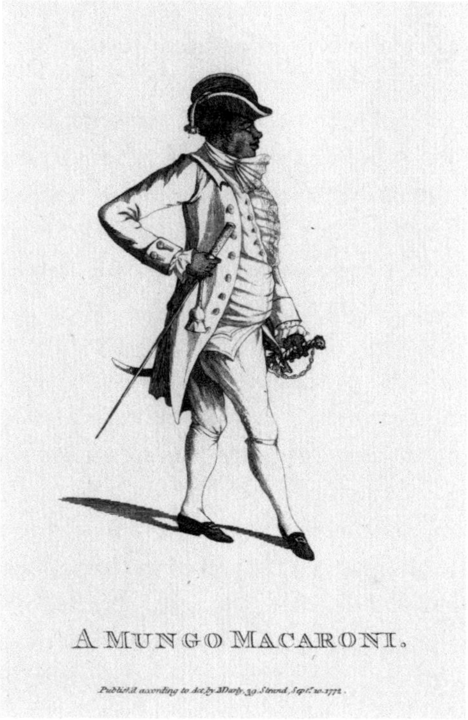

"hidden transcript" outside of the perceptual realm for white people.[21] Ta-Nehisi Coates, contributing editor at the *Atlantic*, writes about codes used by Mr. Obama as president to signal the black community. "These cultural cues became important during Obama's presidential run and beyond. Obama doesn't merely evince blackness; he uses his blackness to signal and court African Americans, semaphoring in a cultural dialect of our creation—crooning Al Green at the Apollo, name-checking Young Jeezy, regularly appearing on the cover of black magazines, weighing the merits of Jay-Z versus Kanye West, being photographed in the White House with a little black boy touching his hair."[22]

Not long before the 2008 election, the phrase *postblack* gained traction in New York media, followed by the illusion of a postracial America heralded by the election of President Obama.[23] What does it mean to be black or, for that matter, postblack? Is postblack merely a rearticulation of New Negro aspirations from a century ago? Is it the same inchoate plea for a validation or recognition of one's humanity outside essentialist ethnic caricatures and characterizations? Does it allow an exit from the panopticon sense of a permanent visibility (and its accompanying invisibility) that is a part of the power of whiteness that has benefited from this panoptic structure?

Double consciousness and other black Atlantic investigations often look at hybridity and creolizations to explain their subject, but there is a dimension to the formations emerging from the cultural collision of Europeans and Africans during the Atlantic slave trade and its aftermath in the Caribbean and the United States rooted in insularity, seclusion, secrecy, and protection.[24]

Two of the major social spaces for the enacting of collective privacy were the dance hall (roadhouse, or wherever people gathered to play and hear music) and the church; secular and sacred spaces for gathering and expressing the communal and spiritual self. To these spaces we might add the barbershop, the beauty salon, the family reunion, and the kind of common experiences found through *Green Book* travel. Fahamu Pecou (figure I.3) has taken the barber chair a step past Kerry James Marshall and signified it with the Asante (of Ghana) gold stool of royal iconography by upholstering it with African cloth and adorning the chair with gold leaf. He has given the barbershop a figurative ancestral link. Onaje Woodbine has introduced the argument that the basketball court has become a sanctuarial space in some ways for young black men.[25] It was in these out-of-view social spaces turned into ritual spaces that authentic identity could be formed safely and performed and that visual/verbal signs and signifiers from those practices and sanctuaries might signal one's membership in that beloved community.

Here we will build on Richard Powell's articulation of a visual blues aesthetic, religious and spiritual performance references, and add to it a pattern aesthetic that includes quilt and cloth forms and their eventual translation into visual art, especially after 1960, when black artists began traveling to Africa and encountering a visual aesthetic that was more symbolic and conceptual than representational.[26]

Does a blues aesthetic ignore jazz and hip-hop as indicators of culture? The short answer is no. Krista Thompson has written a remarkable book, *Shine*, about the visual notion of shine, or light (bling), in African diasporic aesthetic practice. She explores how contemporary consumer culture "dominate[s] how people in the African diaspora experience culture, music, their sense of the world, and their places within."[27] According to Stuart Hall, popular consumer culture, greatly influenced by black American expression, is firmly rooted in capitalism, its assumptions, cir-

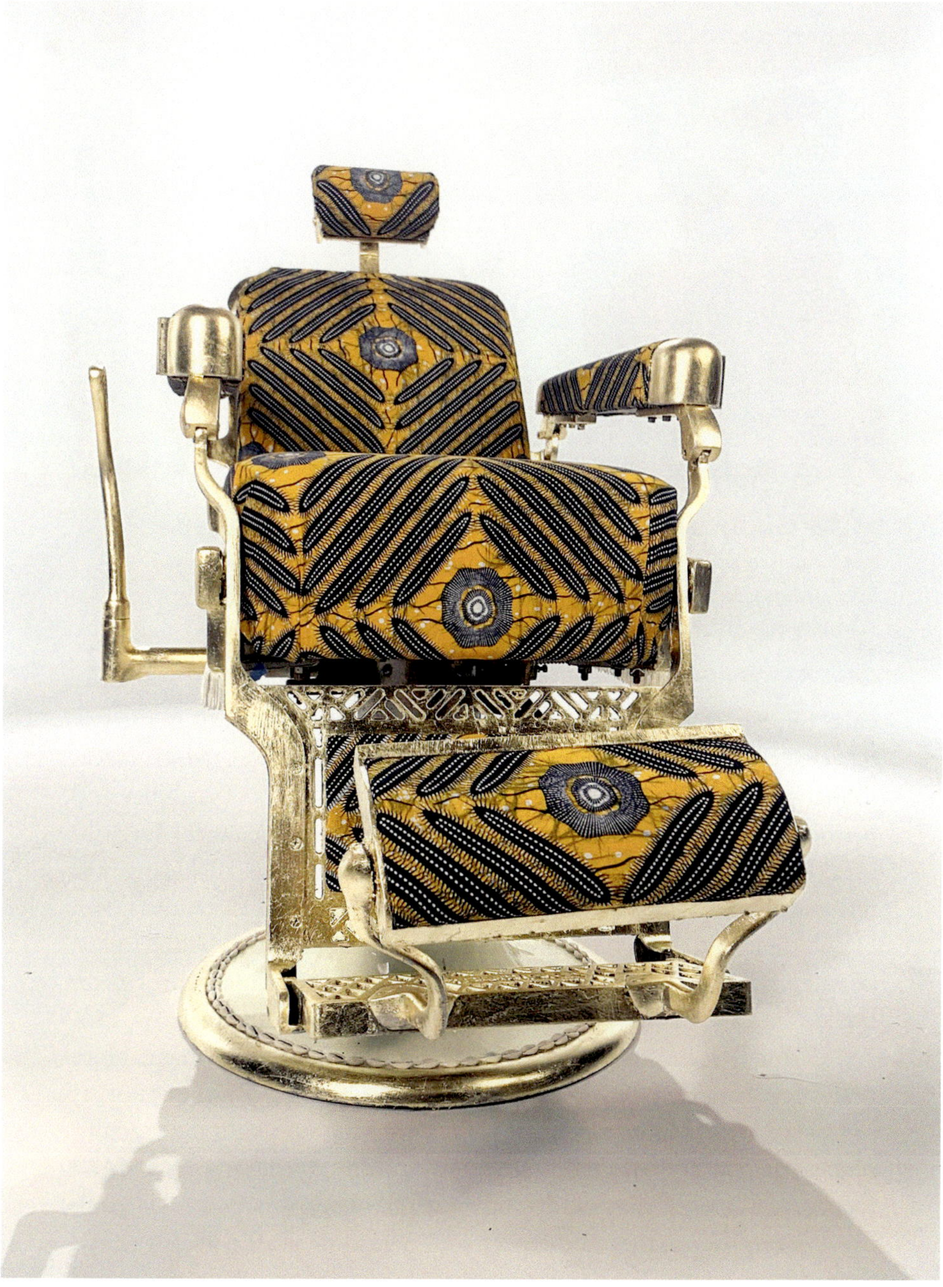

I.3 Fahamu Pecou, *Watch the Throne*, from *Of Crowns and Kings* collection, 2019. Mixed media barber's chair, dimensions unknown. Courtesy of Fahamu Pecou Art/Studio KAWO, Atlanta.

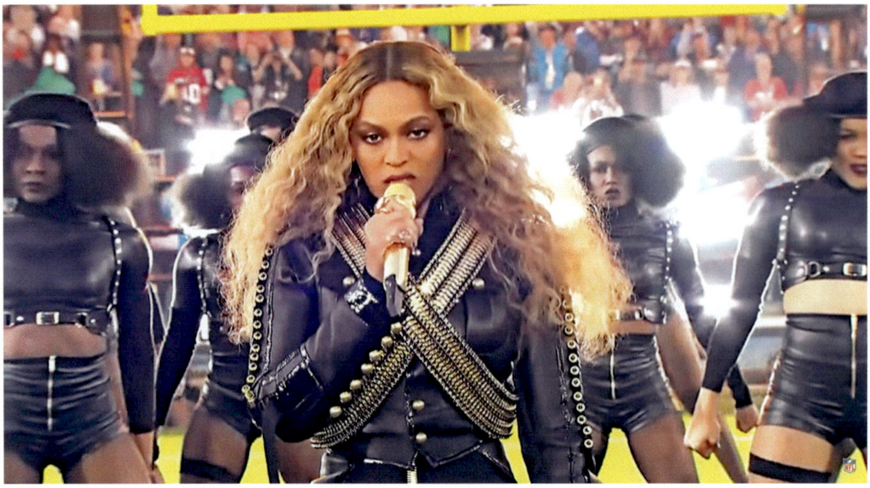

I.4 Still from Beyoncé's halftime appearance in the 2016 Super Bowl at the San Francisco 49ers' home stadium near San Jose, California. "Beyoncé and Bruno Mars Crash the Pepsi Super Bowl 50 Halftime Show," YouTube, February 11, 2016, https://www.youtube.com/watch?v=SDPITj1wlkg.

cular references, and transactions in ways that deeply root us in the system that produced the panoptic relationship and the racialized structures so many seek to escape.[28] Thompson observes strategies of visibility and play with visual technologies in the United States and the nearby English-speaking Caribbean islands of Jamaica and the Bahamas, including new rationales for bleaching the skin. She writes, "Dancehall attendees even bleach their skin (which purportedly prepares them for the video light), all in an effort to become visible—to be made spectacularly present in the lens of the video camera."[29] Youth culture and an emphasis on style and currency seem, to some extent, episodic and of the moment more than they seem foundational. As Thompson observes, "In the 1980s, as hip-hop gained visibility and commercial success nationally and globally, rappers increasingly turned their attention from politics to pleasure and focused on earthly and bodily gratification, hedonism, and even nihilism. . . . Hip-hop artists in the post soul period unabashedly celebrated materialism or a 'radical consumerism,' draping themselves in symbols of wealth from gold chains and medallions to all manner of brand-name goods."[30]

Resistance to and critique of a system that oppresses through outsider status seemingly has become a strategy for visibility and inclusion. During the February 7, 2016, Super Bowl, Beyoncé performed during halftime the song "Formation" while wearing an outfit that seemed to pay tribute to the Black Panthers (figure I.4), prominent in the Bay Area during the 1960s, where the Super Bowl was being hosted in 2016, and to Michael Jackson's outfit worn during his 1993 Super Bowl halftime performance. Her dancers wore black berets or large Afros to further identify with the Panthers. The bandolier of bullets on the singer's arm is reminiscent of those collaged onto AfriCOBRA founding member Wadsworth Jarrell's (b. 1929) notable 1971 painting inspired by Angela Davis, *Revolutionary* (figure I.5). Jarrell was further inspired by his wife, Jae Jarrell, also a founding member of AfriCOBRA, and her 1969 *Revolutionary Suit* (figure I.6). Beyoncé's song and performance implied allegiance to the Black Lives Matter movement, prompting immediate backlash from (panopticonic) authoritarian voices, like former New York mayor Rudy Giuliani, as being disrespectful to the police.[31]

Perhaps this is as serious as the searing Max Roach 1963 album, *We Insist (Max Roach's Freedom Now Suite)*, his collaboration with Oscar Brown Jr. begun in 1959 with a view toward a 1963 performance to commemorate the centennial of the Emancipation Proclamation. A *New York Times* article about Beyoncé and Jay-Z points out that her performance was "the most widely seen act of political art in recent memory" and that Jay-Z and Beyoncé "increasingly use their outsize platform as a tool of social agitation."[32] Her songs have the potential impact of James Brown's 1968 political anthem, "Say It Loud—I'm Black and I'm Proud."[33]

Beyoncé's outfit also included high heels, a swimming-suit-like short top only reaching her hips, fishnet stockings, a leather garter on her thigh, and a blonde hair weave down to her waist, somewhat graphically illustrating the double voicing often present in Africana expression. The surprise release of the music video two days before the Super Bowl performance did nothing to convince that the song and performance were rooted expressions of deep cultural practice or sincere activism rather than savvy marketing. In the current context, however, using a media platform is an effective complement to the street activism of the Black Lives Matter movement and other media-savvy political strategies. The subsequent video project *Lemonade* was an hour-long musical essay about personal pain, black womanhood, and the tragedy of Hurricane Katrina in New Orleans and was populated with a phenomenal series of deep cultural references; in fact, it was brilliant and political in a less direct way. It tied ancestors, African cultural imagery and fragments, black popular cultural

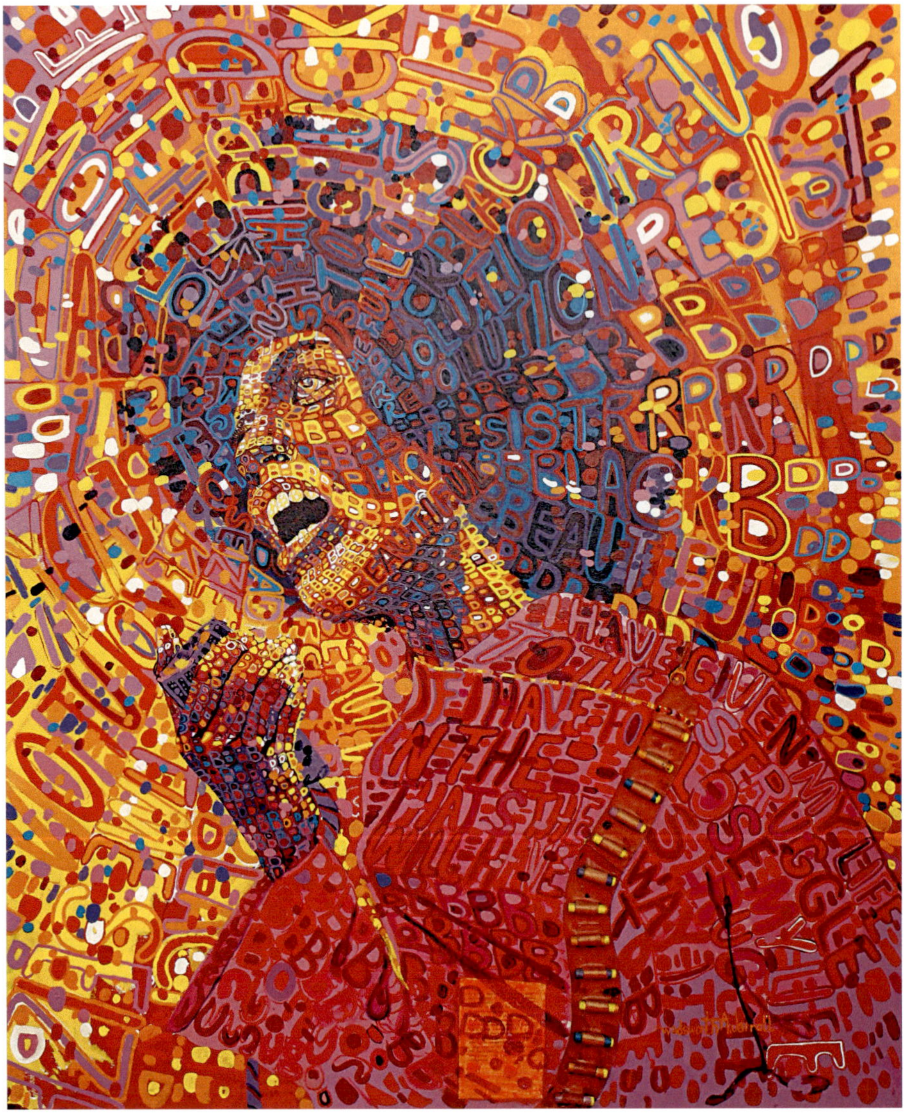

I.5 Wadsworth A. Jarrell, *Revolutionary*, 1971. Acrylic on canvas, 64 × 51 in. Collection of Brooklyn Museum, NY. Used by permission of Wadsworth Jarrell.

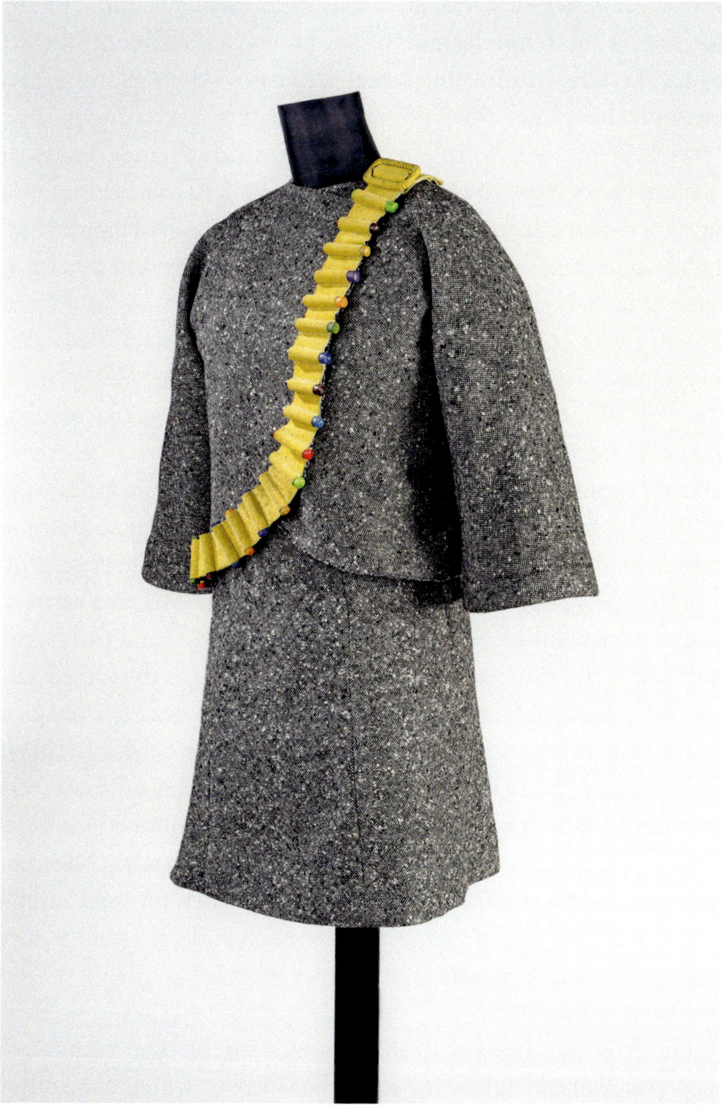

I.6 Jae Jarrell, *Revolutionary Suit*, 1969. Black-and-white wool tweed, suede, silk, wood, and pigment. Collection of Brooklyn Museum, NY. Used by permission of Jae Jarrell.

expression, family and babies, heartbreak and redemption, to what is at stake in personal relationships.

Beyoncé and her husband, Jay-Z, through Tidal, his music streaming service, are trying to build a level of autonomy and self-control through their business while addressing social activism in their expressive work. For example, her Super Bowl performance risked alienating part of her crossover audience with unruly references instead of pandering to them. Can a savvy use of popular culture, social media, and mainstream musical performance—an effective use of the system—actually change that system? Can something based within the system resist or step outside of its panoptic gaze and control? Can it change from within, as the civil rights movement (with complementary pressure from the Black Power movement) accomplished in some significant ways in the 1960s?[34]

Many old West and Central African cultures, such as the Yoruba, the Akan, the Fon, and the BaKongo, are foundational to black (or Africana) cultural formations in the Americas, and those earlier societies were integrative. On the surface, the rhythmic cadences, lyrical asymmetry, performative improvisation, and call-and-response characteristics of African expressivity are present in hip-hop and other Africana expression. However, spiritual ideas were not unconnected to visual forms, public masquerade performances, and musical expression, so the sacred-secular dialectic of a Western Christian epistemology and linear notions of time in the Christian eschatology differ in many ways from the circular and rhythmic structures often found in an African ontological frame. Therefore, vernacular notions of the spiritual often forge connections between blues music and gospel expression. A passage from a novel by Nigerian author Ben Okri perhaps illustrates the fluidity between spiritual and physical realms in a West African conceptual context still a part of its culture's imaginations and assumptions:

> Not far from me, like a skull sliced in half and blacked with tar, was a mask that looked frightening from the side, but which was contorted in an ecstatic laughter at the front. It had eyes both daunting and mischievous. Its mouth was big. Its nose was small and delicate. It was the face of one of those paradoxical spirits that move amongst men and trees, carved by an artist who has the gift to see such things and the wisdom to survive them. . . . Then I picked it up and wore it over my face and looked out from its eyes and something blurred the sun and the forest became as night.

> When I looked out through the mask I saw a different world. There were beings everywhere in the darkness and the spirits were each of them a sun.[35]

It is likely that I am continuing a conversation that surfaced over forty-five years ago about the creation of a vocabulary for talking about and articulating a black aesthetic founded within those New World sanctuaries where we reimagined and reinvented ourselves.[36] In May 1970 Jeff Donaldson organized CONFABA (the Conference on the Functional Aspects of Black Art) at Northwestern University, and conference material stated:

> When we addressed ourselves to the problem of the function of art, it was explicit that the function of art is to liberate man in the spiritual sense of the word, to provide more INTERNAL space. . . .
>
> The heart of the Black Artist's ideology is the dedication of his art to the cultural liberation of his people. It is in this sense that Black art is decidedly functional, politically and spiritually, and it is not to be confused by the alienation concept of "art for art's sake" rather than art for people's sake.[37]

Barred from attending the conference by the US State Department, Elizabeth Catlett gave a telephone presentation (which Jeff Donaldson taped) from Mexico to the conference.[38] Among those in attendance were Margaret Burroughs, Aaron Douglas, Sylvia Boone, Larry Neal, Samella Lewis, Nelson Stevens, Ethiopian artist Skunder Boghossian, the members of AfriCOBRA, A. B. Spellman, Edmund Barry Gaither, Charles White, Sterling Stuckey, Dana Chandler, John Biggers, Lois Mailou Jones, Hughie Lee-Smith, Ed Spriggs, Floyd Coleman, Bernice Johnson Reagon, and David Driskell.

Though the emphasis here is on the United States, the so-called syncretism of African-derived religions behind Catholicism provides evidence of practical continuities across the black Atlantic. Perhaps this is a contemporary chapter in Alain Locke's 1925 discussion of a "Legacy of the Ancestral Arts" that Alvia Wardlaw renovated with her 1989 exhibition and publication, *Black Art—Ancestral Legacy*.[39]

Ultimately, this book emerges from dissatisfaction with the persistence of race as an underlying and unquestioned means of talking about African American art, and the notion of its inclusion in a Western canon often being dependent on an embrace of the panoptic assumptions of exclusion. As musician and scholar Dwight Andrews wrote in 1989, "It would be ridiculous to base an aesthetic model simply on race. To do so would inevitably lead to the same ludicrous assertions and conclusions of other racist cultural theorists and demagogues. . . . We must acknowledge the limitations of race as an appropriate criteria for the formulation of an aesthetic."[40] Within the larger body of work by artists of African descent, we can find insider *cultural* references that speak, or signify, to audiences authenticated by membership inside those protected spaces; those dance halls and churches (and barbershops, beauty parlors, family reunions, basketball playgrounds, backyard barbecues) and places where people gathered safely within their identity and social practices. And, over time, a million more concerns, expressive forms, and elements of artistic freedom found their way into the art. The experience and condition of being black are the geologic pressures that formed black culture, but they are not the culture itself.

> A black face didn't make me kin.
>
> SAIDIYA HARTMAN, *LOSE YOUR MOTHER* (2008)

Why meditate on culture? Because it provides opportunities for understanding black (or Africana) creative expression in ways that racial categorization does not. Composer and musician T. J. Anderson says, "All black music is based upon black speech. That's why the preacher is so important. All of it comes from the church and the bars and all of that, so it is environmental. This is an extension of who we are as a people."[41] The job of the artist, he says, is to do something with that. To this we can add Dianne Stewart's suggestion of prayer as "power speech" to reinforce the generative force of speech as a concept within African and African diaspora cultures.[42]

African American art presently is most often defined racially even when the intention is not to do so. Schwendener's *New York Times* discussion of a "cultural conversation" at the Studio Museum in Harlem is filled with formal, art historical, and racial references, but no cultural terminology or explanation is excavated from the art. Questions found in the exhibitions such as "Is there such a thing as black abstraction?" have little to do with black culture. She also asks, "What does it mean in art to represent bodies that have been marked as property and by racist violence?"[43] These questions can be found in racialized conceptions of being and where the black (racial) body is a signifier of disease and discretization. It is only within a racial concept that the black body exists and must be defended or redefined or reimagined. Questions about racial tension, exclusion, or social histories tend to preserve the assumptions of a racial context and, therefore, are active in continuing the existing racial assumptions.

Culture and ethnic practices would appear to be a better foundation for examining and defining African American (or African diasporic) art as an idiom (or a series of idiomatic expressive forms) instead of the label *black*. It is within culture that we find the lived experiences of expression Robert Farris Thompson mentions above. There are references, subjects, practices, and shared understandings within black cultural/ritual spaces that affect and effect the work of many artists of the African diaspora and, whether intentional or not, provide markers that differentiate that art and, importantly, offer insider evocations allowing black audiences to find emotional and experiential responses to the work. It is within culture that we find normality.

Building on previous brilliant and insightful work by Powell, Alvia Wardlaw, Jeff Donaldson, and others like David Driskell and Samella Lewis, this volume intends to explore Africana diasporal visual expression from some slightly different angles and emphases. Because musical and religious performance have acted as containers and transmitters of African and African American culture and identity, it is worth considering the appearance of those references in the visual expression of Africans in the Americas and the reasons that Amiri Baraka identified us as "blues people" and that Powell rearticulated the notion of a black aesthetic as a blues aesthetic.[44]

Artistically, expression seeking to be a part of the canon, the mainstream of H. W. and Anthony F. Janson's *History of Art*, and even the critique of race and racism, seems to be welcome in the mainstream art apparatus more than art with assumptions and codes of a black audience.[45] Admittedly, this can offer enviable financial rewards and personal recognition. With racial critiques, like those by Kara Walker, white people are a part of the conversation. So Kehinde Wiley's reimagination of classical European paintings, similar to Bob Thompson's paintings of the early 1960s, sometimes called restaging histories or resignifications of the black body, or even Robert Colescott's satirical restatement of Vincent Van Gogh's *The Potato Eaters*, *Eat Dem Taters* (1975), seems to find more support and patronage than work by Jeff Donaldson, John Biggers, or Renée Stout that has been directed more toward a black audience's sensibilities and experiences. Pleas for inclusion in the Western canon are dependent on a position of exclusion being the norm and can reinforce that condition. As Jean-Paul Sartre wrote in 1948, "When the Negro declares in French that he rejects French culture, he takes in one hand that which he has pushed aside with the other."[46] This is not to suggest that counterhegemonic production and critique are without utility, but they can carry the risk of reinforcing on one level what they oppose on another level.

I find Colescott's parody of Willem de Kooning, *I Gets a Thrill Too When I Sees De Koo* (1978; figure I.7), to be endlessly fascinating, inventive, witty, and intellectually savvy. The double entendre of the title implied by the Aunt Jemima/mammy head he has attached to a violently rendered body in the sense of de Kooning's female portrait abstractions ties the mammy stereotype to misogynist interpretations of women, and with tongue firmly in cheek, he signifies about undoing coon stereotypes. Directing such statements at mainstream art targets reinforces one's place in the margins, but Colescott twists and satirizes the mainstream in almost mocking gestures—like a visual cakewalk. He successfully places his work within the genre of artistic social critiques by canonical artists like William Hogarth, Francisco Goya, Käthe Kollwitz, Pablo Picasso, and Andy Warhol while rooting himself in traditions of signifying and the sarcasm and irony of African trickster figures. Though Colescott is addressing the art mainstream, he often does so with an Africana cultural syntax.[47]

I am left wondering if a part of Kehinde Wiley's success is because, in addition to the arresting visuality of his paintings, behind the imagery is the assumption of the primacy of classic Western painting traditions and his institutionalizing of the aspirational position of black people toward inclusion within that tradition. The foundational social critique is the recognition of black humanity and the jarring effect of recontextualizing the classic scenes by repopulating them with contemporary black figures. Wiley's work at the same time disrupts the prevailing narrative with pattern and hip-hop imagery, a strategy that potentially invades the Western canon and transforms it from within. This visual transmutation, at its best, is fascinating and offers a layered agenda that seems effective in a work from his global series inserting black and brown men from other nations as subjects.

Three Wise Men Greeting Entry into Lagos (2008; figure I.8) is effective because it is embedded, intentionally or not, with layers of cultural implications. Three young Nigerian men wearing contemporary African shirts with patterns we associate with African cloth are placed on a similarly patterned background as they make gestures with their fists. This

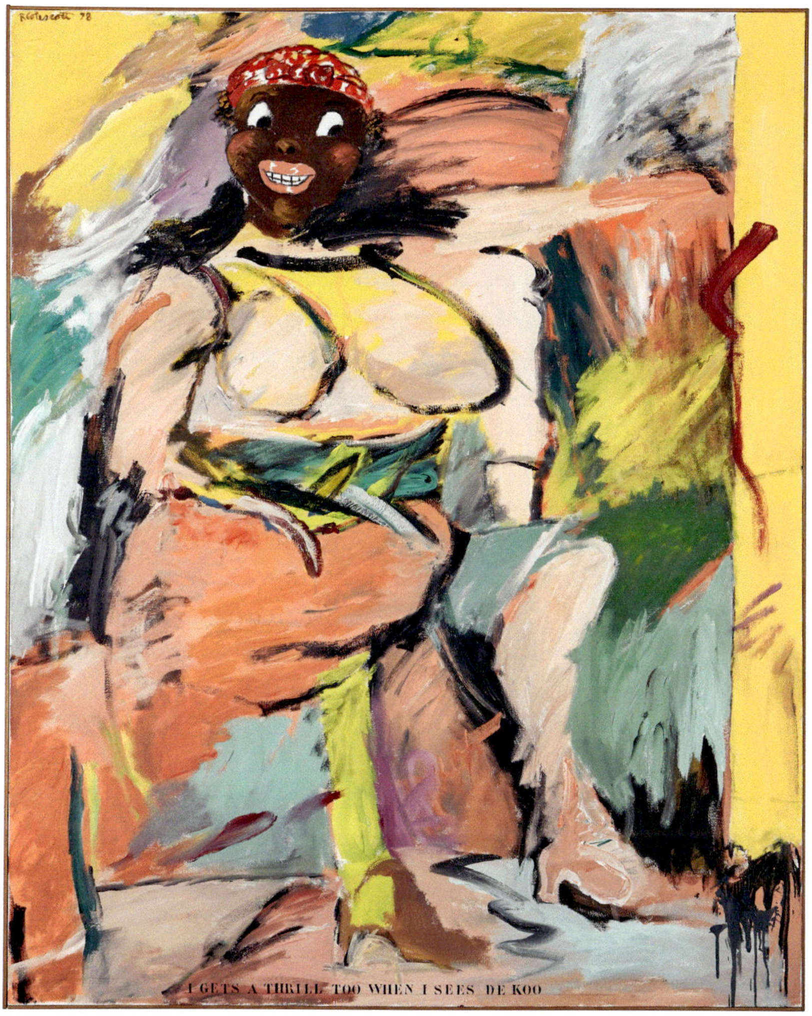

I.7 Robert Colescott, *I Gets a Thrill Too When I Sees De Koo*, 1978. Acrylic on canvas, 84 × 66 in. Used by permission of Rose Art Museum, Brandeis University, Waltham, MA. Gift of Senator and Mrs. William Bradley, 1981.25. Photograph by Charles Mayer Photography.

work suggests the work of Yinka Shonibare, the Yoruba artist living in England who has used African cloth to invade and resignify Victorian iconographic imagery and dress. *Three Wise Men*, at first, seems to have a familiar intimation from European canonical art. However, Sophie Sanders writes that this work instead is inspired by a monumental sculpture, the *Welcome to Lagos Monument*, designed by Bodun Shodeinde in 1991 (figure I.9). Wiley's painting duplicates the gestures of the three figures in the Lagos sculpture, which depicts three Yoruba *babalawo* (diviners or healers).[48]

Sanders appropriately considers Wiley's work in regard to the "colonial textile and decorative arts of Asia, West Africa, and Europe," as well as the common connections to hip-hop style and canon invasion.[49] The background pattern emulates the plant and floral motifs of factory print fabric, but the cloth the men wear draws from the resist dye wax prints that gained a market in West Africa.[50]

The histories behind printed patterned cloth beneath Shonibare's social/political commentary conceptually critique England's colonial history and the invisibility of its subjects by inserting African cloth into Victorian style. The brightly patterned cloth now seen as African in fact is printed in fabric mills in Holland and England and emerged from the colonial period as a replacement for the older narrow loom strip cloth, called Mande day cloth, and is best known in the form of kente cloth. Using this cloth on headless mannequins in works like figure I.10 from 2006, *How to Blow Up Two Heads at Once (Ladies)*, creates a double voicing speaking outwardly about the invisibility of colonial subjects during the height of empire but also has implications about the destruction of the local industry by imports from Europe. Interestingly, this ties into a scene from Beyoncé's *Lemonade* video when she quietly employs Shonibare's transmutation vocabulary by wearing what seems to be an antebellum-styled dress made of African cloth (figure I.11).

Wiley's usual patterns do not deploy the asymmetry found in African cloth or African American quilt tops, or what Robert Farris Thompson has called "offbeat phrasing."[51] Yet there can be something comfortably familiar about Wiley's strategy because it operates from the assumption of black marginality and repeats an old plea for inclusion. It offers no radical proposals for restructuring the Western canon, but it can call for a reassessment of the canon for abnormality, "disorder, theft and extortion."

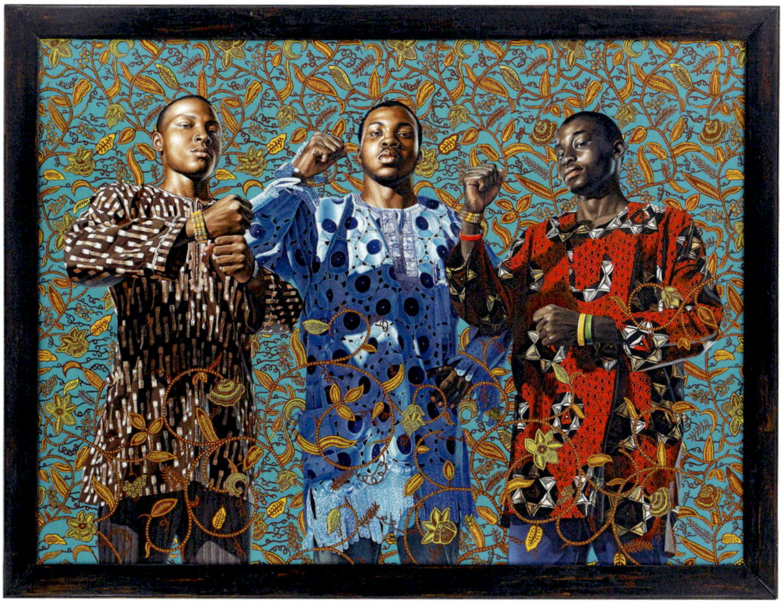

I.8 Kehinde Wiley, *Three Wise Men Greeting Entry into Lagos*, 2008. Oil on canvas, 72 × 95¼ in. Accession Number: 2009.20. © Kehinde Wiley. Courtesy of Pennsylvania Academy of the Fine Arts, Philadelphia. Frances and Joseph Nash Field Fund.

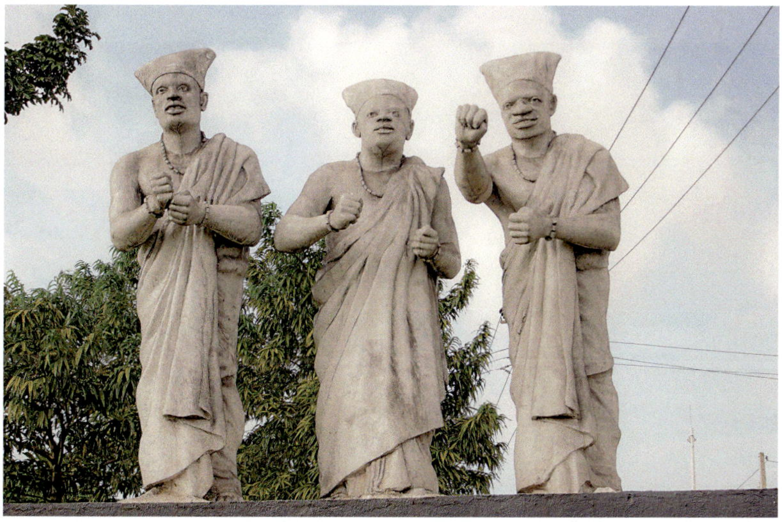

I.9 Bodun Shodeinde, *Welcome to Lagos Monument* (Lagos, Nigeria), 1991. Fiberglass, 12 ft. high. Creative Commons Share Alike 4.0 International, https://creativecommons.org/licenses/by-sa/4.0/deed.en. Photo by Yomi Dauda.

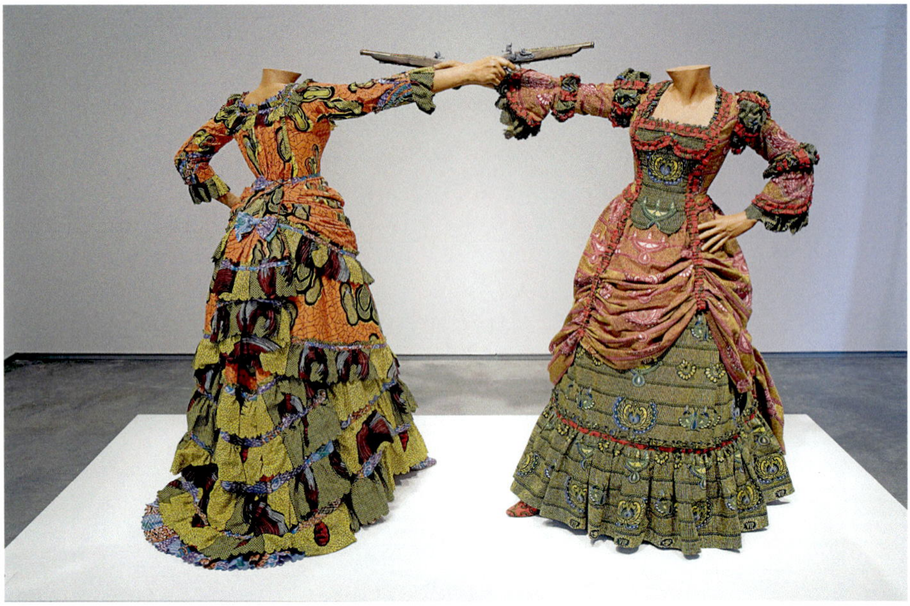

I.10 Yinka Shonibare, *How to Blow Up Two Heads at Once (Ladies)*, 2006. Two fiberglass mannequins, Dutch wax-printed cotton textile, two guns, shoes, leather riding boots, and plinth. 5 ft., 3 in. × 7 ft., 9½ in. × 4 ft. © Yinka Shonibare. Courtesy of Davis Museum, Wellesley College, Wellesley, MA. All Rights Reserved, DAC/ARS, New York 2025.

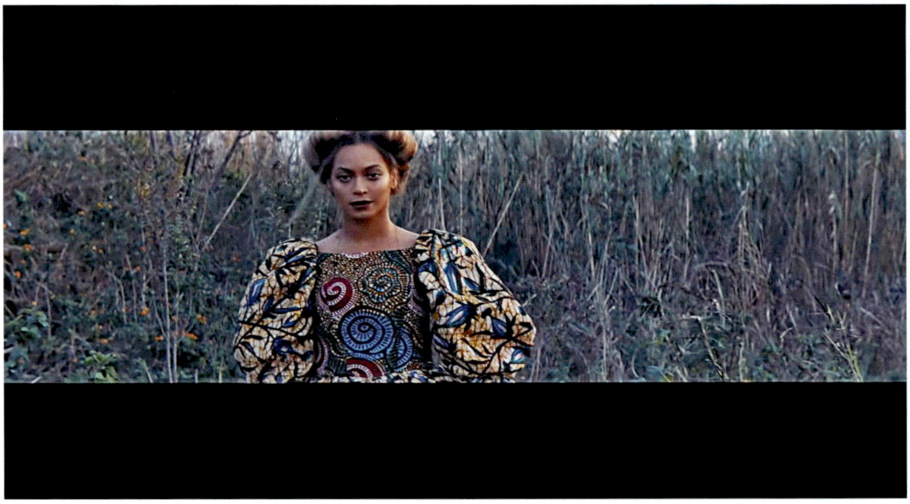

I.11 Still from Beyoncé's "All Night" video from her 2016 visual album *Lemonade*. "Beyoncé—'All Night' (Video)," YouTube, November 30, 2016, https://www.youtube.com/watch?v=gM89Q5Eng_M&list=RDgM89Q5Eng_M&start_radio=1&t=3.

I've wrestled with alligators. I've tussled with a whale.
I done handcuffed lightning. And throw thunder in jail.

MUHAMMAD ALI, "THE RUMBLE IN THE JUNGLE" SPEECH (1974)

The notion of a black or a blues aesthetic conflicts in some ways with younger artists and writers having a perspective rooted in popular cultural references and more stratified class experiences having been born after the murder of Martin Luther King Jr., the passing of the civil rights movement and the Black Arts Movement, and the conservative (and neoliberal) recalibration of American political culture given full motion by the 1980 election of Ronald Reagan and the political forces behind him. In his 1989 essay "The New Black Aesthetic," Trey Ellis calls himself a "cultural mulatto," a term he defines as "educated by a multi-racial mix of cultures" and the ability to "navigate easily in the white world." He suggests that the Cosby girls (of the wildly popular *Cosby Show* of the 1980s) were "equally as black as a black teenage welfare mother."[52]

Ellis's term, *cultural mulatto*, is one of many categorical adjustments in the long search for mooring by folk with uncomfortable fittings in the base stereotypes. It must be considered that black people always have had a clear sense of the "white world" and how to navigate it from various relationships to it because survival has always depended on this knowing.

In a recent *New York Times Magazine* essay, "Can Black Art Ever Escape the Politics of Race?" Vinson Cunningham examined the conundrum of black art and black artists: "How do you make sense of the widespread inability to allow social consciousness and other species of sensitivity to reside within the confines of the same person?"[53] Perhaps the persistent recurrence of black artists wishing to express their existential and human concerns free of racial designations is a by-product of Cunningham's suggestion that "tribal pride has too often meant solidarity with sorrow." He writes, "There exists—there has always existed—a tragic conundrum in the making of black art. The qualities most closely associated with high aesthetic accomplishment, at least in the West—transcendence, a preference for the beautiful over the blunt—are in some ways irresolvable with the details of black life."

African American artists always have negotiated artistic virtuosity and the nature and function of their craft. Cunningham's prescriptive solution is for artists and writers to "split the difference between Enlightenment-era detachment [the idea of art for art's sake] and grim social realism, showing through work and music and love—even laughter, even tears—exactly what a black life might be." Blues music signified its function in the lives of black people in the United States, but within that tradition, there were standards of craft. Form and function cooperated.

In 1963 bluesman Muddy Waters was invited by the Chess brothers of Chess Records to record an acoustic album, *Folk Singer*, to ride the popularity of folk music in popular culture shown by the success of groups like the Kingston Trio and Peter, Paul, and Mary. Not having had a successful song since 1958, Waters was willing to try the Chess brothers' suggestion for a reinterpretation of some old blues classics. Willie Dixon was on bass, Clifton James on drums, but the producers wanted Muddy to go to Mississippi and find an older guitarist to join the session. Muddy told them, "Set the session up for tomorrow, I got him." He brought young guitarist Buddy Guy to play. Guy recalled, "When I walked in the studio, Leonard and them was cursin' at me. Muddy told them, 'Shut up!' and he looked at me, 'Just don't say nothin'.' When I sit down and was playin' the sh__ with Muddy, they looked at me, 'Mother______, you didn't tell me you know that! You older than you say you are!'"[54]

In a world emphasizing the individuality intrinsic to art for art's sake, Africana artists continue to struggle with the lure of that nonracial individuality, what Cunningham calls "the basically illusory imperative for the fine artist to privilege the aesthetic and personal over the social and political."[55] The social realism and racial commentary of many artists can place them within a racialized social position as part of a marginalized group making a plea for inclusion. The racial critiques of artists like Kara Walker, or the creative reimaging of canonical Western art with the presence of black people, are compatible with the existing social structures and can reinforce them.

This book is an attempt to give voice and increased visibility to the experience of the black interior, but as a metaphor rather than a monolith. I wish to relieve it from the panoptic assumptions of the white gaze and its disciplines while acknowledging the presence of this gaze. The book explores the idea that the autobiography of cultural identity and experience, however defined, affects one's art, and recognizing the presence of cultural codes and cues—the dual address—can provide insight into the art and the artist, the intended audience for the work, and provide a much clearer reading of African American art than a racial designation of the artist's identity. In other words, African American art and art by African Americans are not always exactly the same thing. The latter is a racialized definition. The descendant of Baraka's *Blues People* is hip-hop culture, and it is rooted within a racial context, but it is not a racial entity.

CHAPTER 1

The Moan

Calling Forth Culture

I love the Lord, he heard my cry
And pitied every groan.

RICHARD SMALLWOOD, PERFORMER, "I LOVE THE LORD" (1982)

Beware of assuming the sterile attitude of a spectator,
for life is not a spectacle, a sea of miseries is not a
proscenium, a man screaming is not a dancing bear.

AIMÉ CÉSAIRE, *NOTEBOOK OF A RETURN TO THE NATIVE LAND* (1939)

Even at their most challenging moments of history, African captives and their descendants strove continually to keep their spirits alive. . . . They relied on ritualizing spaces in an African spirit in order to survive.

BEVERLY J. ROBINSON, "THE SENSE OF SELF IN RITUALIZING NEW PERFORMANCE SPACES FOR SURVIVAL" (2002)

In the summer of 2014, during a presentation for a National Endowment for the Humanities Faculty Institute at Emory University, Herukhuti Williams conducted a ritual with seventeen people forming a circle facing inward with their eyes closed. He walked counterclockwise around the circle asking them to relax and try to channel their ancestors from the Middle Passage. As he circled the group softly, hypnotically talking them into a penreceptive state, they began to groan, moan, and make nonsemantic sounds, and some cried. Standing outside the circle, eyes closed, involuntarily I was pulled from my thoughts to feelings that diffused certain barriers that normally registered in my mind; values and lines of identity. My realization was that there are conditions that cause people to make sounds that are unrelated to expressive communication but reflect something deeper that is inexpressible in words. The slave ship experience called up into awareness would seem to have generated deeper agonies that, shared, potentially would diffuse dialectical, ethnic, religious, and cultural structures to allow a new commonality.

How did black culture become what it became? How did African cultural and ethnic groups meld into a reformulated classification? According to Ed Spriggs, it started in the bottom of the boat during the Middle Passage with the moan. A moan, it seems, can be primal, primordial, and can transcend ego while expressing a most human, fundamental part of the self. Yoruba scholar and art historian Moyo Okediji indicates, "In Yoruba, you don't speak with the mouth only. You speak with your eyes and *gbogbo ara*—the entire body."[1]

As historian John Henrik Clarke described, the "captives' cries of grief erupted in several different tongues; their moans and wails a common chorus of misery and hopelessness."[2] During this five-to-twelve-week voyage of inhuman treatment, rivalries, nuances of difference, caste or class, and old ethnicities melted into a shared grief and loss.[3] Those who survived this transfer into a new, terrible reality began to focus on their commonalities. This experience is where the root system for a new, adapted culture formed.

In 1627 a voyager described the conditions on the slave ship:

> [The Africans are] so crowded, in such disgusting conditions, and so mistreated, as the very ones who transport them assure me, that they come by six and six, with collars around their necks and these same ones by two and two with fetters on their feet, in such a way that they come imprisoned from head to feet, below the deck, locked in from outside, where they see neither sun nor moon, [and] that there is no Spaniard who dares to stick his head in the hatch without becoming ill, nor to remain inside for an hour without risk of great sickness. So great is the stench, the crowding and the misery of that place. . . . [Nevertheless, most] arrive turned into skeletons.[4]

Folk with dialects and languages unintelligible to one another understood the moan. It marked a misery they shared. Saidiya Hartman argues that on a human level, slavery marked one as a stranger, an outsider, and for Europeans, "race established a hierarchy of human life" and determined "which persons were expendable." For those "chained in the lower decks of a slave ship, race was both a death sentence and the language of solidarity."[5] Spriggs says:

> They couldn't speak to each other. And they couldn't speak to the master. But what they had in common was the fact that they were in pain and they were fearful of what was going on. You put your own imagination to *that*. And they moaned. And they moaned. And that moan became syncopated. You had the boat moving. You had a whole different rhythm of life that kept that moan going.
>
> Then they got to shore, and living in the plantation setting, the moan became a hum. What they could remember, that song they had in them. And they still had the language problem. It's the moan. And their moan became a hum.[6]

While suggesting that moans became a hum can be seen as a part of our lore, the point is to tie the verbal with the cultural and then to the visual. Figure 1.1 offers an arresting illustration of that sequence: the verbal (and preverbal), the cultural, and the visual. Consider this visual image by Tom Feelings: a charcoal drawing of chained figures crying out of their trauma. It commemorates a key dimension of cultural and historical experience represented by Feelings in his celebrated masterpiece, *The Middle Passage: White Ships/Black Cargo.* Here we see how verbal and creative expressions are linked in prior African, and therefore in present African, diasporic cultural formations. Such expressions are a part of the process of re-forming familial kinships as the social and spiritual foundation of identity, a new diasporal identity. Cultural expressiveness and practices, the lived experiences of people in the African diaspora, can be found in various obvious or subtle forms within Africana visual and verbal expression, and those markers provide a means for identifying what might be unique about the art.

Martinican scholar Édouard Glissant wrote that during Middle Passages, "African languages became deterritorialized. . . . The only written thing on slave ships was the account book listing the exchange value of slaves. Within the ship's space the cry of those deported was stifled, as it would be in the realm of the Plantations."[7] Speech, human practices, and interactions were scrambled during that horrible journey. Glissant continued:

> The belly of this boat dissolves you, precipitates you into a nonworld from which you cry out. This boat is a womb, a womb abyss. . . .

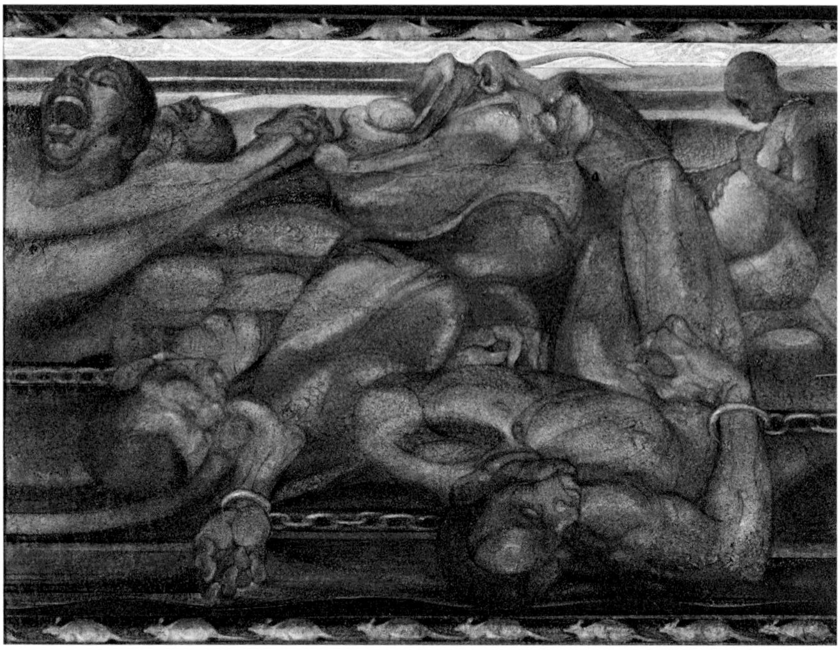

1.1 Illustration from Tom Feelings, *The Middle Passage*, n.p. Courtesy of Tom Feelings Artwork, James Weldon Johnson Collection, Yale Collection of American Literature, Beinecke Rare Book and Manuscript Library, New Haven, CT. Used by permission of Tom Feelings Collection.

> Is this boat sailing into eternity toward the edges of a nonworld that no ancestor will haunt?[8]

During this travel through the abyss, Africans faced "feeling a language vanish, the word of the gods vanish, and the sealed image of even the most everyday object, of even the most familiar animal, vanish. The evanescent taste of what you ate. The hounded scent of ochre earth and savannas."[9]

Here we have another Middle Passage representation: Kara Walker's work that is one of six prints created for her series *An Unpeopled Land in Uncharted Waters* (figure 1.2). The title, *No World*, plays upon the familiar designation *New World* and thus ironically "signifies on" the historical experience of enslaved Africans. The image depicts a slave ship held aloft by black spirit hands. Within the watery abyss of the Atlantic ocean lies prone a large female body also pictured, like the rest of the work, in silhouette; Walker's signature medium of creative expression. But what kind

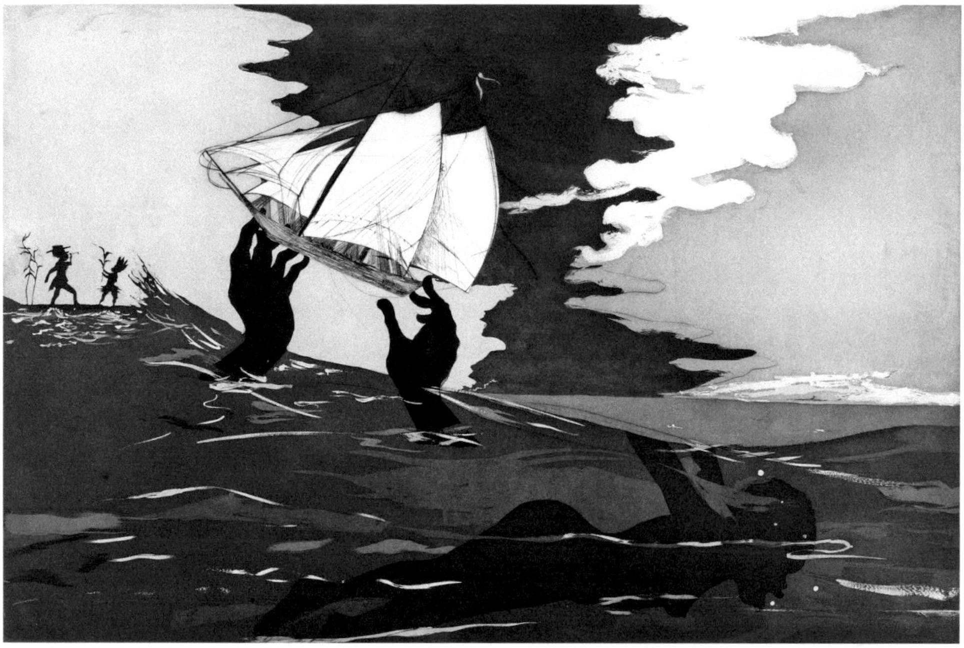

1.2 Kara Walker, *No World*, from the series *An Unpeopled Land in Uncharted Waters*, 2010. Philadelphia Museum of Art. Artwork © Kara Walker. Used courtesy of Sikkema Jenkins and Co., New York.

of creativity could possibly convey the sounds or phonations experienced by such peoples in their shared pathos? In that regard, Clyde Taylor argues that "the major linguistic transmissions from Africa were probably not words at all." He wrote that whenever "a person or a people migrate from one language community to another and learn a new language, a linguistic substratum is held over from their original tongue."[10] Taylor suggests, "Among the cultural baggage that survived the Middle Passage, I would argue, were African 'mythophones,' highly charged symbolizations, in music and language, of entire cultural outlooks. Mythophonic in character, then, would be those orientations to speech, music, dance, and non-verbal communication that could survive that 'tortured passage of flesh' and, as best they could, reconstitute in the new world the values and perspectives of the old."[11]

Moans, Hums, and Intonations: In the Beginning Was the Word

It is possible to think of the moan as an emotional abstraction of speech and as being tied to the generative power of speech and linked theoretically to the primordial concept of the Word. It is a semantic utterance full of meaning and implication. Yoruba and Dogon cultures provide a rich resource for making this contention.

The Yoruba of what is now Nigeria were not a significant population in the antebellum United States, but they have a significant presence in the cultures and religions of the Caribbean and Brazil because they first appeared in the latter portion of the slave trade after American and British legislation in 1807–8 had outlawed the direct importation of captives from Africa.[12] They were a large part of the last phase of the trade when the Spanish and Portuguese speakers dominated, operating largely from bases in Brazil and Cuba.[13] Yoruba orisha (*òrìṣà, orixa*), or their equivalents as saints or spirits, can be found in Brazilian Candomblé, Cuban Santería (or Lucumí), Haitian Vodou, Trinidadian Shango practices, and to a lesser extent in Hoodoo and folklore of the Mississippi Delta region, extending to Louisiana and New Orleans. Also, Yoruba references, in recent years, have become cultural signifiers to many looking for African retentions or reclamations.

If we take the notion of the moan as a verbal act, a verb, expressing one's condition, and elide that act into the cultural intention of a hum, we can link conceptually both orations with the tonal speech and the talking drum found in West African cultures, including that of the Yoruba. In Yoruba culture, expression, acts of selection, and divine intention are linked and are present in their intellectual aesthetic interpretation.

The Yoruba story for disentangling the divine begins with *òrò*, words as an earthly form of sound from God. Rowland Abiodun indicates that Olodumare (Olódùmarè or Òdùmàrè), the Creator, emitted the Divine Word as *Họọ*, a construction of *ọgbón* (wisdom), *ìmọ* (knowledge), and *òye* (understanding). Olodumare realized he "was too charged with energy to come into direct contact with any living thing and have it survive," so he created them as intermediaries. When the verb *rọ* (coming down) was added, it became *Họọ-rọ*, or *Ọ-rọ*, a kind of divine intention as speech.[14] The three concepts are embodied as primordial characters of the same names.

Ogbón (wisdom embodied), *ìmọ*, and *òye* existed prior to speech and, according to Abiodun, disturbed Olodumare "by incessant humming" so he ordered them "to descend (*rọ*) making the sound *họọ*."[15]

Òrò is too powerful—contains too much *ashé*, or divine energy—for human consumption, so it must be modified or cloaked. As Abiodun suggests through verses from Yoruba *Ifá* literature, *òrò* is more than speech. It is a hum before speech, and more:

> *Ọrọ*, the cause of great concern for the wise and experienced elders.
> It sounds *kù* (making the heart miss a beat)
> *Kè* (as a ponderous object hitting the ground).
> *Gì* (making the last sound before silence).
> The *ọrọ* that drops from the elderly
> Is stupendous.
> It was divined for *Ọrọ-ọrọ-ọrọ*
> Who did not have anyone to communicate with.
> And started groaning.[16]

The point here is that speech, sound, tonality, and groans conceptually can be linked to the divine story of creation, and modulated tonalities are important aspects of communication. The incantatory potential of speech is not unlike ancient Judeo-Christian lore in the Bible, where God spoke existence into being. This potential for incantatory transformations may provide a conceptual foundation for the acceptance of conjure and other vernacular forms of metaphysical beliefs and practices.

Speech is animated by breath, and divine breath is personified by Ẹmí, the breath of life personified as Olodumare's daughter.[17] According to Dianne Stewart, kinship relations are a foundation of Yoruba cultural formation, and *Ẹmí* is "affirmed as the foundation of the Yoruba people's most prized social goods, precisely the social good of kinship/family and generativity."[18] As a part of the generative process signified by speech, Stewart argues that human and divine families breathe and vivify the universe together, creating all manner of possibilities. "Yoruba oral tradition and sacred literature offer evidence that Yoruba people have understood familial experience as primordial and ontological, encompassing all of creation. The familial orientation issues from a spiritually—and socially grounded—interdependent existence."[19] She cites a Yoruba poem translated by *Babalawo* Dr. Kólá Abímbólá from the Odù from the *Ifá* corpus in which Orúnmìlà, the orisha of wisdom, asks:

"Isn't it the case that as long as Ẹmí is not lost there is wealth?"
Yes, there is wealth!
"Isn't it the case that as long as Ẹmí is not lost there is a spouse?"
Yes, there is a spouse!
"Isn't it the case that as long as Ẹmí is not lost there are children?"
Yes, there are children!
"Isn't it the case that as long as Ẹmí is not lost all the good things of
life will come?"
Yes, all the good things of life will come![20]

Therefore, an inarticulate hum and a groan of isolation precede the expression of divine intent in human communication. It is breath and life and potential. Abiodun indicates that *ashé*, the vital force of all living and nonliving things, the power to make things happen, is involved primordially with speech: "Without Ohùn ('speech,' 'voice,' or 'the performed word'), neither Èpè (the malevolent component of lifeforce), nor *Àṣẹ*, (the largely beneficent component of lifeforce)—two sides of the same coin—can fulfill its mission."[21]

Abiodun adds the "aesthetic canon" of *ìlutí*—good hearing—to the speech power dynamic and points out that it is very much alive in the cultural practice of call-and-response. "In West Africa, the Yorúbá look for an *òrìṣà* with *ìlutí* to worship, as evident in the saying 'Ẹbra tó lutí là n bọ,' 'We worship and celebrate only deities who can respond when called upon.'"[22]

Ẹmí may be the performed word, speech, as an aspect of the process of creation, but also the hearing and response dynamic, the communal element, energizes and maintains relationships between humans and divine intent. Abiodun has titled the chapter containing this explication "Àṣẹ: The Empowered Word Must Come to Pass," emphasizing the activism implicit in the act of speech.

Perhaps the idea of the moan as a primal expression of that transformational state of death and rebirth through the mid-Atlantic passage can be seen as a small repeat of the creation process. It is the seed of a new culture, a new configuration for Africans and for the world. It is the foundation for a new aesthetic/cultural formation seeded in the holds of slave ships during the Middle Passage in the soil of an African past. It also is tied to familial connections and formations. Stewart reminds us that for the Yoruba, "Familial relatedness is an essence and absolute requirement for all theistic and cosmic operations." She points out, "Yoruba-Orisa devotees in

Trinidad and elsewhere come to experience their deities as family members with roles and responsibilities to children, parents, in-laws and other relatives. . . . A devotee becomes the spouse of her patron Orisa during the initiation process and is spiritually married to the Orisa who has ownership of her Orí [head, personhood]."[23]

This gives added significance to Hartman's statement that slavery caused one to become a stranger, tearing the captive from the bonds of kinship as well as their relationship with the land and their spiritual universe. The ritualized aspects of life, as described by Beverly Robinson and highlighted in my introduction to this book, which held together a sense of self and community, were challenged by the enslaver. Hartman indicates that race is not the basis of kinship but, by implication, suggests that kinship is the foundation of community, culture, and ontology. Reformulation of these things in the aftermath of the catastrophic dislocation of slavery would help recover one's humanity. Race is the catastrophe causing a reformulation, but it is not the *basis* of it.

If we move north to Dogon culture, there are congruencies and consistencies with *òrò* (or Ohùn) and Ẹmí. The Dogon see material reality as *aduno so*, the "word of the world" (or the world as Word), and they have developed an elaborate systemization of their concepts regarding the process of speech and the physical world. They see the physical being or object as the final stage of speech.[24]

In Dogon mythology, the Nummo, the primordial beings who came down as a part of creation, are associated with moisture, which is the life force of the earth, and of the Word or Speech. French ethnographer Marcel Griaule recorded that "when Nummo speaks, what comes from his mouth is a warm vapour which conveys, and itself constitutes, speech."[25] Speech is transmitted from Amma, the Creator, through the Nummo to the world, and physical experience is translated as speech, or *aduno so*.

Rituals, signs, and signifiers are used to express an underlying, cosmological discourse through expressive culture. As Geneviève Calame-Griaule writes, "Among the Dogon, symbolic thinking . . . is an integral part of culture. Individuals learn from childhood to view the world through symbolic eyes so as to decipher its message."[26]

The Dogon levels of knowledge in a ritual context are described in terms of speech and the word. The first is *giri so*, or "fore-word." This is the first layer of explanation in which mythical personages "are often disguised, their adventures simplified or fantasized," and it deals with visible things and deeds. The second layer is *benne so*, or "side-word," which adds deeper explanation of certain rituals and representations. Next is *bolo so*, or "back-word," which completes the preceding knowledge and "furnishes syntheses applicable to greater parts of the whole on the other hand." The last stage is the *so dayi*, or "clear-word," which presents the very secret parts of the knowledge in its "ordered complexity."[27]

In an echo of the process of creation and the generative power of divine speech, the moan is a signifier of the communal act of speech as a transmitter of one's feeling and circumstance in the process of forming or affirming community and re-forming definitions of kinship. Moaning is not culturally specific because all human cultures might use this verbal act to express pain, but in this particular circumstance it can convey a kind of expressed connective tissue as cells of individuality coalesce to become organs of cultural embodiment. And those organs grow to become cultural bodies to inhabit a new environment.

The hum signifies organizing the vocality of African tonal language as a cultural seasoning for a New World entity. It is a transitory act between the primeval moan and the talking drum threading through the cultural expressive forms; an act cloaking the shared *ashé* animating those African captives and their descendants disconnected from the old places and old ways—old ways now re-forming in a diaspora.

Okwui Enwezor wrote about the conflicts and consciousness, actually W. E. B. Du Bois's "double consciousness" that forms in the processes of diaspora.[28] Regarding contemporaneous diasporic studies inaugurated by Du Bois, Enwezor says, "The site of these studies . . . predates the founding of the United States. [Double consciousness] was born in the difficult journey of the Middle Passage across the Atlantic, in the map of a new cultural configuration unique to the conditions of slavery and displacement within plantation society. . . . The challenges, then, were how to build a cultural identity in the traumatic site of the New World and how to negotiate and bridge the gap between the subjugated memory of the African cultures and a dominant European model shaped by slavery."[29]

One of the challenges of building a new cultural identity in a new context was the tension between that identity and the hostility and aggression of the surrounding European one in dialectic with it. While Enwezor uses Du Bois's idea of double consciousness to examine its role as an agent in the "active process of translation, transmission, enactment, and performance," I prefer to look at the interior of that experience, particularly the formations and exchanges rooted in insular, protected spaces, and its shared reactions.[30] Shared experiences and practices formed within insular, sanctuary social spaces grew into codes and recognitions of membership, and, perhaps, the moan was there. The moan showed up in the black church as a divine echo through call-and-response as well as in the music. It showed up in the congregational response to a deacon's prayer. It appeared in the vocal cadences and ecstatic speech of the preacher. It showed up in Sam Cooke's popular song "Chain Gang" in 1960:

> That's the sound of the men working on the chain ga-a-ang
> That's the sound of the men working on the chain gang
>
> All day long they work so hard
> Till the sun is goin' down
> Working on the highways and byways
> And wearing, wearing a frown
> You hear them moanin' their lives away
> Then you hear somebody sa-ay
>
> (chorus) hooh! aah!
> (chorus) hooh! aah!

Cooke ends the song with his own moaning, the kind of emotional expression that has become a staple of African American music, almost a signifier of the genre (even when used more as a technique than heartfelt expression). Always, moans and hums and expressive speech are acts of both communication and expression, or healing incantation. They are Ẹmí at work.

Glissant has written about the significance of language, suggesting that "controlling the substance of one's future would lie in controlling its nomenclature."[31] He argues for the persistence of creolized speech as a fragmented retention of African languages while "feeling a language vanish, the word of the gods vanish, and the sealed image of even the most everyday object, of even the most familiar animal, vanish."[32] The tonalities and intonations of African languages often persist in the cultural vernacular speech of the Americas.

Race and ethnicity have long been competing identity constructions for African Americans. Michael Gomez indicates that Denmark Vesey believed, in order for his insurrection to succeed, a de-emphasis of African ethnicities in favor of "a lone condition, that of blackness, of descent from Africa," was required.[33] Gomez suggests African ethnicities persisted in colonial America more than is commonly assumed, and because "ethnicity's purpose is to dissociate rather than associate," a larger aggregate identity was required for a unified resistance to an already somewhat unified European or white identity of the enslavers.[34] Here my premise is that "Negro" or "black" or "African American" became an ethnicity, a newly formed one, over time, but one formed in the crucible of slavery and race for dissociation with "white" captors. In Hartman's terms, strangers torn from their kinship systems invented new bonds, and racial solidarity "was expressed in the language of kinship because it both evidenced the wound and attempted to heal it."[35] This language humanized strangers who had been turned into commodities, things, or property and who reorganized themselves into a new, larger, coalesced ethnicity.

As suggested by the iconic schematic of the slave quarters on oceangoing ships (figure 1.3), Gomez argues that the Middle Passage was a birth canal that launched a "prolonged struggle between slaveholder and enslaved over rights of definition" but also was "a death canal, baptismal waters of a different kind. At the very least, the African died to what was and to what could have been."[36] Gomez says, "The African antecedent would inform every aspect of African-American culture, not simply music."[37] The links to Africa are found in the facts that from 1790 to 1810 the African-born population in the United States was about 22 percent, after which it declined. Still, "much of the remaining African-based population was only one or two generations removed from African soil."[38] This influence permeated families.

In a diasporal example, Cuban-born artist María Magdalena Campos-Pons said in an interview, "My father talked to me about slavery, and his [great-]grandpa who was a slave that he met. He knew him! He talked to him! He taught him things."[39] Campos-Pons's great-great-grandfather was Yoruba, and her grandmother was a Santería (or Lucumí) practitioner in Matanzas, Cuba. She recalled that her father sang songs to her in Yoruba, and she learned to sing them from memory.

Campos-Pons's 1992 work, *The Seven Powers That Came from the Sea* (figure 1.4), riffs on the slave ship diagram of figure 1.3 but suggests that the African captives brought culture with them. The installation uses seven boards shaped in approximation to a slave ship diagram as well as suggesting ironing boards. This allusion ties the women from these journeys to the domestic labor so many assumed even after the era of enslavement.

Campos-Pons's more recent work *Replenishing* (2003) uses seven photographs arranged to suggest an umbilical connection between her and her mother even across the distance between Cuba and Boston, where

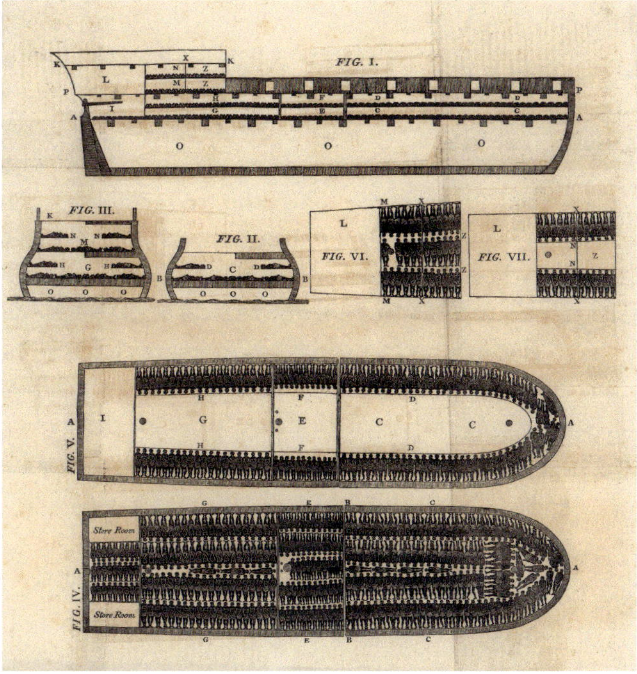

1.3 Diagram of a slave ship showing arrangement of its human cargo, from a pamphlet by Thomas Clarkson, one of England's leading abolitionists. In *Melanges sur l'Amerique*, vol. 19 (London: G. Schulze, 1821). Diagram © John Carter Brown Library, Brown University, Providence, RI. Courtesy of John Carter Brown Library.

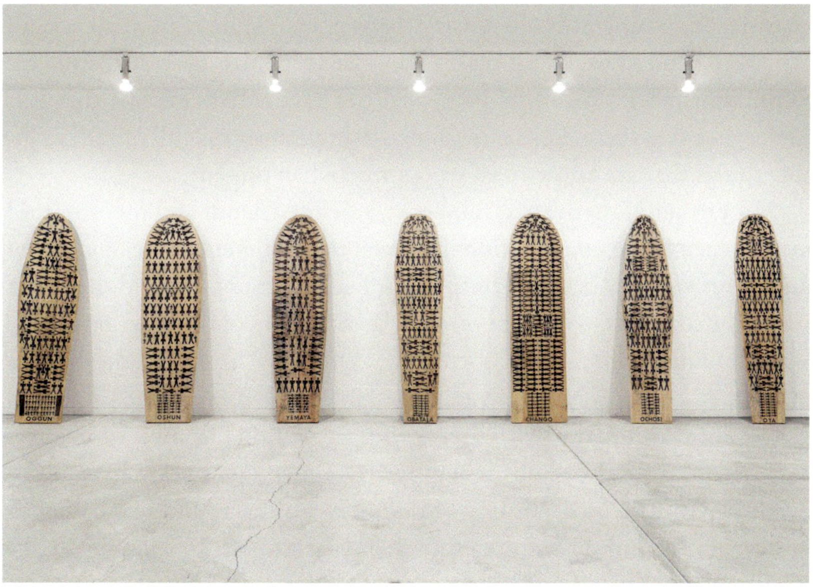

1.4 María Magdalena Campos-Pons, *The Seven Powers Come by the Sea*, 1992. Wood and ink, dimensions variable. A Yoruba orisha is named on the bottom of each slave ship form, each of which also suggests an ironing board. Vancouver Art Gallery, Acquisition Fund.

she resided for many years, despite the more than ten years that she could not return to Cuba to visit her mother after immigrating to the United States (figure 1.5). The quiet cultural reference, for those who know, is the beads between them. Their colors, as well as the dresses each woman wears, indicate Yoruba water orisha such as Yemoja (blue and white), Oshun (cream or tan), and Eshu (red and black), the deity associated with crossroads and the communication between realms. This work rhymes with the earlier *Seven Powers* installation as both stress Yoruba culture and connections across time and space and the retention of familial deities.

The point is that visual expression can be an agent in the articulation or expression of the ontological and cosmological frame discussed here. The verbal and the visual are linked, and like the layers of Dogon knowledge, they are interconnected from the quotidian to the profound. Those with a clear recognition of the signified references, be they cosmological or mundane cultural practices referenced or coded in imagery, can excavate cultural affirmation and shared kinships. They can work in the evocative sense of Clyde Taylor's mythophone.

The moan in the slave ship hold and its link to verbal and musical expression on either side of the Atlantic is as difficult to document as it is to quantify that thing in black music—bent notes, singing "in the cracks of the piano," and so on—that makes what we recognize as "black" difficult to pin down. But those who are a part of the experience know that it is there when it is there. Lore often is mythologized truths full of indescribable things that are known and recognized when present.

Jon Lockard (1932–2015), an artist, teacher, friend, and mentor, told me of remembered conversations between elder women sitting on porches during his younger days in Detroit that had no words. He said they used varied inflections to comment on their observations of the neighborhood: "Um um um." "Um hum." "Uh uhhh." "Uhuh!"[40] In speech these types of sounds are nonsemantic utterances, pauses that are placeholders to give room for thought before returning to speaking. However, in cases like that above, they become semantic utterances, sounds that have actual meaning. There is a vocabulary of shared meanings found in a dozen or more of these sounds that often find their way into black songs, much like whistles, handclaps, foot stomps, grunts, and other nonverbal notations. They all became a part of the lexicon of black cultural performance and, as an extension of the moan, intracultural communication, and they iterate Okediji's notion of *gbogbo ara*, speaking with the entire body.

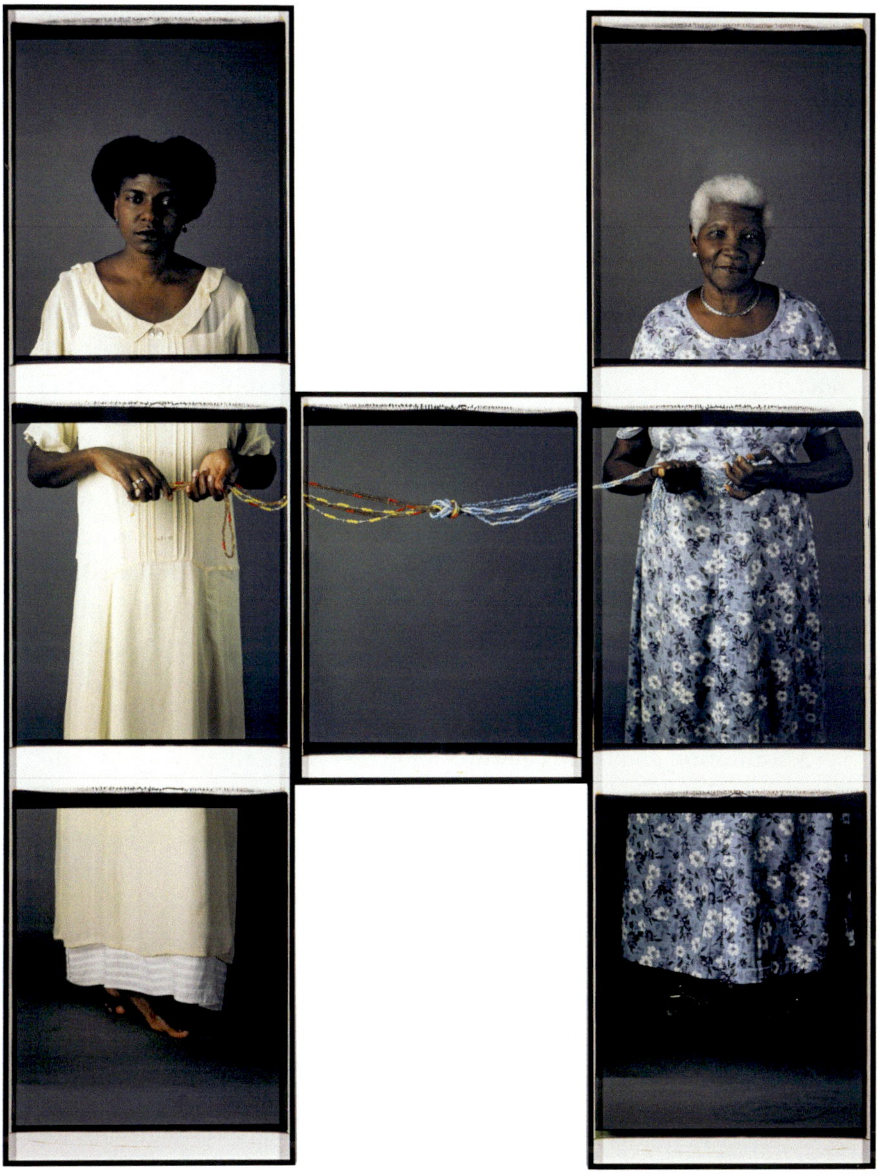

1.5 María Magdalena Campos-Pons, *Replenishing*, 2003. Polaroid photographs, 72 × 60 in. Pérez Art Museum Miami (PAMM). Museum purchase with funds provided by PAMM's Collectors Council. Courtesy of Bernice Steinbaum Gallery, Miami, FL.

Additionally, we are talking about the kinds of vocalization and emphases that come out of oral cultures. Many African languages were not written before the nineteenth century or later. For example, the Yoruba language was not written until the 1850s, when Samuel Ajayi Crowther (1809–91) translated the Bible into Yoruba and began to compile a Yoruba dictionary. One of the functional values of oral culture is that access to knowledge is controlled by how one's readiness for it is perceived by the keepers of that knowledge. In African and African-diaspora cultures, coded communication (the hidden transcript mentioned previously) can take place in front of outsiders effortlessly through signifiers and symbolic references and evocations, and it became a necessary tool of protection in the presence of white people.

Robert Toll, writing about black minstrel performance in the nineteenth century, suggests it often used "symbolic indirection" and some sort of victory, however small, for the black characters.[41] Toll continued, pointing out that black people frequently expressed their resistance and displeasure with the social order, often with allusion or coded references white audiences usually missed. Toll wrote that black culture sensitized people "to hear and enjoy . . . surreptitious barbs, while most whites might not even have noticed them."[42]

Vocalization and bodily gestures and expressions are important indicators in African and African American communication, and idiomatic phrases and metaphoric, rather than literal, expressions fill verbal communication. For example, the Yoruba often use human acts rather than abstract phrases to instruct. *Fí eti sile* (put your ear to the ground) is an instruction to listen, to pay attention. *Fí okan bale* (put your heart on the ground) instructs one to be patient.

Yoruba is a tonal language with a sort of do-re-mi scale with tonality and its orthography rather than spelling often changing the meaning of words. This tonality allows for a blending of language and music in the playing of the talking drum. Imagine a drum playing to announce the arrival of a visitor to a palace and the host being apprised of who has arrived and, perhaps, for what reason. Another example is the banjo, an instrument with Central African origins, which has percussive potentials when turned over.[43] What is a moan or a hum other than, like certain drumming, the vocalization of communicative tonality?

There is a communal sociology with oral cultures. Walter Ong, in writing about orality and literacy, says, "An interlocutor is virtually essential: it is hard to talk to yourself for hours on end. Sustained thought in an oral culture is tied to communication."[44] Communication, particularly in oral cultures, is not what Clyde Taylor indicates is the "broad blast of human communication" and the literary tendency to "fix or freeze speech."[45] Tone, gesture, and visual signs, Taylor indicates, function as "mythograms." Consider as well the mythophonic symbolizations in movement; music and dance; verbal play; misdirection; and subsequent tendencies for musical expression to intimate or mimic speech: All these developments translated African communication practices into diasporal settings. Citing the work of French anthropologist Andre-LeRoi Gourhan, Taylor says a mythogram "would be a visual symbolization in abbreviated form of familiar, traditional ritual and myth. In its concentrated form, such a sign would serve to reactivate mentally an entire myth and its appropriate ritualistic celebration, dance, music, sacrifice, and feast."[46]

I suggest that orality, vocalization, and cultural expressiveness were intertwined in the formation of insular aspects of African American culture that resisted, and often became counterhegemonic to, the violence and oppression of slavery and its aftermath. This insularity formed a thread of continuity across African American vernacular culture. From those sanctuary spaces, actual and virtual, an intelligible cultural lexicon of sounds, gestures, and phrases developed, forming and affirming black culture. A call-and-response interlocution occurred, a vocalized dialogue that took place underground, out of sight, and is intelligible fully only to those with access to such safe social and conceptual spaces and familiar with their codes.[47]

References or representations of that cultural lexicon, including folklore, trickster figures, and the practices of signifyin', are found in African American visual art as signs of insider knowledge; in much the same way, they provide recognition and identification for African American audiences within vernacular music or religious expression. Imagine the dialogue, the call-and-response, between a preacher as he begins a singsong cadence in a sermon and the congregation with affirming or acknowledging grunts, moans, "amens," handclaps, and, eventually, ecstatic hollers as a select few are "filled with the spirit!"

Collective Privacy and the Need for Sanctuary

Africana expressivity within a communal context communicated an emotional and spiritual conversation that could only authentically occur within a collective privacy. This is what was performed in sanctuaries, cultural safe houses within a matrix of violence—physical, emotional, psychological, mental, and economic—that, like geological pressures, formed the cultural gemstones of black life. The references to this emotional bling can be found in a stream of African American art and function as codes of belonging, often adding a dimension hidden in plain sight within the art. We might think of these sanctuarial spaces as ritualized spaces for reinforcing community and being in the sense Robinson describes in the introduction.

A million indicators, both large and small, generated the need for safety; acts of violence that were physical, sexual, social, and psychological. A permanent exhibition of Civil War medicine, *Broken Bodies, Suffering Spirits*, opened at the Mütter Museum in Philadelphia in the fall of 2013. A review of that exhibition pointed out that African American soldiers who fought in the Civil War "were given inferior food, supplies and medical care, and as a result had higher rates of disease than whites." Because of this, black soldiers were "seven times as likely as whites to contract smallpox, probably because they were less likely to have been vaccinated. And one black regiment had 150 deaths in a single summer from scurvy, or vitamin C deficiency, caused by a lack of fresh food."[48]

Hale Woodruff's 1935 linocut, *By Parties Unknown* (figure 1.6), is one of the more notable artworks from the first half of the twentieth century directly addressing the murderous violence that threatened and claimed so many black lives in the American South. This work presents the toll on the victims from a black perspective and iterates the need for protection from exposure to this terror and risk. The victim's tattered clothing in Woodruff's work, rather than being a trope for black poverty, suggests the physical violence that accompanied his lynching.

Woodruff's work presents a faceless victim whose body was left, ironically, on the steps of a small church. The image was printed with a preponderance of black areas, creating the sense of a night setting. The lynch rope still in place around his neck testifies to the life-ending events preceding this moment. The placement of the body on the steps of the sanctuary implies this space to be at the center of the black community and a place to effectively leave a terrorist message for that community as well as for the victim's family. The door of the church itself forms a cross in the image, implying the martyrdom of the victims of this ongoing racist carnage. Billie Holiday's 1939 song "Strange Fruit" (first published in 1937 as a poem by Abel Meeropol) testifies to how widespread the practice of lynching was at that time.[49]

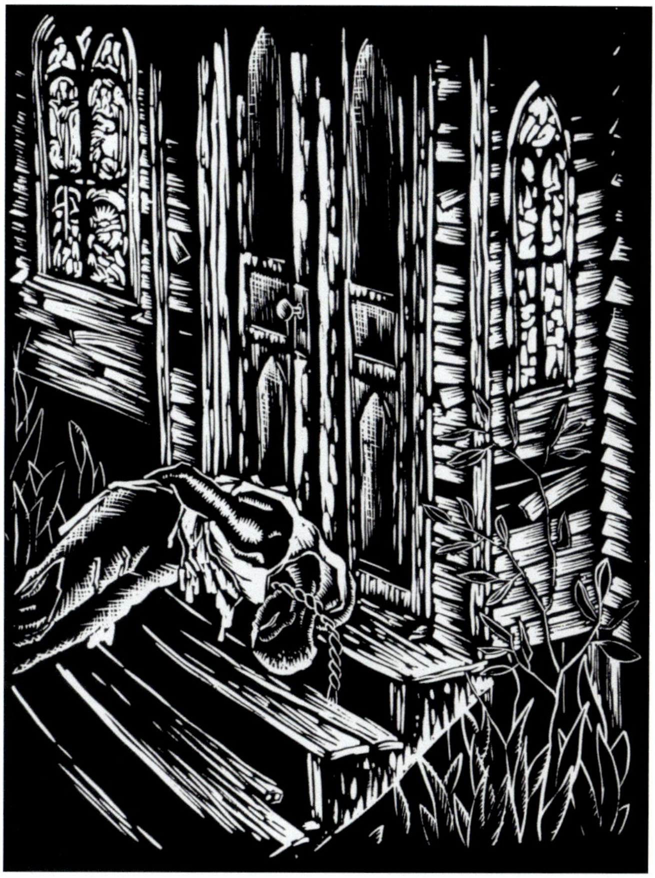

1.6 Hale Woodruff, *By Parties Unknown*, 1935 (printed by Robert Blackburn). Linocut on Chine collé, 19⅛ in. × 15 in. Accession number 2000.1.005. © 2023 Estate of Hale Woodruff/Licensed by VAGA at Artists Rights Society (ARS), New York. Courtesy of Spelman College Museum of Fine Arts, Atlanta. Gift of Kathryn C. and Kenneth I. Chenault.

To make a shift to the external gaze, James Allen's 2000 book, *Without Sanctuary*, reproduced dozens of vintage postcards showing lynched and murdered black people, often along with the white mobs who attended the spectacle of the public execution. In the 1911 image in figure 1.7, we see a woman, Laura Nelson, who was murdered in Oklahoma, hanging above a river. The fact that so many of these horrifying photographs were taken is astonishing. It is incomprehensible that they became commodities to be sold as postcards.

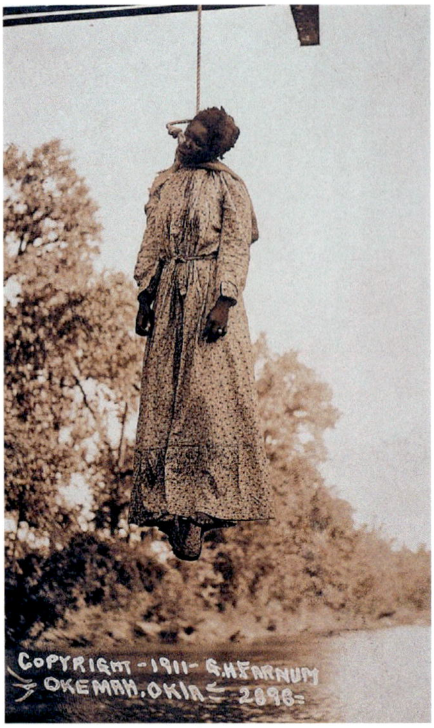

1.7 Barefoot corpse of Laura Nelson, Okemah, Oklahoma, May 25, 1911. From James Allen, *Without Sanctuary*, 100.

Figure 1.8 shows a 1920 image with number of white males of varying ages gathered around the bodies of three young men who had been murdered in Minnesota. In the case of Laura Nelson, District Judge John Caruthers charged a grand jury to investigate the lynching of the woman and her son with these instructions: "The people of the state have said by recently adopted constitutional provision that the race to which the unfortunate victims belonged should in large measure be divorced from participation in our political contests, because of their known racial inferiority and their dependent credulity, which very characteristic made them the mere tool of the designing and cunning. It is well known that I heartily concur in this constitutional provision of the people's will. The more then does the duty devolve upon us of a superior race and of greater intelligence to protect this weaker race from unjustifiable and lawless attacks."[50]

Leon Litwack, in "Hellhounds," an essay named after a Robert Johnson blues song, wrote that on April 23, 1899, more than two thousand white people from Georgia "assembled near the town of Newman [Newnan] to

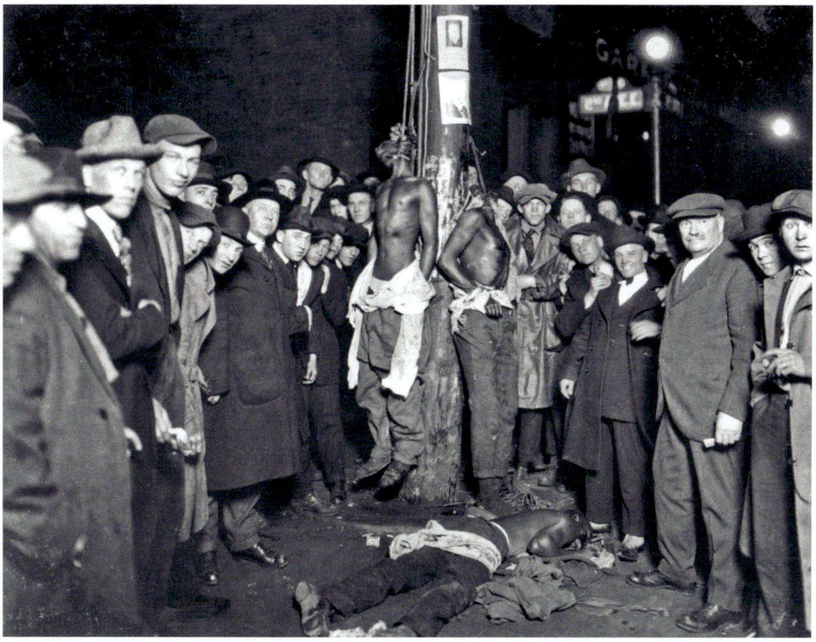

1.8 The lynching of nineteen-year-old Elias Clayton, nineteen-year-old Elmer Jackson, and twenty-year-old Isaac McGhie, Duluth, Minnesota, June 15, 1920. Racial violence was not located only in the South. From James Allen, *Without Sanctuary*, 88–89.

witness the execution of Sam Hose, a black Georgian. . . . The guilt of the victim had not been proven in a court of law. As in most lynchings, no member of the crowd wore a mask, nor did anyone attempt to conceal the names of the perpetrators; indeed, newspaper reporters noted the active participation of some of the region's most prominent citizens."[51]

The title and subject of Allen's book perfectly indicates the need for sanctuary of African Americans and suggests the potential for the formation of cultural codes understood by black folk and their use as an acknowledgment of a shared risk. Verbal play, metaphors, signifiers, semantic utterances, gestures, and coded references often conveyed meaning by "hitting a straight lick with a crooked stick." Masking, codes, signifyin', double entendre, and cultural bilingualism were among the ways folk hid in plain sight while resisting their dehumanization. As Paul Laurence Dunbar wrote in 1896:

We wear the mask that grins and lies,
It hides our cheeks and shades our eyes,
This debt we pay to human guile;
With torn and bleeding hearts we smile,
And mouth with myriad subtleties.[52]

Yvonne Chireau, writing about post-Emancipation black religious preference, indicates that many white people were surprised "that independence had brought such a powerful sense of religious autonomy to black people, as was evidenced by their hasty and conspicuous departure from most biracial southern churches. As they wrested control of their own places of worship or withdrew from racially segregated congregations, African Americans publicly acknowledged aspects of their spiritual lives that had been concealed within the confines of bondage."[53] At the time, black spiritual practices, hidden because of their suppression, were thought to be immoral and heathen.[54] The formerly enslaved Emily Dixon remembered, "On Sundays, us would git tergether in de woods an' have worship. Us could go to de white folks' church, but us wanted ter go whar us could sing all de way through, an' hum 'long, an' shout—yo' all know, jist turn loose lak."[55]

Other cultural dynamics were in process at the same time as black cultural re-formations were evolving in black homogeneous spaces. As Enwezor claims, "It is also about the remaking of African memories and reconciling them with the Euro-American experience of their new home in a way that gives form to an entirely new self-understanding, one neither purely African nor wholly European or American."[56] Enwezor argues that double consciousness "with its creolized juxtapositions" is the foe of ethnocentrism, that it, in part, "relates to how the black subject negotiated the cultural boundaries between Africa, Europe, and America."[57]

Robert Farris Thompson, writing about Jean-Michel Basquiat, says, "We recognize a major source of power: Self-creolization. This simply means being fluent in several languages and knowing how to fuse them to effect." He then asks, "Can you transform self and heritage into something new and named?"[58] Glissant suggests an answer: "In opposition to [the abyss of slavery] they propose the rhizome, an enmeshed root system, a network spreading either in the ground or in the air, with no predatory rootstock taking over permanently. The notion of the rhizome maintains, therefore, the idea of rootedness but challenges that of a totalitarian root."[59]

Perhaps this root system is the persistence of African and Africana culture. African American and African diaspora culture grew out of the social deracination of the Middle Passage during the slave trade. Glissant describes the process, writing that "their ordeal did not die; it quickened into this continuous/discontinuous thing: the panic of the new land, the haunting of the former land, finally the alliance with the imposed land, suffered and redeemed. The unconscious memory of the abyss served as the alluvium for these metamorphoses. The population that then formed, despite having forgotten the chasm, despite being unable to imagine the passion of those who foundered there, nonetheless wove this sail (a veil). They did not use it to return to the Former Land but rose up on this unexpected, dumbfounded land."[60]

Articulating this process in terms reflective of religious creation mythology, the generative power of breath, speech, and the word was instrumental in the reconfigured familial and cultural formations that now populate the Americas, including the Caribbean. Allegorically speaking, Africana cultures are born-again reformulations of antediluvian Middle Passage existence. Voiced expressivity (the moan) in effect represents the incantatory conjure of called-forth creations. The specifics of the slave context required that people of African descent express themselves fully in sanctuarial or safe spaces. Coded expression became necessary given the surveillance and control imposed by European and American slave cultures, but insider experiences in sanctuary settings, both secular and sacred, often affirmed new kinship bonds. Those experiences can be found through references, codes, signifiers, symbols, gestures, and all sorts of indicators in the music, language, performance practices, and visual expressivity of Africana cultures. This matrix of meaning and creative expression is the basis of an Africana aesthetic. So we continue to moan, hum, code, and mask.

> At the bottom of the Atlantic Ocean
> there's a railroad
> made of human bones
>
> Black ivory
> Black ivory
> Black ivory
>
> AMIRI BARAKA, performance of "Why's/Wise," Sanctuary for Independent Media, Troy, New York (2009)

CHAPTER 2

Etymologies and Black Love

> In fact, music provides an ideal site for exploration of the shifting terrain and process of black ethnicity.
>
> GUTHRIE RAMSEY JR., *RACE MUSIC* (2003)

> The black preacher does not simply speak . . . [but] often "sings" . . . as well. Within this tradition, the sung word is radically more powerful than the spoken word . . . [and] the metaphysical powers of sound . . . [characterize] the "tuning" preacher as one example of the empowerment concept.
>
> DWIGHT ANDREWS, "FROM BLACK TO BLUES" (1989)

People in the African diaspora have worked to maintain subtle, often coded references to those practices and patterns evocative of sanctuarial spaces. Music persisted throughout oppressive racialized experiences and operated, like rituals, as a great container and preserver of culture. Subtle and obvious references to musical performance can be found in visual art, particularly since Henry Ossawa Tanner's notable 1893 painting *The Banjo Lesson*.

A few years ago in Washington, DC, I spoke with Alfred Smith, the artist and professor who directed my MFA thesis at Howard University in the late 1970s. He talked about rhythm, its visualization in his own work, and how Romare Bearden structured the equivalent of musical "jump space" in his compositions. This is the way Charlie Parker created a rhythmic, percussive structure in his horn solos with a run of notes. Those notes, he explained, were creatively altered with a triplet in the space that contained a single quarter or eighth note. Then, adding another complexity, Parker might leave the center note in the triplet blank, creating a "jump" space where the negative space (or sonic absence) itself marked the time. In Bearden's work this meant the elimination of the transitional middle ground between the foreground and background in a composition creating a visual jump that was the equivalent of Parker's marking rhythm with both the presence and the absence of form. Smith also talked about visual time signatures with large, flat forms playing slower, like half or whole notes, while textured or patterned areas seemingly filled the same time with more notes.

Ruth Fine wrote that the visual structure of Bearden's work used the call-and-response aspects of jazz as well as having "call and recall" embedded "in his repetition of motifs, always with variation of one sort or another."[1] She also tells of how Bearden "often mentioned discussions with [Stuart] Davis about interval in the music of jazz pianist Earl 'Fatha' Hines. He also acknowledged Davis' advice to 'always remember about color that in a painting it has a position and a place, and it makes space . . . not as a separate entity but color also as form, as space, and not as decoration.'"[2]

The translation of the sonic and visual, a process of evocation and cultural signification, and aesthetic identification, was innovatively articulated by Robert Farris Thompson in his 1983 book, *Flash of the Spirit*. Thompson indicated that the "organizing principles" of African musical performance in song and dance mingled with New World and European elements to create what he calls a black Atlantic visual tradition.[3] Thompson finds organizing principles and gestural patterns in black religious and vernacular practices in the Atlantic world that have foundations in Old World African cultures.

Among the principles he identifies are the dominance of a percussive performance style, multiple meter (competing meters sounding all at once), overlapping call-and-response, an asymmetrical organization he calls "offbeat phrasing," and "songs and dances of social allusion" that are danceable and swinging but that "remorselessly [contrast] social imperfections against implied criteria for perfect living."[4] Thompson roots the black Atlantic visual tradition to a great extent in Yoruba, Kongo, Fon, Mande, and Ejagham art and philosophies.

James Phillips, an artist, friend, and colleague, complemented Smith's ideas and Thompson's principles with details of how his own work, full of complicated, colorful symbols and patterns on a flat picture plane, using seeming transparencies to simulate depth or space, acted as a musical synonym. Patterns filled every inch of Phillips's canvases (see figure 2.1) in the

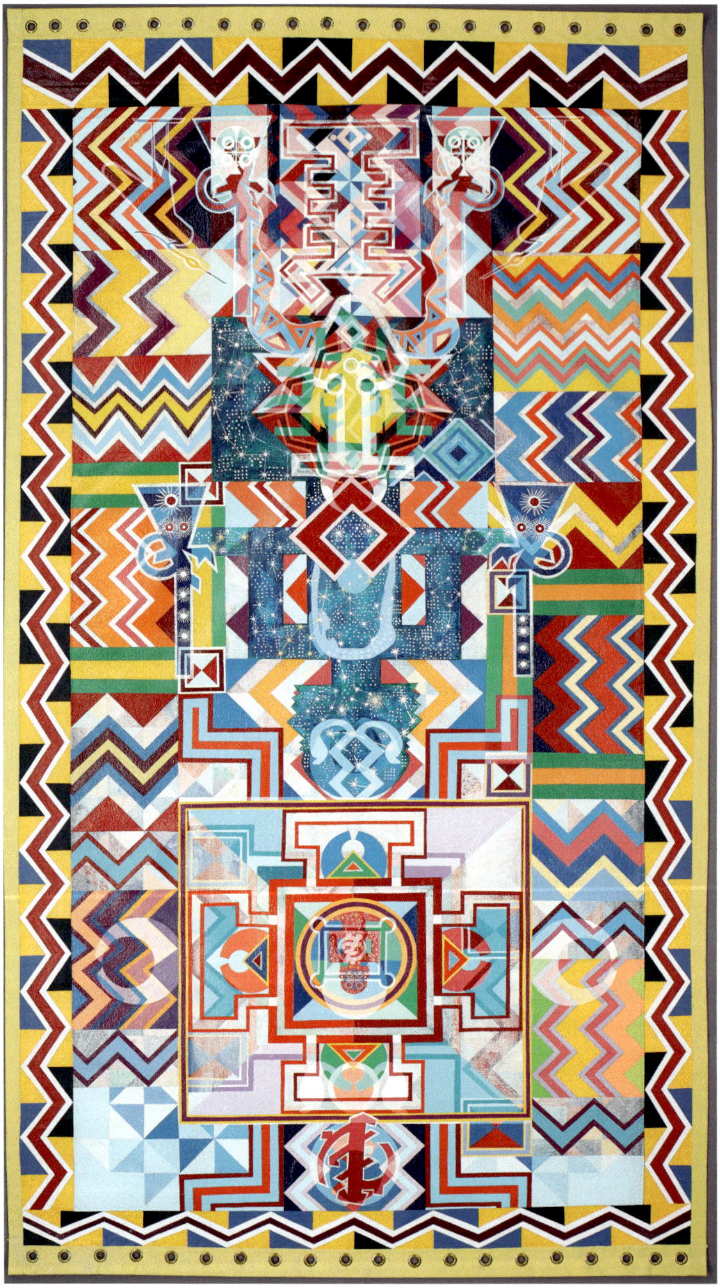

2.1 James Phillips, *Mojo*, 1987. Acrylic paint on canvas, 114 × 66 in. Dallas Museum of Art. Used by permission of James Phillips and Dallas Museum of Art.

way that John Coltrane filled the air with sheets of sound and in the way that his tonal and modal improvisation on chord structures harkens back to the muscular piano of McCoy Tyner with its overtones and waves of energetic sound. Phillips talked about how his work, despite the appearance of precision and geometry, used color and its relationships to create a sense of musical structure and free jazz improvisation in his imagery. Phillips's complicated use of meter and shifting, asymmetrical color relationships within the patterning evokes the tonal qualities of exploratory and free jazz expression in the work of Cecil Taylor, Coltrane, Eric Dolphy, Don Cherry, and others.

What appears to be symmetry in the structure of *Mojo* is, in fact, asymmetry as patterns on either side are moved upward or downward on the opposite side, and color (tonal) relationships change from right to left. Yet the patterns and colors are unified by a yellow ground appearing beneath the patterns and symbols. This is an example of Thompson's principles for black percussive musical style with "offbeat phrasing" and "multiple meter." The center strip of imagery contains a number of symbols such as a Janus-headed figure in the center reminiscent of an African sculptural form and, like the Kongo *nkisi* two-headed dog nail figure (figure 2.2), indicates an ability to see into two worlds. The title suggests the vernacular folk term *mojo*, which can be a charm and/or spirit energy, also called *gris-gris* in some contexts.

Thompson continuously writes about the term *mojo* having origins in the Kikongo term *ki-mooyo*, a concept of opening our eyes to hidden dimensions, expression that brings spirit and image together. It is the idiom of the soul.[5]

In 1956 Muddy Waters recorded the powerful and popular song "Got My Mojo Working":

> Got my mojo working but it just won't work on you
> Got my mojo working but it just won't work on you
> I want to love you so bad I don't know what to do
> Going down to Louisiana to get me a mojo hand
> Going down to Louisiana to get me a mojo hand
> I'm going to have all you women, getcha under my command
> Got my mojo working[6]

In *Mojo*, the metaphysical tenor of Phillips's work is set by the circular symbol at the very top of the central column, called *gye nyame*, an

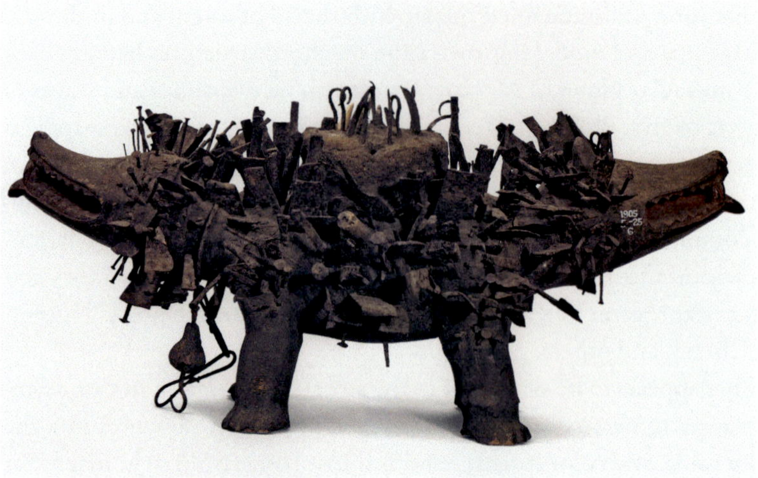

2.2 Kozo Kongo *nkisi* figure, late nineteenth or early twentieth century, Democratic Republic of the Congo. From Wyatt MacGaffey and Michael D. Harris, *Astonishment and Power*, 40. Originally published in R. Verneau, "Le fétichisme à travers les ages: Les grandes idoles à clous des Nègres du Loango," *La Nature: Revue des Sciences et de Leurs Applications aux Arts et à l'Industrie* 44, no. 2221 (April 22, 1916).

Adinkra symbol from Ghana meaning "fear none but God." It is repeated in yellow about two-thirds of the way down this column, just above a complex of Adinkra and Egyptian symbols and an improvisation on the Kongo cosmogram known as *tendwa nzá* (or *dikenga* cross) often cited by Thompson as charting the "four moments of the sun," or the cycle of life from birth to death to the spiritual underworld and implying a reincarnate return to life.[7]

The symbolic references in this work as well as the title open up levels and layers of meaning and reference for those who know and positively regard the world of vernacular spiritual practices as well as forming a kind of histogram of African American cultural heritage. The patterning in the top layer of the work suggests a three-dimensional graph of the cultural and historical complex contained within jazz hidden as abstraction and performative virtuosity.

Alfred Smith has great interest in rhythm, to the point of learning to play drums, and often creates imagery and sculptural forms expressing rhythmic concerns and interpretations in his visual structures. His 1994 work *Bembé Clavé* (figure 2.3) combines repetitive, rhythmic vertical ele-

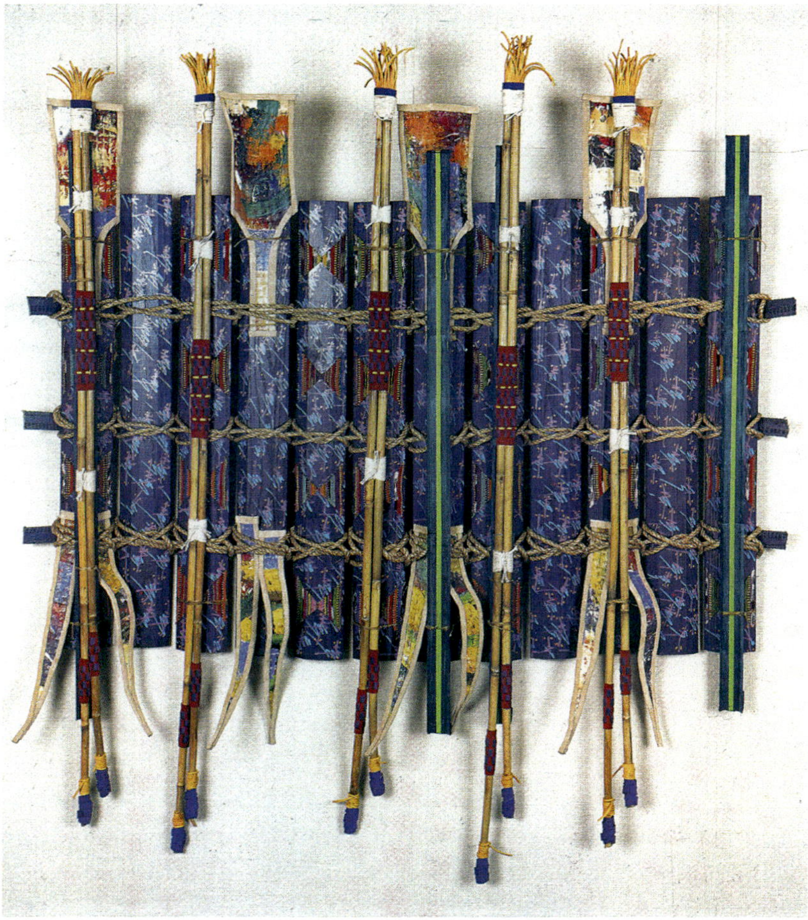

2.3 Alfred Smith, *Bembé Clavé*, 1994. Mixed canvas, bamboo, wood, leather, rope, and acrylic, approx. 48 × 48 × 3 in. Used by permission of the artist.

ments and bright colors, which create the kind of tonal/chordal implications found in Phillips's work, but Smith uses organic marks to suggest the gestures of percussive playing of drums and claves. The title refers to a West African drum and a Cuban percussive instrument. Horizontal lines of braided rope help organize the structure of the work into something implying a musical chart filled with notations of varied time signatures.

Smith's work emblematizes the notion that an object is, according to Thompson, "more than a musical instrument." Thompson writes of a Cuban "*palero* (a priest in the creolized Kongo religion of Cuba)" who was playing a rumba box (*mar'mbula* in Cuba, *marimba* in Haiti), an instrument emerging from the thumb piano, with "spiritually named keys: bird (*núni*), skull (*konzóngolo*), and earth (*nsí*)." Thompson wrote, "Touching the bird key feathered his music with allusion to heaven. This mixed with horizon aspects when the earth key was sounded. Hitting the skull key called on the ancestors."[8]

Smith's work insinuates these traditions, their creolized instruments, and the performative movements associated with playing them. Colorful calligraphic marks across the surface of Smith's work suggest gestural notation, as if he has mapped the movement of a player's hands striking surfaces in a performance with this "instrument." Smith began using these marks to indicate movements used during tai chi and transfigured them into musical gestures in his art.

Both Phillips and Smith listen intently to jazz music, study its history and form, and are very open about the importance of musical expression for full understanding of their work.[9] Thompson wrote that the musician in Cuba was "outwardly 'musicking,' [but] was inwardly tracing a line from God to the ancestors."[10] It is from these philosophical and aesthetic discussions and ideas that the seeds of this book were sown.

Musical references are prominent in this art because music has been so essential to African American culture in its articulation and as an expressive social lubricant. So much of what is/was collective and communal is contained within musical performance, whether in work songs, spirituals, gospel music, blues, jazz, rhythm and blues, and recently hip-hop and rap. Religion and spirituality, both Christian and African derived, have been an essential part of Africana culture, and at some point in the twentieth century, secular and sacred music frequently became interchangeable because they shared the same structure and emotional expressiveness. Singers Aretha Franklin and Patti LaBelle, as examples, for decades have had their gospel singing foundations as elements of their artistic bios.

Music

As she left the site of her enslavement in Maryland for a free existence in the North around 1844, Araminta Ross, the granddaughter of an African,

> wished very much to bid her companions farewell, but was afraid of being betrayed, if any one knew of her intentions; so she passed through the street singing—

> "Good bye, I'm going to leave you,
> Good bye, I'll meet you in the kingdom,"—
>
> and similar snatches of Methodist songs. As she passed on singing, she saw her master, Dr. Thompson, standing at this gate, and her native humor breaking out, she sung yet louder, bowing down to him—
>
> "Good bye, I'm going for to leave you."[11]

She is well known by the name Harriet Tubman as well as Moses. Her husband, a free colored man named John Tubman, married her in 1844, and she kept his surname after they parted ways. Like so many of her contemporaries, Tubman performed her identity in part through music. During slavery, folk often sang about their personal and collective misery, hopes, and aspirations and found many of their pleasures there. Often in songs and religious ecstasy, people found agency for their lives, transforming or transcending difficult circumstances—impossible circumstances—in the experience of enslavement. Music often functions for people today in the same way.

Guthrie Ramsey argues, "Cultural forms such as tales, stories, and music (especially the performative aspects of such) function as reservoirs in which cultural memories reside. These memories allow social identities to be knowable, teachable, and learnable."[12] Ramsey places this idea within a larger argument about the performance of ethnicity and the congruency of ethnic performance and musical performance. He argues that ethnic identity operates, or is "performed," in much the same way as musical practice.[13] In essence, blackness exists when it is performed in the world.

Musical and religious performances are great containers, transmitters, and preservers of culture. Culture is intended here to coincide with Lawrence Levine's argument that it is a process rather than a fixed condition. He says that culture's "toughness and resiliency are determined not by a culture's ability to withstand change, which indeed may be a sign of stagnation, not life, but by its ability to react creatively and responsively to the realities of a new situation."[14] What diasporic Africans contained and transmitted were for the most part, ways of doing things and ways of understanding and relating to the world, not static practices or material forms. James Snead argues that culture "as a reservoir of inexhaustible novelty is unthinkable." Therefore, every culture maintains "a sense of continuity about itself. . . . A basic self-identity must not be altered."[15] He contends cultures have methods of self-perpetuation even as they evolve.

One of the structures or processes used by Africana culture is repetition, often in the form of rhythm. Snead suggests that "periodic ceremonies are ways in which black culture comes to terms with its perception of repetition, precisely by highlighting that perception."[16] The rhythmic forms of music, and the repetition in rituals or social gatherings, the call-and-response repetitions of black music and black preaching, are methods or processes of perpetuating the culture. Repetition also is a rhetorical device and points to the importance of the voice in African and African diaspora cultures.

Many African cultures were primarily oral despite the presence of graphic communication systems like Ethiopian Geez and Amharic, West African Vai script, Ghanaian Adinkra, Nsibidi signs, and, of course, the ancient glyphs of Egyptian and Nubian writing systems. Oral cultures use repetition and rhythm as structural devices for memory, the construction of historical narratives, which commonly shift to improvise new information and interpretation within the larger structure of the narrative, and to emphasize points and organize the speech for the audience. One notable aspect of West African drumming is the talking drum's ability to approximate human speech—something that is very plausible when one considers the importance of tonality in defining words and meaning in the Yoruba language, as discussed in the previous chapter. The nexus of language and music is also found in the Americas.

What I am suggesting here is that Africana, or black, culture is an interesting mix of performative and oral cultural traditions and literary culture. Oral thought produces different rhythms and practices and a greater dependence on gestures than literary thought. Walter Ong writes that orally based thought "tends to be highly rhythmic, for rhythm aids recall, even physiologically."[17] Orality is a human-based rather than thought-based, existential activity and emphasizes communal and communicative relations. Repetition is tied to mnemonics, and mnemonic patterns in rhythmic verse, for example, allow for the retrieval of memory and thought, the preservation and recall of ideas and histories. In literal culture, this function is moved outside the mind through texts.

Africans, mainly from oral cultural traditions, for more than circumstantial and pragmatic reasons, were able to maintain cultural patterns and practices through oral stylizations, rhetorical cadences in preaching or performed folklore or repeated figures in music. We should consider the primacy of the voice, its centrality in the performance of blackness, and its approximation in art. This is consistent with T. J. Anderson's assertion, previously elaborated in my introduction, that all black music is based on black speech. Robert O'Meally says jazz "is the instruments talking to one another, now with intoxicating allure, now with prophesy."[18] Portia Maultsby tells us that "in Africa and throughout the diaspora, black musicians produce an array of unique sounds, many of which imitate those of nature, animals, spirits, and speech. . . . Black instrumentalists produce a wide range of vocally derived sounds—'hollers,' 'cries,' 'grunts,' 'screams,' 'moans,' and 'whines,' among others." She also suggests that "African retentions in African-American music are defined by the sharing of conceptual approaches to the music-making process" rather than the . . . instrumentation, or melodic structures of African music.[19]

During a conversation about photographer Ming Smith's work, Arthur Jafa and Greg Tate discussed what Tate called "the visual fields that Black people occupy in the world." Jafa mentioned how this was based in the structures of "Black phonic expressivity" and its affirmations of "certain kinds of things that Black people take for granted, in terms of them affirming what we consider beautiful."[20]

Jafa indicated that certain musicians, including Albert Ayler and Jimi Hendrix, performed "aspects of Black sonic beauty or taste, which would be considered, at best, on the margins of appreciation in other musical modalities. Vibrato. Undertone. Overtone. Things like this. It's on the edge of those things. In other words, it becomes like the space in which a Black person in the space of other values, or maybe dominant values, nevertheless will hold the line in foregrounding schemes in their work."[21]

African captives arrived in the Americas without most of their material culture, though some African instruments were carried on slave ships to encourage the captives to sing and dance for exercise during the long Atlantic voyage. However, the captives carried within them understandings and interpretations of the world and their roles in it, as well as, in many cases, a knowledge of tools and instruments that were useful. Their identity was performed far more than being dependent on material culture. The pervasive oppression of slavery and its racial nature kept Africans fundamentally separated from their white captors in ways that helped them retain African ethnicities, folkways, and certain cosmological beliefs and practices. As historian Michael Gomez shows, during the colonial period, this was true even for small black populations:

> The black New England community resonated with its own cuisine, dance, style of dress, songs, implements of industry, games, funeral

> rites, and medicinal practices, all based upon African models. . . . In these and other ways, black New Englanders successfully achieved a life-style that conformed to the basic contours of African cultural patterns.
>
> . . . The black population accounted for only 2 percent of the New England total at the beginning of the eighteenth century and reached only 3 percent by 1750.[22]

Cultural and psychological sanctuary often was manifested in actual performance spaces where music was shared, or within the circles of a ring shout or at a baptism by the riverside. Sculpture, masks, shrine paintings, and masquerade costuming were no longer a material aspect of African cultural expression in the Americas; therefore, oral, aural, and gestural forms did the cultural work. Visual expression in the antebellum period was found in ceramics, quilts, and other craftwork. However, as African American artists adopted European forms of drawing, painting, sculpting, and printmaking, eventually a uniquely African American idiom emerged in that realm as well.[23] The stream of visual art rooted in deep cultural reservoirs might be the equivalent of the blues in the sense that Dwight Andrews suggests as representing "a particular worldview—a way of looking at life and of understanding life" and that there is a "blues aesthetic."[24]

This is a stream of African American art concerned, like the blues, with a black story—with all the folk idioms, nuances, pathos, signifyin', singsong preaching, Vaselined legs, hot-combed hair, scat singing, stylish dancing, profiling, and front-porch-sitting familiarity found in performed black ethnicity. As Andrews points out, unlike the novel, prose, or the short story, "the blues form evolved unfettered by any aesthetic obligations outside of the African-American traditions and the community it was destined to reflect and serve."[25] Importantly, Andrews also points out that the "concept of self-empowerment, which is often overlooked, is the most significant of all the probable African adaptations/retentions in African-American music."[26]

Consider here William H. Johnson's 1941 painting *Jitterbugs (II)* (figure 2.4), one of a series of six panels evoking the Savoy Ballroom and other nightspots in New York's Harlem community. The work is organized around three large rectangles in the background; two vertical ones atop a horizontal one at the base. Their static geometry, accentuated by vertical lines and brushstrokes, is countered by the leaning angularity of the two dancers in the foreground and the musical instruments in the background.

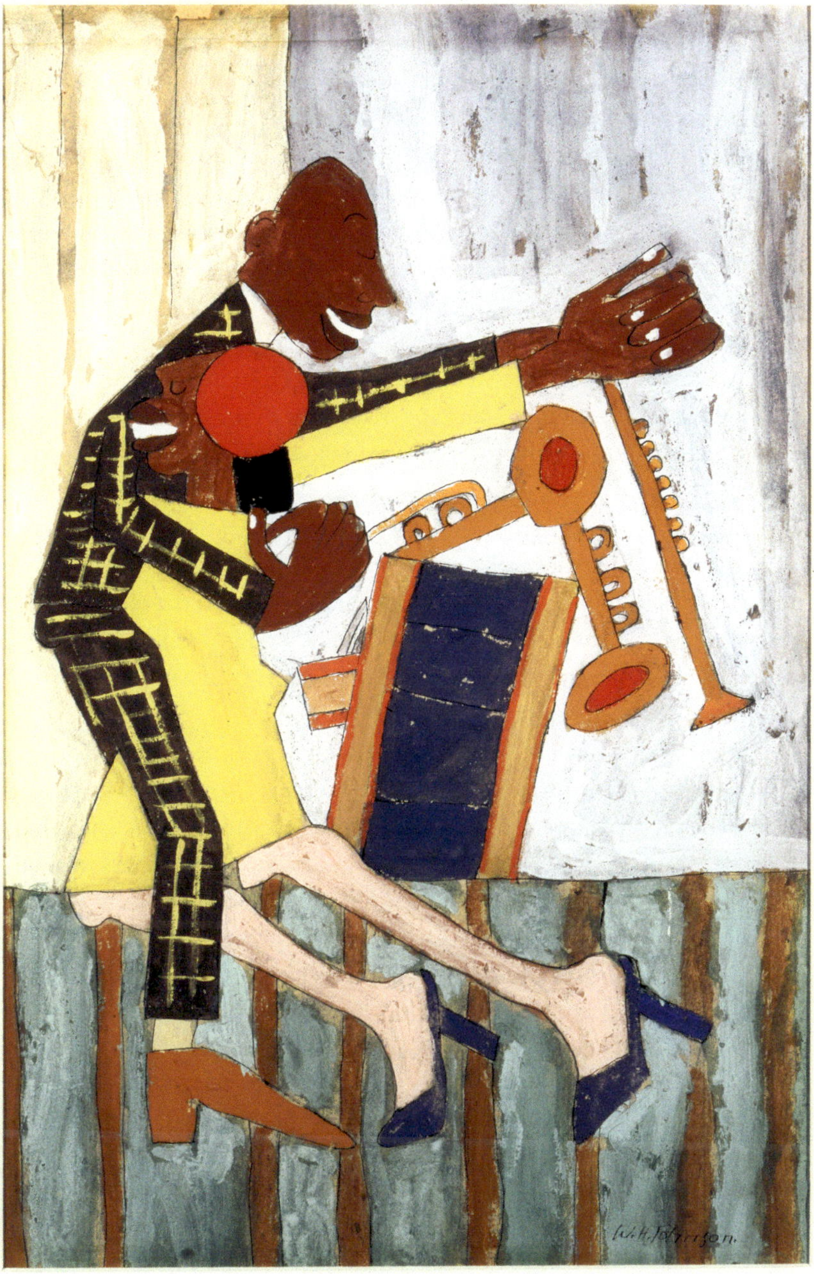

2.4 William H. Johnson, *Jitterbugs (II)*, 1941. Oil on paperboard, 24 × 15⅜ in. Smithsonian American Art Museum. Gift of Harmon Foundation. Photo: Smithsonian American Art Museum, Washington, DC/Art Resource, New York. Used by permission.

Johnson humorously nuanced the legs of the female to indicate the light sheen found when black women wore stockings lighter than their skin tones, something fairly common in the 1940s and 1950s before manufacturers began acknowledging the richly varied hues of black women.

This small painting on paper, according to Richard Powell, "records a broad, choreographed dip by a female Jitterbug while her male partner dramatically supports her." The work indicates that Johnson "fully understood that the hyperkinetic dances and fashion extremes of contemporary black culture were appropriate inspirations for a modern African-American art."[27] The woman seemingly has been dancing separately from the male, connected only by her right and his left hand, and he has spun her into his arms in a stylish lean captured by the artist. The jitterbug, as is implicit in its name, was not a cheek-to-cheek dance, but one of energetic, athletic, rhythmic movements.

There is no transitional middle ground or implication of perspective space in the work. Structurally we are looking at stabilizing backbeats or rhythms beneath quick, swinging solos. The dancers and the band and the music are one and the same. The painting is not a dancehall narrative but rather a symbolic abstraction not unlike the patterned musical abstraction with embedded codes of James Phillips.

The modernist execution of the painting placed it within the contemporary stream of the period and conveys the expressive aspirations of the artist as a painter exposed to European avant-garde artistic ideas of the 1930s, but the subject matter emerges from Johnson's visit to Harlem nightspots during a return to the United States in the late 1930s. He has not articulated the Cotton Club, where black performers entertained a white audience they could not join, but he gives a glimpse into a gathering spot like the Savoy Ballroom. The stockings of the woman are a nuanced reference that many white people would miss by being outside of that experience.

Roy DeCarava's dark photograph *Dancers* (figure 2.5), from 1956, captures the creative, athletic movement of two male dancers in motion at a social club on 110th Street and Fifth Avenue. In the large, dimly lit ballroom we see only the dancers' silhouettes, their bodies composed of sharp, energetic angles. The photograph was taken during intermission, and the men became the entertainment, dancing to jazz music. The creativity, fluidity, and rhythmic excellence of dancers resonate with viewers familiar with such social settings. DeCarava captures the mood and emotion of the setting as he freezes a moment during a dancehall narrative.

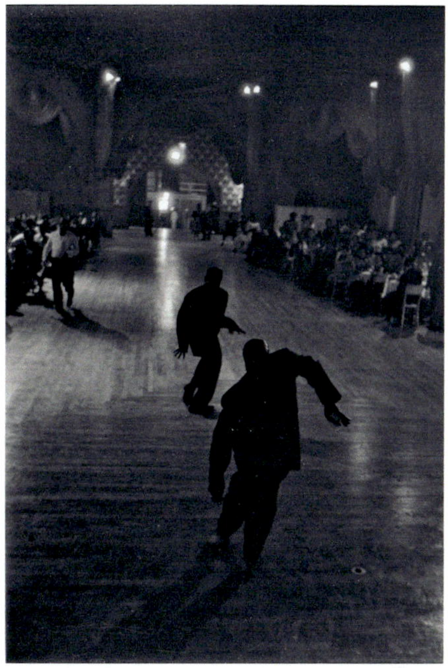

2.5 Roy DeCarava, *Dancers, New York*, 1956. Gelatin silver print, 13⅙ × 8¾ in. (image); 13¹⁵⁄₁₆ × 10¹⁵⁄₁₆ in. (paper). Art Institute of Chicago. In DeCarava's photograph of two men dancing in a large, dimly lit ballroom we see only the dancers' silhouettes. The work is distinctive for showing how artists of the time developed a unique style to suit certain "underlit" spaces (Arthur Jafa's term) that black people have claimed as cultural sanctuaries.

DeCarava's specialty with the dark half of the gray scale in photography makes his work especially adept at capturing a sense of night play in clubs and dance halls, or the virtuosic intensity of jazz players like John Coltrane. Jafa and Tate, building on the ideas mentioned above suggesting modalities on the edges of mainstream expression, talk about photographers who use darkness and obscure faces to indicate those edge spaces and as a means of countering the ever-present threat of surveillance. Jafa says that black people often occupy spaces that are underlit. "Because they are underlit, and because they are secret spaces and things like this, they require technical approaches to be aligned with those spaces." He is discussing sanctuarial spaces. He indicates that photographers like Ming Smith and Roy DeCarava counter mainstream photography methods and enter the underlit spaces black people have claimed and tune their techniques to those spaces:

> You see a lot of consequences of this commitment to going into the spaces Black people occupy, or are forced to occupy, or left to occupy. For example, we know one of the more egregious aspects of the very mechanism itself, photography, is surveillance. Right? . . . There's

> always a danger that the photograph can be used as evidence against you in some fashion. But as soon as you say, "I'm going to go into the spaces in which Black people feel comfortable that they're not being surveilled"—meaning dark spaces, underground spaces, spaces in the woods—the photographer is now introducing into that space the instrument par excellence of surveillance.[28]

Visually, what we see in *Dancers* is a dark space and faces that cannot be identified. "What you're left with are things like the line of a person's body, a person's postural semantics, things like that, which cannot be used as evidence."[29]

In *Coltrane on Soprano* (figure 2.6), Coltrane, in the midst of a frenetic solo, emerges from a dark background as if he is a primeval force emerging from the abyss. His face, barely identifiable with an eyes-closed grimace, seems to be forcing the energy of some visceral emotion through the soprano sax in motion on his fingertips. There is a vibrato quality to this image that relates to one of the sonic modalities Jafa indicated above, and suggests the idea of motion, which is a commonly found aspect of African artistic expression, with masquerades and objects that are not static but have agency because of their motion.[30]

Those of us who enjoy Coltrane's solos, and shout at virtuosic, energetic horn solos at jazz concerts, can see this image as an evocative trope of those experiences shared in commune with fellow travelers on artistic nights. DeCarava has preserved one of those moments when the soloist seemingly begins creative levitation, rising onto his toes, or onto one foot, lifted by the emotional heat streaming and screaming in a gravity-defying improvisational fire. In these cases, a full description is not possible or necessary; only an evocative reference and acknowledging assents link us, through call-and-response, as cultural conspirators.

So many conversations and memories pivot on musical settings and performances. Many friends and acquaintances from Cleveland, Ohio, still talk about the weekend battle between the local O'Jays and Detroit's Temptations (of Motown) at the nightspot Leo's Casino in the mid- to late 1960s. The O'Jays, led by Eddie Levert just before they rose to national attention on the strength of the "Back Stabbers" single, performed at a level of intensity and excellence that caught the Temptations by surprise and forced them to elevate their own performance.[31] Word spread through the neighborhoods after the first show Thursday night, and by Friday it was the talk of the town. Forty-plus years later, those who were fortunate

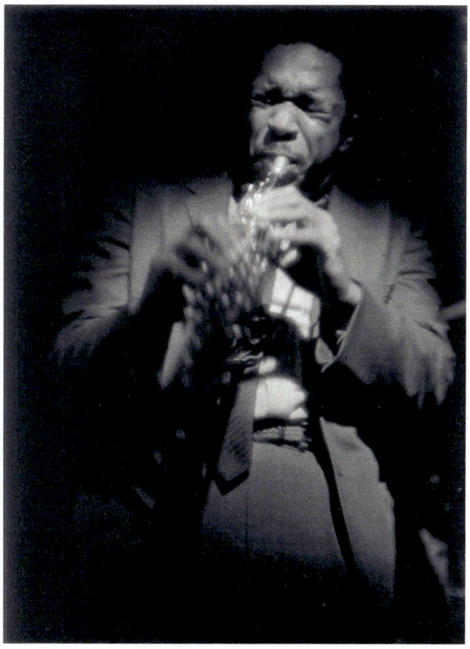

2.6 Roy DeCarava, *Coltrane on Soprano*, 1963. Gelatin silver print, 13⅛ × 9¾ in. (image); 14 × 11 in. (sheet). In this photograph there is high contrast between jazz musician John Coltrane's illuminated face and instrument and the dark backdrop. The blurriness of the image suggests movement and agency, which in African American art often emerge from within enclosed and secret spaces and are commonly associated with masquerades in African art.

enough to attend one of the shows that weekend need only a verbal nudge to share the understanding and a taste of the emotion again. It is in this way that many African American artists give a visual nudge to viewers to evoke a deep cultural experience shared in black cultural and emotional sanctuaries, those spaces and places where identity and self-empowerment form and are shared.

Sanctuary

> A secret place filled with mirrors. . . .
>
> JON LOCKARD, VISUAL ARTIST, IN CONVERSATION WITH THE AUTHOR (JULY 17, 2012)

A sanctuary is a place of refuge or safety. It also is a holy place, the inmost recess or holiest part of a temple or church. Immersed in a racist, oppressive society that routinely defeated, denigrated, and violated them, African Americans often sought refuge—sanctuary from these conditions and the people who created and maintained them. Black people retreated to their own communities and cultural patterns and practices and gathering places where people came together and creatively expressed themselves. During slavery, these places and occasions might be religious services in the woods or musical gatherings. In the twentieth century, many folk gathered and got "real" in churches and dance halls, which might have taken the forms of roadhouses, nightclubs, house parties, backyards, and the like.

These were places to find, exchange, modify, and enhance African and, eventually, African American identity and culture. Additionally, there was an underground social space where one could find and express African cosmological ideas through Vodou, Hoodoo, charms, gris-gris, mojos, roots, ecstatic religious worship, and the myriad ways people attempted to affect those unseen forces they believed could impact their lives. African transformative or trickster personas such as Papa Legba, Br'er Rabbit, Aunt Nancy, Dr. Buzzard, Baron Samedi, and others populated this spiritual underground along with, in some places in the diaspora, African deities (often called *orisha* or *loa*) such as Shango (Xango), Oshun (Oshum), Ogun (Ogum), Yemanja, Eshu Elegba, Oshoosi, and Osanyin. In some cases in the Caribbean, Brazil, and New Orleans, people came home from Catholic masses and attended to shrines dedicated to their underground saints.

Within these physical and psychological spaces, fundamental survival processes took place: acts of personal and corporate or communal transformation, or conjuring. Jim Perkinson theorizes that a form of shamanic struggle occurs when "techniques of ecstasy are solicited to force affliction to yield healing and vitality," transforming the experience of "being made black in America."[32] He theorizes that the violence of slavery, in the sense of classical shamanistic form, "dismembered and recomposed the slave body in everyday practice." He also implies that the Middle Passage in some ways mimicked the creation story with a sense of the African's "initial fall away from wholeness and into pain." From this dismemberment of the black social body, and its accompanying psychological fissure, articulated by W. E. B. Du Bois as "double consciousness," we find in religious and musical practices a sort of collective conjure and re-creation. There is a "mythic epiphany made palpable, given voice, full of scent and sound."[33] The black experience, configured by slavery, is congruent with shamanic models of death and dismemberment, travel to the underworld, an ecstatic journey, transfiguration and transcendence, and return. The shaman, or in the social sense, the shamanic experience, learns or teaches the ecstatic technique for the dramatic epiphany, rebirth, and transcendent reconfigured identity. Perhaps this process in some way explains the important presence of figures such as Eshu and other mediators between realms in African/black folklore.

With Du Boisian double consciousness, Perkinson successfully argues that Du Bois is consistent with an implicit Hegelian theme of recognition by another as the curse, and the spiritual insight—"second sight"—as its transformational gift. The white slave master's view of the enslaved was as a physical body under the enslaver's control. The blackness of that body was a sign of internal depravity to be rehabilitated through domination and control.[34] Therefore, the experience of enslavement was a form of death and dismemberment. "Double consciousness as a positive critical awareness emerges only when the slave can say emphatically 'I am my own body.' Only when the victim refuses any longer to see the body in a detached fashion does the oppressive dichotomy between body and mind . . . begin to be overcome."[35]

In the black experience, the body and mind are cleaved, and the mind splits into two consciousnesses with the preeminent awareness of the demeaning external view. Creative and religious expression were survival forms providing a view of the world beyond the transformation and rebirth, and a view of the black body as something other than its symbolism in the white imagination. Perkinson suggests that black music offers "transcendent glimpses of a world far different than the one defined by segregation" and that there is a "form of incipient and anonymous shamanism at work in the very core of black musical creativity." He refers to black British social critic Paul Gilroy to make a complicated case for the role of music as an agent in cultural and psychological transformation. "Blues, jazz, gospel, reggae, soul, funk, and hip-hop are all interrogated in form and function [by Gilroy] as complex re-creations of communal identities under the duress of modern structures of oppression that *transfigure violence into beauty*."[36]

There was significant agency to be found through this transformation enabling survival in a toxic environment, and the shamanic, transformative aspects of music were not significantly different from those of religious expression and belief. Consistent with notions of dismemberment and reunification, the sanctuaries and what took place there functioned not only to preserve the culture but also to heal and psychically protect the individual.[37] Guthrie Ramsey discusses "the cultural work performed by music in the processes of African-American identity making." He suggests black music's social ubiquity: "As I recall, a variety of music—jump blues, rhythm and blues, soul, and jazz—accompanied virtually every family gathering. Soul food and, most important, dance were central to these events and charged each with an air of communal celebration in which everyone—the young and the not-so-young—eagerly participated."[38]

Sanctuary secured space for black ecstasy, an emotional expressiveness coded in the improvisation of gospel music, dancing emotional utterances as one was filled with the spirit, the sensuous hip rolls in slow dances, and octave jumps in saxophone solos; orgasms in another mode. Sanctuary was a space and a process for healing the fissures in the black consciousness. The interior black life lived there was patterned and performed and was a vernacular reservoir for African American artists seeking to touch cultural relevance in their work.

Beginning, perhaps, with Henry Ossawa Tanner's iconic 1893 painting *The Banjo Lesson* (discussed in chapter 3), African American art became recognizable and distinct from mainstream American and international art. This does not mean that all artists of African descent have undertaken an approach that made their art visibly African American. Many artists, including Tanner's predecessors and contemporaries such as Robert Duncanson, Edmonia Lewis, and Edward Bannister, addressed similar themes and used similar techniques as did their mainstream contemporaries, preferring to emphasize their individuality apart from their racial or cultural identity. However, there is a stream of work within the body of art by African American artists that can be identified by the use of references to cultural and religious performance. Initially the work used subject matter from the sanctuaries of black life, those places where the black interior could emerge, where we could be, as Langston Hughes famously suggested, "free within ourselves."[39]

The complex social layering and nuanced understandings necessary to decipher the abstracted references that evoked the visceral performative practices of black life are found in artist Murry DePillars's description of his youth in Chicago. DePillars spoke of seeing musicians work and practice their craft, some even practicing outdoors in the summer (sans inside air-conditioning). People spoke with them routinely and would never ask for an autograph from even the most well-known musicians. "Space on the stage is public space. Space on the street is private space," he said. And everyone recognized the difference.[40] The musicians lived in, performed in front of, and remained a part of the larger community. And that community itself formed a sanctuary.

Cultures adapt and change, so while the patterns, structures, and orality of thinking in African American culture in many ways remained

African, the subjects of songs and folk tales became increasingly American. Specific African ethnicities were preserved in the Americas, but they began to give way to a new formation called *Negro* or *black*.[41] Their shared experiences in the Americas melded African ethnicities together to some degree, and their common folkways merged. Music and religion reflected and articulated these changes. Langston Hughes wrote that the black community furnished "a wealth of colorful, distinctive material for any artist because they still hold their own individuality in the face of American standardization. . . . And they accept what beauty is their own without question."[42] Visual art relevant to these people often referenced their music, folkways, and religious practices. Often it spoke to them and for them and with them. And it loved them.

CHAPTER 3

From *The Banjo Lesson* to *The Piano Lesson*

Reclaiming the Song

> What he wanted was your song. He wanted to have that song be his. He thought by catching you he could learn that song.
>
> AUGUST WILSON, *JOE TURNER'S COME AND GONE* (1988)

> It was always the music that explained things.
>
> SIDNEY BECHET, *TREAT IT GENTLE* (1960)

Amiri Baraka in his classic text *Blues People* suggests that "if the Negro represents, or is symbolic of, something in and about the nature of American culture, this certainly should be revealed by his characteristic music."[1] Baraka cites the blues as "one beginning of American Negroes," a point when we stopped being captives and began to be a new entity in this culture with concerns and referents addressing this experience.[2] The music was a part of a new language, an American language for speaking to or about American stories. Yet the function of the music as a carrier and articulator of culture persisted from earlier incarnations.

In his play *Joe Turner's Come and Gone*, August Wilson shows that the music that black people used to define themselves, paradoxically, placed them in jeopardy.[3] A white character in the play (set in 1911), Joe Turner, tried to kidnap black people into slavery to possess their song. In *The Piano Lesson*, a play set in 1936, a white man, always offstage, is still trying to capture their song "by buying the instruments that produce it—there are several references in the play to a mysterious white man who is 'going around to all the colored people's houses looking to buy up musical instruments.'

The process of trying to rob the black man of the source of his identity—and his power—continues."[4]

The banjo functioned as a sign in nineteenth-century American culture for things black. The name of the instrument came from an African designation variously named in the Caribbean as *banza* (Martinique), *bangil* (Barbados), *banshaw* (St. Kitts), or *bonja* (Jamaica) and found as *bangio* in South Carolina and *banjou* in Philadelphia as early as 1749.[5] The name most likely was derived from the Kimbundu *mbanza*: a plucked string instrument.

Because the instrument originally was made with a gourd and was African in origin, it became a trope for black performance during the antebellum period. Black people (or white people in blackface) playing the banjo in minstrel performance, and in visual representation, came to signify stereotypical black plantation performance for many white people. Black performance was characterized as intuitive and natural, so imagery depicting a black musician, and especially a banjo player, reinforced notions of a happy slave performing his ethnicity. The banjo-playing black—comic, intuitive, happy with circumstances—was a staple of the minstrel show in the United States from the 1840s to the Civil War. After Emancipation many people, both black and white, sought to integrate freedpeople into society through education. Education became a liberation strategy. When Henry Ossawa Tanner became one of the first African American artists to engage banjo imagery, he used pedagogy to undermine the trope. His simple image *The Banjo Lesson* (1893) was counterhegemonic and joined a liberation discourse already decades old, and he reclaimed the stolen song that had been misused and distorted for so long.

When Romare Bearden created *The Piano Lesson* nine decades later, he was reprising the pedagogy as a strategy and cultural continuity. By 1983, when Bearden completed *The Piano Lesson*, African Americans were no longer a generation removed from slavery. Many felt deeply American, having spent generations sweating and bleeding and singing their songs in this society. The banjo had been reclaimed, and black musicianship redefined, so a piano, an instrument more associated with parlors and middle-class aspirations, replaced the folk instrument long associated with the plantation and minstrelsy. An urban jazz history begins, perhaps, with the "professors" of New Orleans's Storyville at the beginning of the twentieth century. Their ranks, replete with pianists like Fats Waller, band leaders such as Duke Ellington and Count Basie, and the virtuosos of the 1950s and 1960s, Thelonious Monk, McCoy Tyner, Bud Powell, Art

Tatum, and so many others, were deeply endowed with notions of black music and cultural expression. The fierce musicianship and artistic complexity of post–World War II jazz music undermined old notions of intuitive or natural musical ability in black people, and Bearden's important work suggested a new set of assumptions and instruments for the song, the cultural patrimony, so long contested.

Tanner's painting, in my mind, was one of the first by an African American artist to depict a genre scene that represents our point of view. The agenda of the work is dependent on racial characterizations, but it gives a glimpse into the black interior as conceived by Elizabeth Alexander.[6] It shifts the perspective from the external observer to that of the subject. We begin with a bit of historical context.

Eastman Johnson's *Negro Life at the South*

The banjo was certainly not the only instrument fraught with racial considerations in nineteenth-century American visual culture, but the instrument's African origins probably added a point of emphasis, an element of authenticity, to any given picture. Eighteenth- and nineteenth-century farms and plantations were isolated places, and entertainments were welcome events. Roger Abrahams writes in *Singing the Master* that enslaved people provided evening amusements. Tasks often were set for them behind the Big House, "and there the playing broke out as well, the singing and the ring-play dancing that were later to be elaborated into the 'plantation scenes' of the American stage," or minstrelsy.[7] Abrahams suggests white people lived in close proximity with black people and "so far from other whites" that "the planter families came to rely on slave singing and dancing displays regularly for their entertainments."[8] Black performance was entertaining, exotic, and provided another, albeit somewhat symbolic, type of black labor for white benefit, and it offered the added benefit of confirming in the planter's mind the happiness of the slaves. "Singing and dancing were regarded as signs of happiness, in spite of the fact that many whites could understand that the songs were often about the agonies of separation and alienation. . . . For the working seemed to go better when it was accompanied by singing, and the play that broke out provided the planters with home entertainments."[9]

Abrahams argues performance was an aspect of black style. Certain kinds of team labor, especially when tools and movements were in unison, created regular sounds that could be incorporated into the music. Sacred and secular music were not rigidly separated. Songs sung while working often were spirituals. Patting Juba became a signature of black performance style, "for, through clapping hands, patting legs, arms, and armpits, snapping fingers, and other such rhythmic effects and countereffects, an individual could use his or her whole body to create multiple rhythms simultaneously," and "those not actually playing banjo or fiddle were considered 'accompanists' who patted with their hands and kept accurate time with the music."[10]

White fascination with this style and its exotic, even mysterious aspects undoubtedly became foundational for minstrel performance. Black performance might be captured and controlled through imitation and translation. W. T. Lhamon complicates this notion with the interesting argument that blackness itself was a signifier in minstrelsy for the mark of Cain. Cain was the first angry young man who took action against "preferential differentiation." As an outsider bearing a mark of discreditation, he came to be linked to black performers but also became the signified of blackface signification that allowed white people metaphorical identification with minstrels.[11] The black figure became a metaphor for the outsider, a means for working-class white people to resist the downtown Knickerbockers and stiff necks. The black face became a symbol of resistance to the power structure because blackness was emblematic of exclusion.[12] Black people became signs in a discourse that, at first, critiqued certain class tensions through minstrel mockery, but as minstrelsy developed, it became a space for racial and antislavery arguments rather than a means for the unwashed masses to ridicule the bluenoses.

In addition, white people found liberation behind the minstrel mask because, just as Mardi Gras in New Orleans, or Carnival in the Caribbean and Brazil, allows people to mask and enact normally unacceptable behaviors, masking in blackface allowed poor white people to escape their dreary lives and to say and do things they normally could not. By stealing the song, they freed themselves, while giving voice to their social conditions. However, this theft muted the black voice.

Similarly, in the twentieth century with the blues, Daniel Lieberfeld suggests that blues (read: black) culture "offers an antidote to toxic emotional repression." Within a bounded space like the minstrel stage or a blues bar, white people can "transgress safely, loosening the dominant culture's constraints like an overtight necktie, and adapt a peripheral culture's imagined exoticism to their own emotional needs."[13] The excursion into primitive culture liberates white people while reinforcing the subaltern role for black people as perennial underdogs. As Lieberfeld suggests, whether "in an oppressor or emancipator role, however, white people remain the subjects, and black people the objects, of their fantasies."[14]

The raging debate over slavery in the nation, something that seemed to rise in temperature and sharpen in tone after the publication of David Walker's radical *Appeal to the Colored Citizens of the World* (1829–30), kept black people in the public discourse and on the nation's mind.[15] From this environment minstrelsy emerged; images of black people playing banjos and amusing white people began to spread.

Imagery in the nineteenth century was commonly read with an awareness of complicated subtlety and visual tropes. Patricia Hills writes that Eastman Johnson's 1860 painting *Negro Boy* "would have probably appealed to the other Academicians, since he plays a flute, an instrument of artistic expression."[16] Johnson's notable painting *Negro Life at the South* (figure 3.1) not only established his career but also subtly began to undermine the banjo-playing stereotype of black people with nuances that became fully developed in Henry Ossawa Tanner's important painting *The Banjo Lesson* just over thirty years later.

Negro Life, according to Hills, is notable because of the range of skin tones it shows in the African American subjects, "which coded the reality of slave and free-black life." Also, there is a mixed-race couple courting on the left who "make explicit to a white audience the reality of love between African-American men and women," something that was "dimly recognized, if at all, by the majority of the white middle classes, conditioned by years of blackface, minstrel-show stereotypes."[17]

Importantly, the banjo-playing man near the center of the scene is closely watched by a boy on his right and another youth sitting in front of him. The musician is not playing to entertain anyone, and the only white audience is the woman entering the yard on the far right, who turns to gaze at him (capturing the song?). The man is playing a banjo, not a violin or flute, giving credibility to the sense that this scene provides the viewer, like the white woman, a chance to observe the interior life of enslaved people inside the yard behind the house, and inside their personal lives when they are supposedly no longer wearing the behavioral masks worn for the master and mistress.

Negro Life was, in fact, a commentary relative to the debate about slavery in Washington, DC, in the 1850s. John Davis writes that the painting depicts "some of the black inhabitants of [Johnson's] father's block on

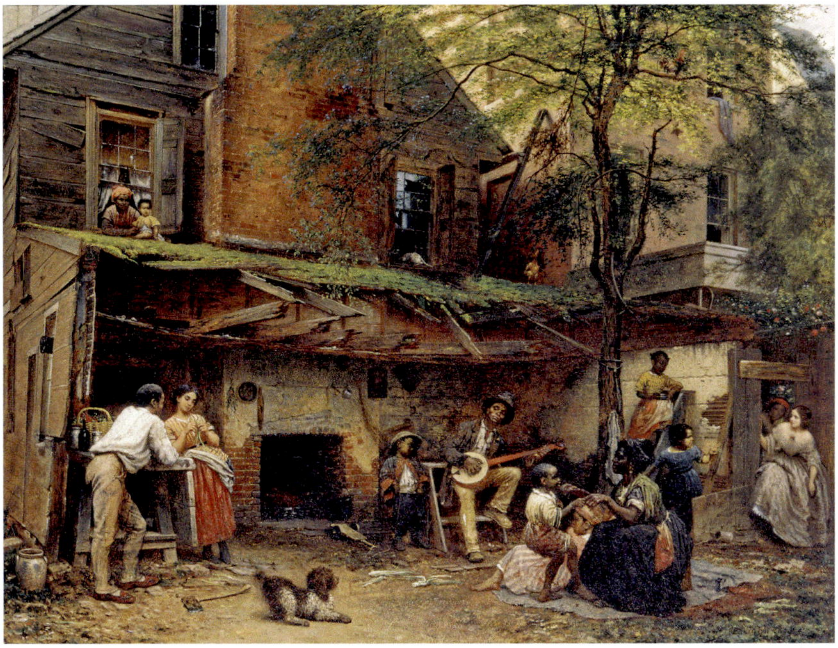

3.1 Eastman Johnson, *Negro Life at the South*, 1859. Oil on linen, 36 × 45¼ in. New-York Historical Society, Robert L. Stuart Collection, S-225.

F Street [in Washington]." The work joined a controversial discourse about slavery in the district that had gone on for nearly thirty years. Some people felt slavery in the nation's capital was an embarrassment and should be abolished, but some Southerners felt that the abolition of slavery in the district represented a dangerous "entering wedge" and that giving way on the issue would mean the loss of their cause in the end. The issue was further inflamed by a practice in the city of Washington of capturing free black people and selling them into bondage in the South. Enslaved people were held in areas hidden from view in interior alley spaces, and their cries and moans were muffled. Johnson's painting depicts one of these spaces.[18] In 2014 this practice—and Washington's holding spaces for black people being sent South back to, or into, slavery—were given visibility in popular culture in the film, *12 Years a Slave*. The film is based on the 1853 memoir of Solomon Northup, who documented his experiences as a free person kidnapped and sold into slavery.

The banjo player in Johnson's painting twisted and complicated the existing stereotype, but the image functioned as a trope so easily for viewers of the day that many missed the nuance and the antislavery critique and assumed the work to have been a plantation view in the South. It functioned as such for many white people, and the scene evoked stereotypical notions of black people despite Johnson's enlightened sensibilities.

As Judith Wilson writes, white artists, "whether they meant well or ill . . . generally pictured Blacks patronizingly," and their works "seldom threatened racist beliefs in the innate inferiority of people of African descent."[19] The works often observed more than understood black people and culture, and many saw them as Negroes more than as individuals, a fact confirmed by the title of Johnson's painting. It is only at the end of the century that an African American artist, Henry Ossawa Tanner, is able to challenge this orthodoxy.

The Banjo Lesson: From Stereotype to Pedagogy

Thirty-four years after Johnson's painting was first exhibited, Henry Ossawa Tanner returned to the United States from Paris to recover from typhoid fever and to renew his funds. He attended the Chicago Conference on Africa, which opened August 14, 1893, and lasted a week. Tanner's father, Bishop Benjamin Tanner, was very prominent in the African Methodist Episcopal (AME) Church and was a participant in the conference. The AME church had a reputation of promoting black pride, self-help, and self-determination. The church also worked to develop ties between people of African descent internationally. Judith Wilson suggests Benjamin Tanner's "views on racial matters, then, exhibit a tension between assimilationist and Black nationalist ideals that was prevalent in his denomination."[20] Bishop Tanner gave his son the middle name Ossawa, a shortened version of Ossawatomie, the name of the town in Kansas where John Brown in 1856 killed proslavery vigilantes who were attacking antislavery homesteaders. Henry's participation in the conference (he gave a talk titled "The Negro in American Art") came through his father.

During the summer of 1893, Henry Ossawa Tanner painted *The Banjo Lesson* (figure 3.2). It was first exhibited at a Philadelphia gallery in October 1893. The painting develops and improvises on a theme found in the work of Thomas Eakins, Tanner's teacher at the Pennsylvania Academy of Fine Arts, whose 1878 work *Negro Boy Dancing* (figure 3.3) depicts an elder supervising a young man playing the banjo for a boy apparently learning to dance. The pedagogical aspects only hinted at in *Negro Life at the South* become more explicit in this work with the elder man's supervisory posture, and intergenerational familial relations are suggested by a framed photograph of Abraham Lincoln and his son Tad in the upper left corner of the painting. The image implies black agency because of the absence of any white figures, and the teaching aspects of the work began to fray widely held assumptions about the "natural" performative and musical abilities of African Americans.

In *The Banjo Lesson*, Tanner performs the delicate task of reclaiming the banjo from its sad work as a sign of demeaned blackness and restores it as a cultural icon. This is the power and significance of the song and the tragedy of its theft. *The Banjo Lesson* (and the related *The Thankful Poor* from the same period) expands on the pedagogical elements of the Johnson and Eakins paintings and works within an African American context of education as liberation. Eastman Johnson's painting, despite its sympathies, succumbed to what Wilson describes as white artists' tendency "to depict Blacks as . . . anonymous figures in group scenes."[21] They seemed to imagine African Americans, whether free or enslaved, as "a nation of servants, musicians and rural laborers."[22] Tanner's work individualizes the two subjects, undermines prevailing stereotypes about the nature of black performance, and ties in to the discourse about education playing "a central role in shaping Black selfhood."[23] The intimacy of the interaction between the grandfather and the young boy humanizes them and offers an emotional and intellectual life not present in *Negro Life* or *Negro Boy*.

Tanner's important painting begins what Daphne Brooks, discussing stage performers, describes as a nineteenth-century counterintuitive articulation and redeployment of "the discourse of socio-political alienation. Wedding social estrangement with aesthetic experimentalism and political marginalization with cultural innovation, these resourceful cultural workers envisioned a way to transform the uncertainties of (black) self-knowledge directly into literal and figurative acts of self-affirmation."[24]

Tanner created a work that was counterhegemonic in its destabilization of stereotypical imagery, its challenge to the banjo trope, and the humanization of folk commonly dehumanized into "negroes" or types. Tanner countered notions about the natural musicianship of African Americans with an emblematic moment of teaching. As Robert O'Meally

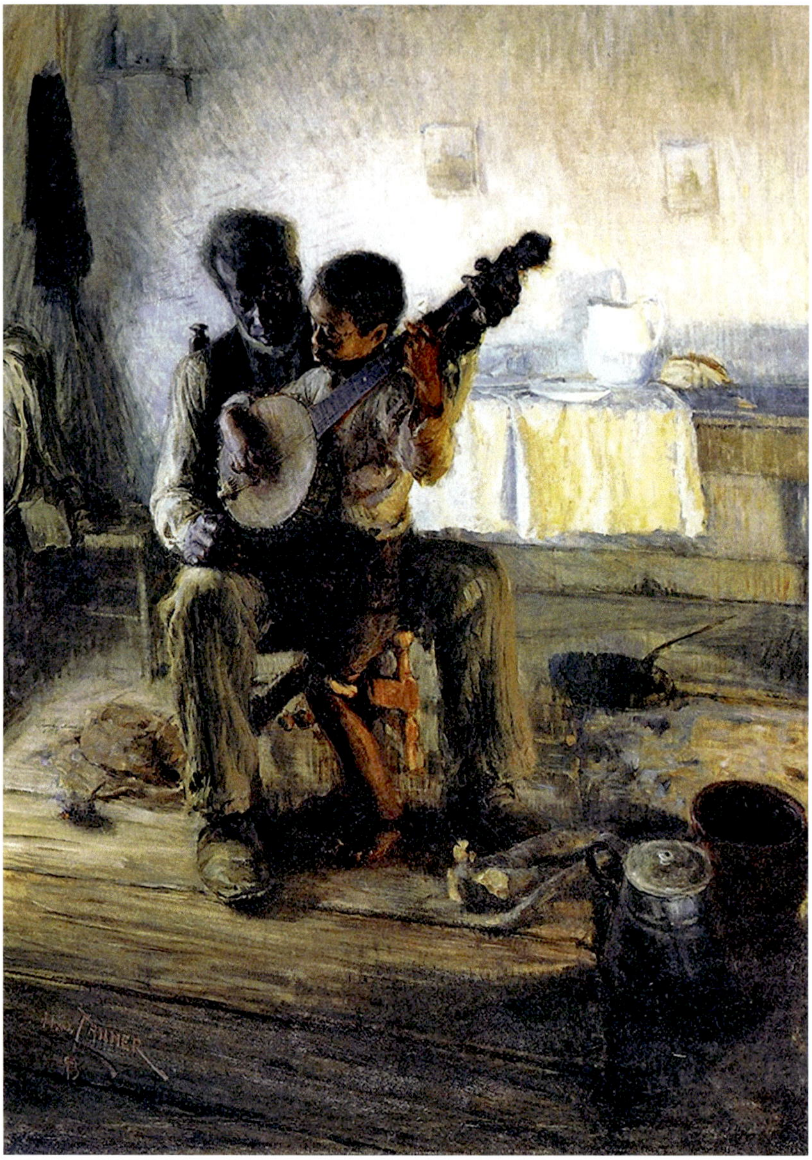

3.2 Henry Ossawa Tanner, *The Banjo Lesson*, 1893. Oil on canvas, 49 × 35½ in. Positioned securely in his grandfather's arms, the boy gazes toward his fingers on the banjo's strings, as does his teacher. In this intimate moment, grandfather and child are united through the music lesson and are portrayed not as "Negro" types but as individuals with agency and purpose. Collection of Hampton University Museum, Hampton, VA.

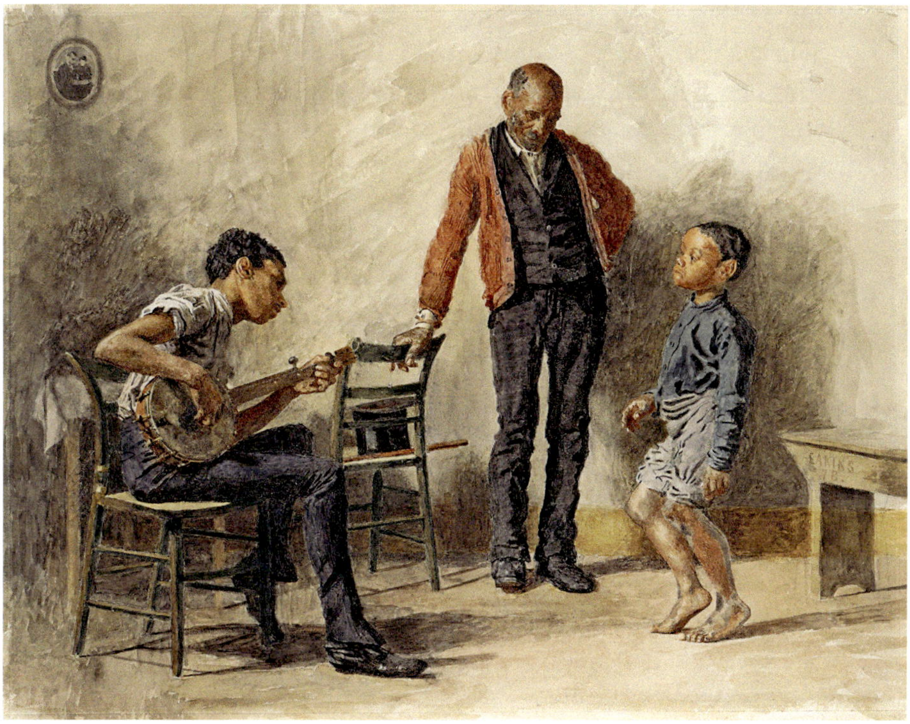

3.3 Thomas Eakins, *Negro Boy Dancing*, 1878. Watercolor, 18 1/16 × 22 9/16 in. Pennsylvania Academy of the Fine Arts, Philadelphia, Charles Bregler's Thomas Eakins Collection, purchased with the partial support of Pew Memorial Trust and John S. Phillips Fund.

appropriately writes, "*Jazz* [black music] is a definable set of musical forms, transmissible not by blood transfusions or magic codes but by careful, painstaking study (at the nexus of work and play) within its particular ritual testing grounds and classrooms."[25] Teaching introduces intellectual exchange into the discourse, and the intergenerational exchange produced an image of black male responsibility.

Tanner also spoke from within African American culture as an insider, not as an observer. He began to reclaim the song, the heritage of performed culture that had been disfigured by its distortion into stereotype. He, himself a target of stereotypes, had an emotional stake in the work. The harsh racial climate that developed after the collapse of Reconstruction and solidified with the 1896 *Plessy v. Ferguson* decision of the Supreme Court abandoning black people to segregation, racial violence, and virtual reenslavement in the southern sharecropping system reinforced the sense of a need for sanctuary where one was safe from white people. Quite often these havens were found in private spaces like the one in Tanner's painting, or in public homogeneous settings. The figures in Tanner's *Banjo Lesson* are not minstrel performers preparing for that stage but suggest an old player preparing a successor. The work is at once a document of protest, liberation, and transformation.

The Piano Lesson

Henry Ossawa Tanner's important painting opened a new discourse in African American art and began the formation of a new artistic vocabulary of black visual representation. Ninety years later Romare Bearden was a master of that vocabulary, and he articulated a blues and jazz version of Tanner's *Banjo Lesson*.

Around 1980 Bearden and his wife, Nanette, were in Atlanta to receive an award from the Atlanta chapter of the NAACP (National Association for the Advancement of Colored People). Richard Long, who was a good friend of the Beardens, recalled the event.

> Another honoree was Mary Lou Williams. She was then living in Durham at the time at Duke University. . . .
>
> I don't think the Beardens had met her previously at all, but they fell into conversation. Of course, Mrs. Bearden had a dance company, ultimately called "The Nanette Bearden Contemporary Dance Company," and she was always looking for things to make her company

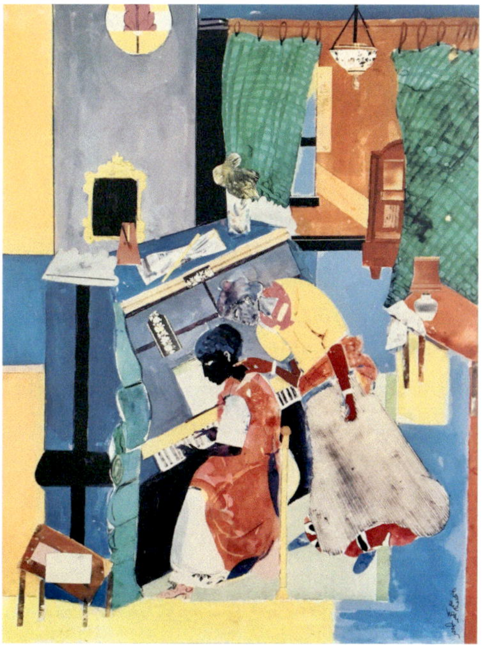

3.4 Romare Bearden, *The Piano Lesson*, 1983. Color lithograph, 29½ × 20½ in. *The Piano Lesson* incorporates watercolor and collage to show a woman seated at a piano with another woman (presumably her teacher) behind her. The collage includes materials of various colors and textures, illustrating the complexity and hybridity of black visual representation in the last quarter of the twentieth century with blues and jazz idioms.

> interesting and distinctive, and so it occurred to her right then and there to ask if she could use some of the music that Mary Lou Williams had to create an evening of dancing. . . . At any rate, as they got ready for the program, Romy created a poster for it, and the poster started off with the collage, *The Piano Lesson*.[26]

Long points out that Mary Lou Williams (1910–81), though born in Atlanta, moved to Pittsburgh when she was five. Romare Bearden lived there during his high school years. So *The Piano Lesson* (figure 3.4) "was inspired by Mary Lou Williams; by Mary Lou Williams as a young piano player in Pittsburgh."[27] (In fact, an alternate title of the lithograph of this work is *Homage to Mary Lou*.[28]) This might have been more than coincidental when August Wilson later became inspired by the artwork and created his play by the same name, which had Pittsburgh as its setting.

By the time Bearden completed *The Piano Lesson*, the stereotypes Tanner undermined so precisely in *The Banjo Lesson* were no longer the prevailing notions and images signifying African Americans, but the lessons in each work remained related to each other. Bearden completed works with banjo players, but they signified folk musicians rather than racial archetypes or their negation.

Throughout his career, musicians—folk, blues, and jazz—appeared in Bearden's work. He was very aware of art history, and many works were based on, or responded to, the work of other artists. He also revised his own work and translated it into different media and sizes. His 1941–42 painting *Folk Musicians* (figure 3.5) has three figures facing the viewer, the central one with a guitar, and a redbrick wall forming a rectangular block behind the men on about two-thirds of the right portion of the painting. The work is beholden to similar work by Pablo Picasso with its robust, cubistic figures.

A small 1964 collage and oil, *Trio* (23 × 28 inches), reprised the composition, abstracted it, and gave the figure on the left a guitar, and the figure on the right a banjo. Photo collage was used as a part of the new work. All three figures have wide-open eyes looking at the viewer, something that changes in the larger 1967 version, *Three Folk Musicians* (figure 3.6), now grown to 50⅛ by 60 inches. The eyes in the central musician and the banjo player are more downcast and introspective than in the earlier works, and the banjo player has a head and face that suggest a self-portrait. The banjo player is left-handed in both works, providing an angular counterpoint to the rightward thrust of the guitar neck and bringing the viewer's gaze back into the center of the composition. The monumental hands in *Folk Musicians* were reduced in the later works, giving way to the prominent, light, solid shapes of the instruments.

The banjo player is no longer a trope but merely a blues/folk reference, and an interesting artistic subject. Clearly less is at stake here than was the case with Tanner's work, or even with Eastman Johnson's 1859 painting. The rural folk references so assiduously avoided by generations of African American artists because of their nearness to plantation stereotypes are sought out by Bearden here, and in a number of works during his career. His North Carolina origins founded a series, *Mecklenburg Autumn*, of which Myron Schwartzman suggests *The Piano Lesson* is a part. While visiting Bearden to discuss the series, Schwartzman was struck by the work and wanted to see it again. "Bearden took out all of the completed collages which were stacked in a corner of the studio: he named them as he set them side-by-side on the floor against the bookcase. He loved to do this when he had finished a number of pieces, and he named them with pride, although some of the titles have been changed since that day. He set *The Piano Lesson* right next to us so that we could see it easily as we talked about it."[29]

Schwartzman saw in the work similarities to Henri Matisse's *The Piano Lesson* from 1916 and Matisse's *Music Lesson* from 1917. But he notes, "These allusions notwithstanding, Romare's flower-patterned Aeolian

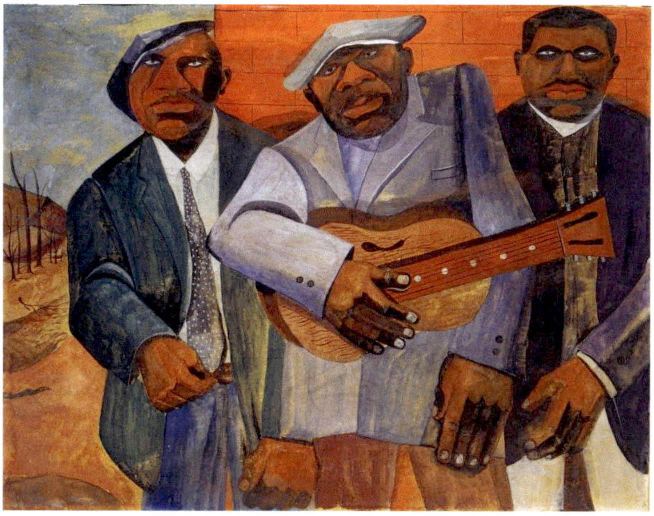

3.5 Romare Bearden, *Folk Musicians*, ca. 1941–42. Gouache and casein on kraft paper, 35½ × 45½ in. In *Folk Musicians*, the features of the men are exaggerated in a cubist style, and the artist uses realistic colors and the bold stances of each figure to create a folk aesthetic that engages the viewer.

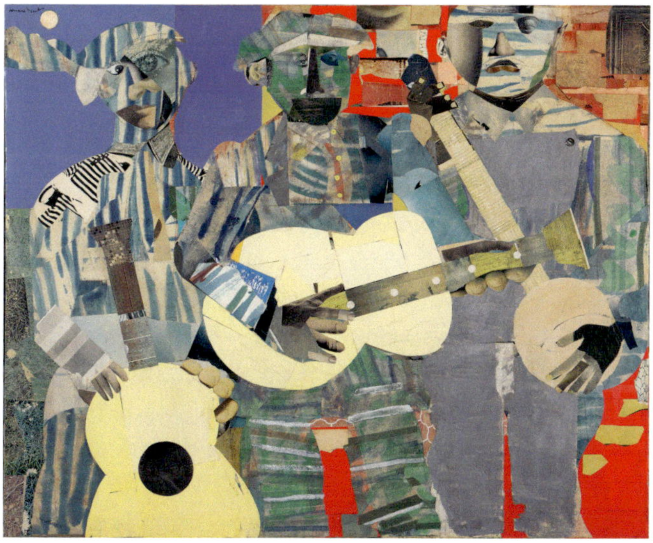

3.6 Romare Bearden, *Three Folk Musicians*, 1967. Collage with paint and graphite on canvas, 50⅛ × 60 in. © 2025 Romare Bearden Foundation/Licensed by VAGA at Artists Rights Society (ARS), New York. Used courtesy of Virginia Museum of Fine Arts, Richmond. Arthur and Margaret Glasgow Endowment, 2016.336. Photo: Travis Fullerton. © Virginia Museum of Fine Arts.

windows, the chandelier, the furniture, the piano, and each detail of costume are unmistakably from a Southern parlor."[30] Bearden, in the same conversation, revealed his remarkable awareness of art and art history, discussing how Francisco Goya, Édouard Manet, and old masters "painted on what they called red or brown bolas grounds" and the techniques they used to let some of the ground play through in their works:

> I've seen some of Goya's paintings where the underneath ground predominated over half the painting and then he would, say, weave a certain blue color here and then develop those things he wanted to be highlighted. This was an Italian technique from the Venetian painters—Tiepolo, Veronese, Tintoretto painted very much in that way. So I let the ground play through. . . . And then in this, I did something I don't usually do. You see I tipped it to lay the piano in a kind of perspective going this way, and to compensate for that I had to . . . bring things back on the frontal plane—you see the blue?—because this is going this way and the other blue is for that reason: to carry you back to the front.[31]

The southern qualities of the details in the work are not necessarily set in the South. The work easily could have been set in Pittsburgh, as Long indicates, because Mary Lou Williams and her family were among millions of African Americans who migrated to the North, in her case from Georgia. These blues travelers carried within them the sensibilities and cultural affinities of their southern lives. In the foreword to Schwartzman's book on Bearden, playwright August Wilson described his Pittsburgh encounter with that transplanted southern world. "In 1965, as a twenty-year-old poet living in a rooming house in Pittsburgh, I discovered Bessie Smith and the blues. It was a watershed event in my life. It gave me a history. It provided me with a cultural response to the world as well as the knowledge that the text and content of my life were worthy of the highest celebration and occasion of art."[32] Wilson indicates that the next watershed event was his first encounter with Bearden's work. He was shown a copy of *The Prevalence of Ritual* by a friend one evening after dinner and experienced something akin to an epiphany. "What for me had been so difficult, Bearden made seem so simple, so easy. What I saw was black life presented on its own terms, on a grand and epic scale, with all its richness and fullness, in a language that was vibrant and which, made attendant to everyday life, ennobled it, affirmed its value, and exalted its presence. . . . I don't recall what I said as I looked at it. My response was visceral. I was looking at myself in ways I hadn't thought of before and have never ceased to think of since."[33]

Bearden's work *Mill Hand's Lunch Bucket* inspired Wilson's play *Joe Turner's Come and Gone*, and *The Piano Lesson* spawned the play of the same name. Two of Wilson's characters, Seth and Bertha, were taken from another Bearden painting, *Mr. Seth and Miss Bertha*.

Wilson indicates that his play, set in 1936 Pittsburgh, is a lesson focused on two related questions: "What do you do with your legacy, and how do you best put it to use?"[34] Wilson has said he "got the idea from the painting that there would be a woman and a little girl in the play." The woman "would be a character who was trying to acquire a sense of self-worth by denying her past. And I felt that she couldn't do that. She had to confront the past."[35] Wilson wrote this play in the midst of a ten-play chronicle of African American life and culture with each set in a particular decade. Plays set in earlier decades, such as *Joe Turner's Come and Gone*, deal with the migration from the South to the North, but *The Piano Lesson* began to contemplate the movement back to the South to claim legacies and heritage there.[36]

Sandra Shannon argues that the lessons are complex in the play: "In considering what one should do with a legacy, the play reveals more than one teacher and more than one lesson. For example, the teacher-pupil relationship portrayed in Bearden's collage models the relation between Wilson and his audience. . . . Also, each of the cast of characters teaches both directly and indirectly, as their words and their actions signal their regard for their legacy."[37] The foundation of the play *The Piano Lesson* is about heritage, dignity, and intergenerational legacies transferred. Shannon suggests that the impulse driving all of Wilson's plays is his "desire to change attitudes about the importance of one's culture and heritage."[38] Beginning with Tanner's *The Banjo Lesson*, artists from within the culture extol the folk cultural legacies and foundations that root and define African American life. In Wilson's plays, blues music often functions metaphorically to articulate the soul struggle folk faced. Pereira indicates that "the blues is the seam that threads the themes [in the plays] together. It also casts an emotional aura over the characters, uniting a group of seemingly diverse personalities with a bond forged in a common past." The tension comes because the music keeps alive the pain of a brutal experience, but "in one magnificent leap it elevates black people from the status of slaves to the level of artists."[39]

In Tanner's work, the folk instrument founded in Africa is lifted to an instrument of art, and the process of art is shown. The instrument and the music are studied and complex, and there are traditions and techniques to build on, just as with any art form. Tanner is synchronically creating art, building on past art, beginning the foundations of a uniquely African American art, and visually wiping the cork off the blackface minstrel. He is speaking from and about the black interior.

Bearden's *Piano Lesson* presented black life, as Wilson says, on its own terms. There is no posturing for sanction and approval by white people as a part of an integrationist effort. The work is rooted in the experience of conjure women, trains and train whistles signaling migration potentials and movement. There are quiet rural moments and blues songs, jazz clubs, and urban streets in this work. Yet there is a call to reclaim the song, to embrace the banjo and the blues, and that southern soil, dark with black blood. It is from this foundation, this heritage, that Bearden engages Goya and Picasso and Matisse.

On more subtle and symbolic levels, art historian Maude Wahlman pointed out Bearden's use of collage and its approximation with fragmented imagery. In her description of Bearden's collage *Ritual Bayou* (1972), Wahlman observed that this work drew from "the African American tradition of newspapered walls to protect against evil spirits."[40] Images cut from books, magazines, and newspapers and applied to walls worked in a double entendre protection of homes, insulating walls from the cold and occupying neglected spirits, preventing their mischief "for it is believed that they must read everything before they can do any harm."[41] Slowed by the complicated imagery, the spirits would not be able to complete this task prior to dawn. In some ways, the fragmented imagery approximated the pieced-together qualities of improvisational African American quilts and their encoding with cultural knowledge, messages, and, perhaps in some cases, the insider esoteric equivalent of Masonic codes.

The Piano Lesson was a part of a creative enterprise that included music, dance, art history, quiet pedagogy, and classical artistic sensibilities and techniques. It is the matrix of complexity and hybridity that was African American reality in the last quarter of the twentieth century. The trope had been trumped, and the banjo, again, was a part of culture, not a sign of its mockery. The subjects were no longer rural and impoverished but were urban dwellers who carried southern decoration and histories with them in the details of their lives. August Wilson's play *The Piano Lesson*, inspired by Bearden, became a sort of backstory for the artwork, and the lesson of the banjo, long learned, moved to a second verse in a different key. The stolen song has been recovered, and the banjo is ours again.

CHAPTER 4

Fish Fry Music

A Blues Aesthetic

> White folks don't understand about the blues. They hear it come out, but they don't know how it got there. They don't understand it's life's way of talking. You don't sing to feel better. You sing 'cause that's a way of understanding life.
>
> MA RAINEY (NÉE GERTRUDE PRIDGETT) AS PORTRAYED IN AUGUST WILSON'S *MA RAINEY'S BLACK BOTTOM* (1982)

> Ain't but one kind of blues. And that consisted between male and female that's in love. . . . Love hide all faults; make you do things you don't want to do. Love sometime will leave you sad and blue. I'm talkin' about the blues, now. I ain't talking about monkey junk.
>
> SON HOUSE, BLUES MUSICIAN, IN *BLACK SNAKE MOAN* (2006)

> Back to the mine
> You coal black shine,
> There'll be no rest today . . .
>
> FOLK SAYING REMEMBERED FROM YOUTH BY AFRICOBRA ARTIST NELSON STEVENS, IN CONVERSATION WITH THE AUTHOR (MARCH 11, 2016)

Sometime around 1865, a photographer took a picture of the black people who had been enslaved by Joe Davis (1784–1870), older brother of Jefferson Davis, in front of the library pavilion of his Hurricane Plantation near Davis Bend in Mississippi (figure 4.1). The photograph is signed "eddie" on the back. More than forty men, women, and children are spread around two sides of a large one-story building surrounded by columns and topped

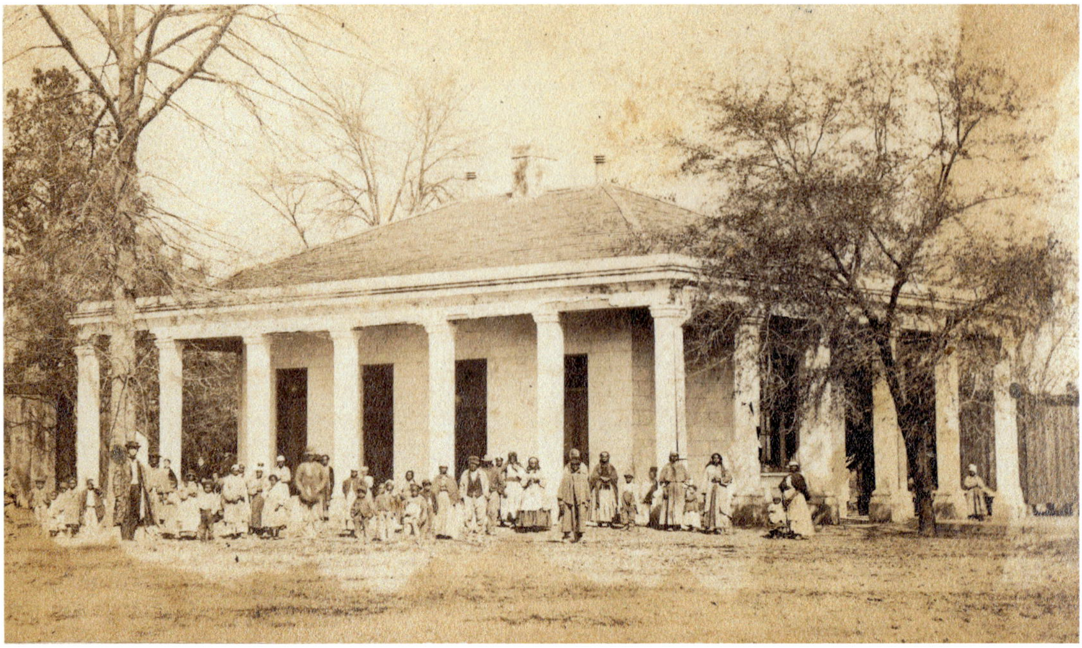

4.1 Freedmen in front of the library pavilion of Hurricane Plantation, owned by Joe Davis, older brother of Jefferson Davis. Mississippi, ca. 1865. Albumen photograph carte de visite, photographer unknown. Milbourn J. Crowe Papers, 1889–2005. Stuart A. Rose Manuscript, Archives, and Rare Book Library, Emory University, Atlanta. Manuscript collection no. 1084. Box no. 5. Courtesy of Stuart A. Rose Manuscript, Archives, and Rare Book Library.

by a low, sloping hip roof without dormers or gables. The Davis brothers owned plantations about twenty miles south of Vicksburg.

Hurricane Plantation held 350 slaves and became a site for Joe Davis to explore the utopian socialist ideas of Robert Owen (1771–1858), a Welshman whom he met when Owen traveled in the United States in the mid-1820s. Davis intended to create a model slave community on the plantation, encouraging self-leadership and providing a higher-than-normal standard of medical and dental care. That settlement, Davis Bend, became a free black community when Davis sold the property to the formerly enslaved Benjamin Montgomery, a prominent figure in the community.

A prolonged agricultural depression, falling cotton prices, and white hostility led to the failure of Davis Bend as a black settlement, but Isaiah Montgomery (1847–1924), son of Benjamin, led the 1887 founding of Mound Bayou, Mississippi, one of the first incorporated black towns in

America. White hostility led to the founding of a number of black towns such as Rosewood, Florida, or thriving black communities in places like Tulsa, Oklahoma, and Wilmington, North Carolina, which were later subject to catastrophic white mob violence sparked, in part, by white jealousy and resentment fueled by the remarkable economic and commercial success of those communities. So successful a refuge was Mound Bayou, founded by formerly enslaved persons recovering from white-controlled environments after the Civil War, that it served as a sanctuary even decades later, in 1955, when Mamie Till-Mobley found support there during the trial of her son's notoriously brutal killers.[1] Freed from slavery on the Davis plantation, these people sought the sanctuary of their own community.[2]

Mississippi's pressures helped produce the cultural gemstone known as the blues, a practice formed in response to harsh post-Reconstruction realities to give voice and inner light to a common experience. Perhaps the blues can be thought of as the moan complicated and updated; a transformative lexicon, born of shared misery and oppression, giving hope and catharsis.

James Cone suggests the blues "depict the 'secular' dimension of black experience." He wrote that blues and gospel do not offer "artistic creation for its own sake" but rather tell "us about the *feeling* and *thinking* of African people, and the kinds of mental adjustments they had to make in order to survive in an alien land."[3] Amiri Baraka also argues for the functionality of blues music, saying, "Form and content are expressions of each other," and the "highest thought is a doing, a being, not an abstraction."[4] Dwight Andrews writes that the blues "represents a particular worldview—a way of looking at life and of understanding life. Most important, it represents a way of participating and interacting with life."[5] However, Andrews has told me that there isn't just one kind of blues.

Willie King (1943–2009), who ran the Freedom Creek Blues Festival in Old Memphis, Alabama, was interviewed for the 2003 Martin Scorsese documentary about the blues. King said the blues "help give a vision of a brighter day way up ahead. Get your mind off what you're in right now."[6] He pointed out how signifyin' worked in the culture and in the blues:

> They would use a lot of these songs in which they would talk about they woman, but they was telling about they boss man. Talking about the woman, "Oh my baby, she's so mean, she just won't treat me right. She take all my money."

Well, you talking about the boss man. This is a way that they have to give the message undercover.

King suggested that given the conditions, naming names and being direct might "find you hanging from one of them trees before day in the morning."[7] It was hitting a straight lick with a crooked stick; a way of telling insiders what they understood while outsiders missed it. Of course, this was not always the case. As Son House suggests, the songs often were about male-female relationships but also meditations on the difficulties of black life and poverty. They played with the ironies and pains of life, but also with a wink. Muddy Waters in 1963 sang:

You say you love me, darlin'
Please call me on the phone sometime. . . .

I hear my phone ringing
Sounds like a long distance call
I hear my phone ringing
Sounds like a long distance call
I picked up my receiver
The party said, another mule is kicking in your stall.[8]

Early on, the blues was performed on or near large cotton plantations in the Delta region.[9] Robert Palmer writes that Robert Johnson played in the Clarksdale area, "mostly on the huge cotton plantations outside town that employed thousands of black tenant farmers and day laborers," and he was among a number of blues musicians who drifted from "plantation to plantation and town to town, moving in circles local white people neither knew nor cared much about."[10] The workers lived a hard life and liked to come together on weekends to find the pleasure of "drinking white lightning, gambling, dancing the snake hips, and looking for casual sexual liaisons."[11]

McKinley Morganfield, known as Muddy Waters, lived on the Stovall plantation outside Clarksdale in a cabin that doubled as a good-time place, a juke house, on weekends, and he made good moonshine whiskey. It was a way to clear a small regular profit to supplement the 22.5 cents an hour he made driving a tractor on the plantation. And he played some blues.[12] He was a part of the sharecropping system that developed from a sort of mutual dependency after the Civil War into a "a kind of modern-day feudalism."[13]

Muddy Waters migrated north to Chicago, and Wadsworth Jarrell (b. 1929), who also migrated to Chicago from the South (Athens, Georgia), recalls meeting him in 1961 at Pepper's Lounge. Jarrell preferred jazz, and urban blues by singers like Jimmy Witherspoon, Jimmy Rushing, and Bobby "Blue" Bland, and said that he initially did not like Waters's music. However, Jarrell says, "When he took the stage and started singing and playing I was overwhelmed by his musical intelligence (his timing and delivery and spellbinding magic that held the audience captivated). . . . From that moment on, I became a fan of Muddy and visited Pepper's and the Checker Board Lounge many more times to hear Muddy, Little Walter, Buddy Guy, Junior Wells, and that whole contingent of country blues players."[14]

In 1985 Jarrell returned to Muddy Waters in his painting *Juju Man from the Delta* (figure 4.2). He used that title because "he represents a conjure man who can conjure up magic with his music and extend it to other areas, like casting spells by working roots, and having control of his woman. He is capable of creating magic singing and playing on his guitar."[15] Jarrell colored his stained canvas with middle-value tones, creating a sense of muted light. The warmer orange-brown coloration at the top left gives a sense of stage lighting blending with the cooler greens and browns in the rest of the work. In certain ways, this painting is reminiscent of the muted and colorful scenic light found in Chicago artist Archibald Motley Jr.'s Bronzeville nightlife scenes of the 1930s.

The figures in this work have rounded, asymmetrical masklike faces and are built with rich, expressive colors; textured (combed) impasto paint; and various patterns, leaf shapes. The musician on the far right—seemingly Little Walter blowing the mouth harp—has a cap made of cowrie shells. There is a black cat walking to the lower left of the painting, indicating superstition and country lore. Jarrell says that if the cat is going to the left, it is bad luck, and to remove it, "you turn around three times and spit."

Jarrell has said that he doesn't paint the musicians or the music but tries to convey the feeling of hearing the music. He tried to "capture the aura of country-funk that oozed from Muddy like sweat," which included "gold teeth inscribed with designs, leather bracelets on his wrists, rings and thimbles on his finger to lay against the strings of the guitar to achieve the titillating bottle-neck sound."

He feels that a blues singer is "one who understands that the blues is derived from living; if you haven't lived it, you cannot sing or play it. The blues is a demon, a spiritual epiphany that not only represents sadness, but also represents happiness."[16]

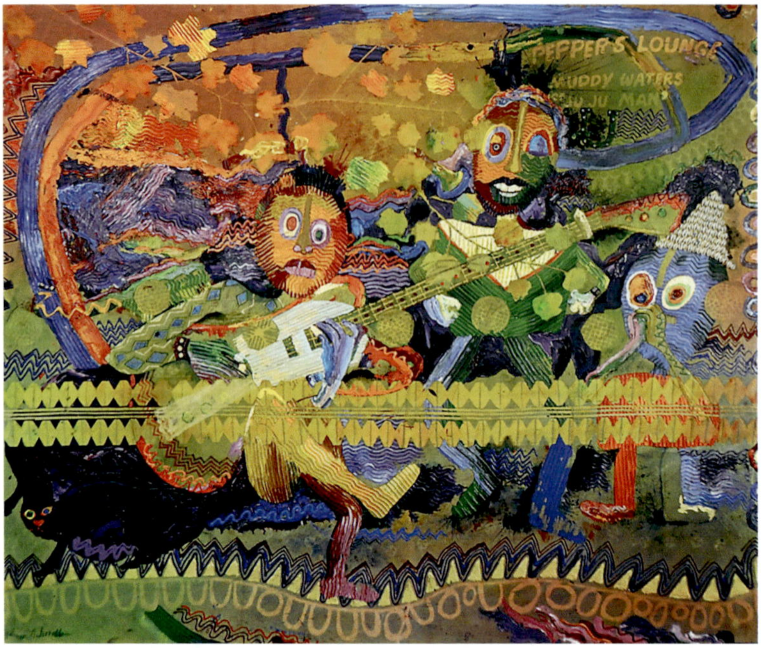

4.2 Wadsworth A. Jarrell, *Juju Man from the Delta*, 1985. Acrylic on canvas, 68 × 90 in. Collection of the artist. Used by permission of Wadsworth A. Jarrell.

Nubia Kai wrote in a 1990 essay about AfriCOBRA, the artist collective Jarrell helped found in 1968 in Chicago, that the "elongated stem of the guitar stresses a continuum of ancestral knowledge and values that move beyond material limitations into the heavenly world of archetypes."[17] With its smooth stained areas playing off corrugated impasto textures, lines of patterns flowing across the image, expressive rather than natural colors, abstracted images, and unexplained leaf imagery across the top half of the work, the painting is more an abstraction than the kind of stylized Bronzeville scenes of Motley.

Richard Powell in his 1989 work *The Blues Aesthetic: Black Culture and Modernism* opened an inquiry about a cultural reading of African American art via the blues while suggesting the blues is a signifier of black life. Powell argues convincingly that the blues

> whips up a panorama of extra-musical associations that, whether one chooses to acknowledge them or not, situate it in Afro-American life of this century.

Does this mean the blues is equivalent to modern Afro-American life? In one way of thinking, yes.[18]

Powell continues by suggesting the blues "was not just musical, but cultural."[19] He argues that if one knows African America—"its history, its traditions, its geography, its verbal and visual codes, its heroes, its demons, its ever-changing styles, and its spiritual dimensions—then one knows the blues."[20] Jarrell's rich painting *Juju Man*, when unpacked, layers these elements in the image. Importantly, by defining the blues culturally and, to a lesser degree, stylistically and idiomatically, the racial stigmas, dogmas, and strictures that the postblack idea seeks to evade are relegated to a contextual significance instead of being a part of an essentialist identity.

Dwight Andrews points out that without racism to respond to, "African American culture would have evolved in quite a different way."[21] Importantly, he argues, "the roots of black music lie not only in the adaption and synthesis of various African musical practices but also in the African conceptualization of music as power." Music, therefore, becomes a means of self-empowerment tied to the voice, but in this frame "the sung word is radically more powerful than the spoken word." So, when the black preacher rises to his singsong cadence in preaching, he is, in effect, singing the sermon and exploiting the metaphysical powers of sound as perceived within an African and, by extension, African American ontological and cosmological framework.[22] Blues culture was rich with metaphorical and metaphysical implications.

In the 1960s several Mississippi bluesmen were rediscovered and recognized by a larger public, including Son House (1902–88) and Robert Johnson (1911–38), in figures 4.3 and 4.4 respectively. Their life stories became a part of their legends and added to their appreciation. Robert Johnson was recognized as an accomplished bluesman and influenced young rock and roll musicians such as the Rolling Stones and Eric Clapton. More recently, several of his songs have been reinterpreted and recorded by Jackson, Mississippi, native Cassandra Wilson.

The persistent lore about Johnson indicates that he was a mediocre player but disappeared for a year and emerged as a master guitarist whose blues lyrics were outstanding. Folklorist Bill Ferris said in an interview, "It is said that the Blues singer could possess women and have any women they wanted. And so when Robert Johnson came back, having left the community as a mediocre musician, with a clear genius in his guitar style and lyrics, people said he must have sold his soul to the devil. And that

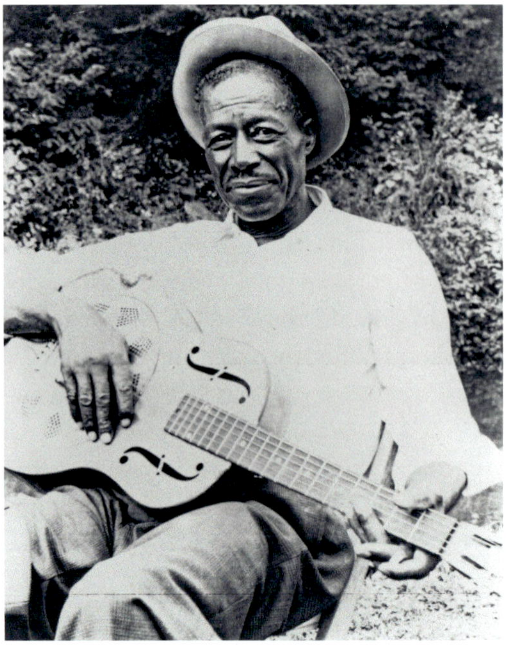

4.3 Blues singer Edward James "Son" House Jr., New York, 1965. He is holding a resonator guitar. Son House was determined to become a Baptist preacher but became attracted to the blues in his twenties.

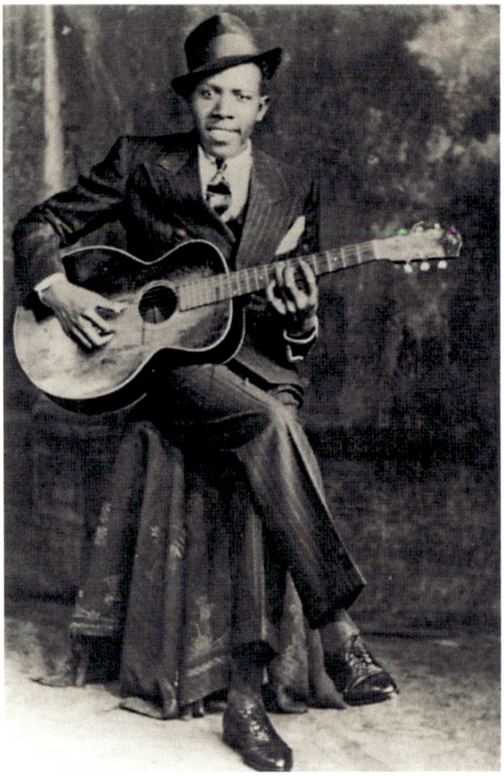

4.4 One of the few known photos of Robert Johnson, ca. 1935. He is holding an acoustic guitar. The images and life stories of forgotten bluesmen like Johnson and Son House added to the public's appreciation when the musicians were later rediscovered in the 1960s. From Marla C. Berns, *Dear Robert, I'll See You at the Crossroads*, 38.

fits with this old African association with the crossroads where you find wisdom: you go down to the crossroads to learn."[23]

Rather than a Faustian bargain with the devil, this loric scenario suggests an encounter with Eshu (Èṣù), the epic trickster figure also called Papa Legba, Elegbara, and Eshu Elegba, among other names.[24] Johnson was twenty-seven when he died, reportedly by drinking poisoned whiskey, an *ice course*, as the result of an encounter with the wrong woman.[25] Some of his more famous songs were "Cross Road Blues," "Me and the Devil," and "Hellhound on My Trail." Additionally, Johnson's forsaking the church for secular blues music was seen as a sort of deal with the devil at the time.

The crossroads symbolically is a place where one can encounter the spiritual realm; it is a place of crossing over and meeting the Yoruba orisha Eshu, a figure who intercedes between humans and the gods. One must pay him through an offering or "dash" for delivering one's desirous prayers to the appropriate deity or spirit (angel?).

We find the crossroads to be of significance in Central Africa as well. It shows up in cosmograms. Robert Farris Thompson tells us, "Crossroads or forks in a path are viewed in many Bantu cultures of the Kongo-Angola region as virtual cosmogram *trouvés*. These points of literal intersection were where one might go to offer sacrifice or prayer to the ancestors."[26] Thompson indicates the correspondence with Yoruba ideas suggesting that the crossroads "functioned as a powerful symbol in African-American folklore. . . . It was where one went to ask favors of the cosmos."[27] Kongo-Angola cosmograms have a compelling presence in Haitian Vodou ceremonies with the ground emblazons called *veve*. These graphic signs drawn on the ground during ceremonies often have a cross at their center and suggest an indication of invitation for spirits, or *lwa*, to visit through possession.

In folklore, people in the dark, secular world—particularly musicians and gamblers—were thought to have made deals with the devil or shady, trickster characters at the crossroads to gain some metaphysical edge. Film director Martin Scorsese says in his foreword to the published screenplay by Alan Greenberg, *Love in Vain: A Vision of Robert Johnson*, "The thing about Robert Johnson was that he only existed on his records. He was pure legend."[28] This elusive, indeterminate quality of Johnson approximates that of Eshu himself, adding force to his legend in folklore.

Early country blues musicians, as itinerant figures constantly on the road, elusive, and sources of emotional and social transformation through performance, had loric qualities resembling Eshu. Abiodun writes that Eshu represents "the force that can belong in two different places without showing any signs of discomfort," and he "looks in two opposite directions, embodies two bodies, and inhabits two spaces at the same time."[29]

As Son House mentioned above, the blues does relate to "a lonely and terrifying sense of personal betrayal and anguish," but it reflects also a larger sense of black life in the South. Leon Litwack indicates that Robert Johnson's blues playing "suggested a society impossible to change or overcome and a new generation of interior exiles like himself, exiles in their own land, empty of belief or hope, vulnerable without sanctuary."[30] The lyrics of Johnson's "Hellhound on My Trail" give emotional insight into itinerant musicians and migrating black people heading north:

> I got to keep moving, I got to keep moving
> blues falling down like hail
> blues falling down like hail
> Uumh, blues falling down like hail
> blues falling down like hail
> and the days keeps on worryin' me
> there's a hellhound on my trail,
> hellhound on my trail
> hellhound on my trail.[31]

Hellhound, as Willie King mentioned above, had to be a reference to the virulent and violent white male, including the boss man, who terrorized black people in Mississippi and for whom an open direct reference might be a capital offense. Between 1930 and 1950, more than fifty thousand black people left Mississippi heading north, carrying with them, and within them, a lexicon of cultural references they collaged into their new urban lives.

The life and career of Robert Johnson and all the implications about trickster figures, black life in the South, cultural invention, and their cultural persistence show how the lore of black folk is a sign evoking a deeper sense of the culture to those who know. Renée Stout implies a good deal of this in her art, particularly through the multipart work and exhibition *Dear Robert, I'll See You at the Crossroads*.[32]

Stout is known for her use of symbols and references to spiritual and cultural practices associated with Hoodoo in the Gulf Coast and Delta areas of Louisiana and Mississippi and, ultimately, their origins in the

Kongo region of Central Africa. The 1993 work *Louisiana Love Icon* (figure 4.5) evokes mystic, spiritual, and transformative ideas associated with accessing the supernatural to effect love in this world. A small heart prickly with pins placed in it lies bloody on a small altar space at the bottom of the stele-like object. In African art, accumulation such as the sacrificial residue of dried blood or layers of small, attached objects often accompanies rituals of secrecy and spiritual effectuation.

Hidden among the various accumulated objects in this work is a cross form in the center just above the median. This marks the work as a crossroads for spiritual encounter and hints at Kongo cosmograms and Haitian *veve*.

Some disparate African examples are the BaKongo *nkisi* objects, notably the nail figures of the late nineteenth century (such as figure 4.6), and encrusted Bolu and Dogon/Tellem figures from the Senufo and Dogon peoples of the Sudanic area in Mali and Burkina Faso (see figure 4.7). The accumulation of sacrificial material, like blood or millet beer in the case of the Dogon, emphasized the utility of the objects as a part of practice. With the Dogon/Tellem example, the formality of an elongated body and the arms-raised gesture is extended through the surface evidence of functionality into an aesthetic incorporating both aspects.

Stout's *Icon* is the materialization of a plea for love and implies the underground system, openly feared and quietly practiced, that also causes admonitions about keeping one's hair clippings or fingernails from falling into the wrong hands and making a person susceptible to spells or bad effects. For example, if a bird uses a woman's hair to make a nest, it causes madness. Men have been told to burn their hair after a haircut because a woman could use it to cast a love spell. In indigenous African aesthetic practice, hair or feathers often worked as signifiers of the symbolic or conceptual ideas behind the material—the hair—more than as material objects. Behind this aesthetic approach is a sense of the physical world manifesting, or mapping, unseen relationships and forces. Dogon and other Sudanic regional affinities in blues culture are more conceptual than actual, but Kongo practices are linked more directly to the large captive populations brought to the Americas during the slave trade.[33] In addition, *minkisi* (plural of *nkisi*) can function as sacred medicines that embody and direct the energy of spirits for harm or cure. For example, the caption at the base of figure 4.6 reads, "Congo No. 17. Le grand Fetish Mabialla Mandembe." The 'fetish' power of these objects can function both metaphorically and metonymically for good or ill.[34]

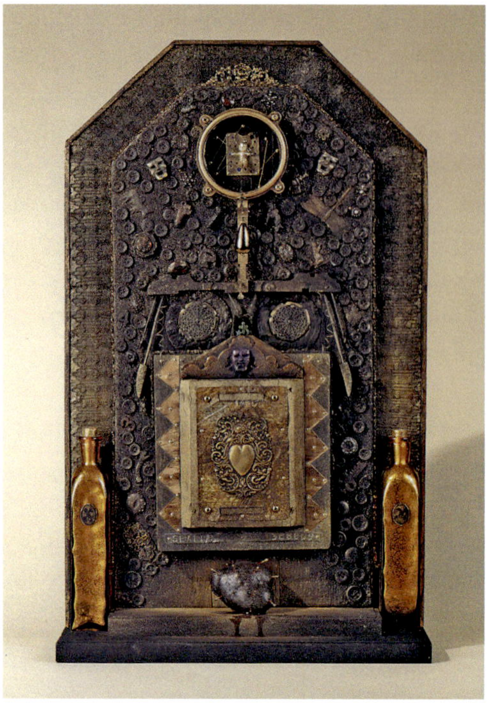

4.5 Renée Stout, *Louisiana Love Icon*, 1993. From Marla C. Berns, *Dear Robert, I'll See You at the Crossroads*, 22. Courtesy of the artist.

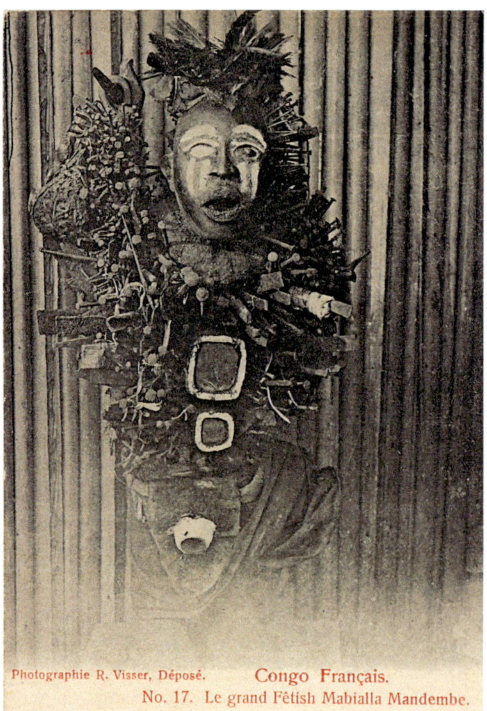

4.6 Nkisi Mabyaala Ma Ndembe. Postcard, Loango, French Congo, 1882–94. No. 17. *Le grand Fetish Mabialla Mandembe* (The great Mabialla Mandembe fetish). Photograph by Robert Visser, ca. 1900. Eliot Elisofon Photographic Archives, National Museum of African Art, Smithsonian Institution, Washington, DC. EEPA Postcard Collection, Congo Francais, cf-03–02.

Small acts like bodily gestures, verbal phrases, aphorisms, metaphors, and loric parables (like John Henry) became indicators of meaning and serve as spiritual systems and outlooks in black life. This matrix of meaning, gestures, symbols, and metaphysical or social relationships animates the blues and is the aesthetic foundation of black, or blues, culture. Signifyin' as a social practice and verbal play also translates into the blues aesthetic, where things indirectly can mean much more than what they overtly seem to mean.

Stout has done similar work pertaining to Marie Laveau, the famed nineteenth-century Vodou priestess from New Orleans whose grave site still is visited by those who wish to leave offerings, homages, and requests (figure 4.8). This is the system in which we find the lore of the crossroads, Papa Legba, and Robert Johnson. This is blues culture with African survivals and cultural rhyming, sanctuarial references, and extra-Christian metaphysical supplications. In a sense, these practices might be seen as African syntax expressed through a New World lexicon. Stout says, "To me, the crossroads is that place where the mortal plane meets the spiritual plane, and you can access the power of the ancestors and the guidance of the ancestors. The crossroads basically is the place that functions as the *nkisi*. It's an *nkisi* but of the environment where you go and get access to the spirits of the ancestors."[35]

Stout's installation *Wylie Avenue Juke* (1994–95; figure 4.9) intimates those black cafés and juke joints where folk congregated, drank, and listened to blues music. Places like this had their own codes, jargon, and safety from white violence and oversight. The work is not an illustration of a juke joint but intends to evoke a sense of the space and its context in the viewer. The black interior experience and its associative emotional and psychological freedoms add a layer of intensity for audiences. Many art installations move viewers through an experiential sensation from the particular interaction they have at the moment with the work, but Stout, like María Magdalena Campos-Pons, adds memory and cultural association to the experience of the art.[36]

What easily can be overlooked in considering blues and gospel music as a secular and sacred dialectic is the presence of the sacred and spiritual in the underlying cultural assumptions of blues culture. Intimations of Eshu at the crossroads reveal threads of Africana spiritual ideas in the cultural fabric. Vodou and conjuring sit consistently in Stout's work with her references and attention to Marie Laveau and her Hoodoo love charms, and they often are found in blues lyrics, as we shall see shortly. Because of

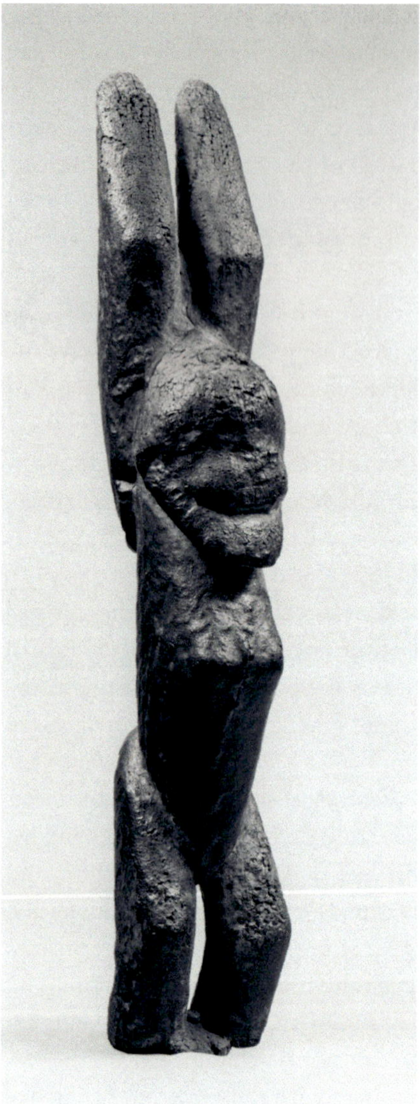

4.7 (*left*) Tellem figure from the Dogon region of Mali, encrusted with sacrificial materials. Date unknown. These objects, many of which were found in caves by the Dogon when settling in the Bandiagra escarpment area of Mali in the thirteenth to sixteenth centuries, often were incorporated into Dogon rituals. This particular object presents a slender, humanlike figure with arms upstretched to bridge the sky and the earth in supplication for rain.

4.8 (*below*) Marie Laveau's grave with offerings and marks left by contemporary pilgrimages and requests. New Orleans St. Louis Cemetery No. 2, date unknown. Photograph by Michael D. Harris.

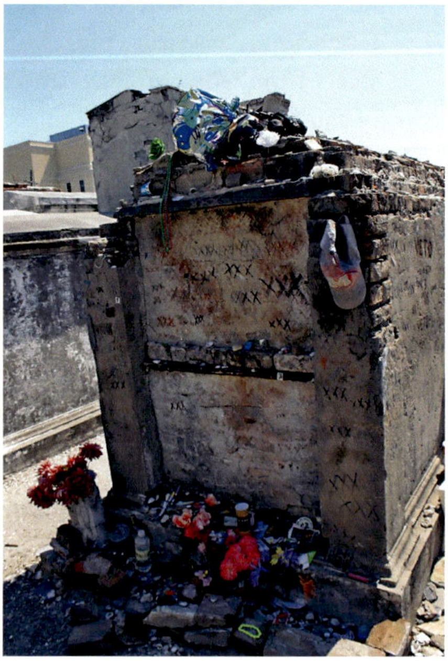

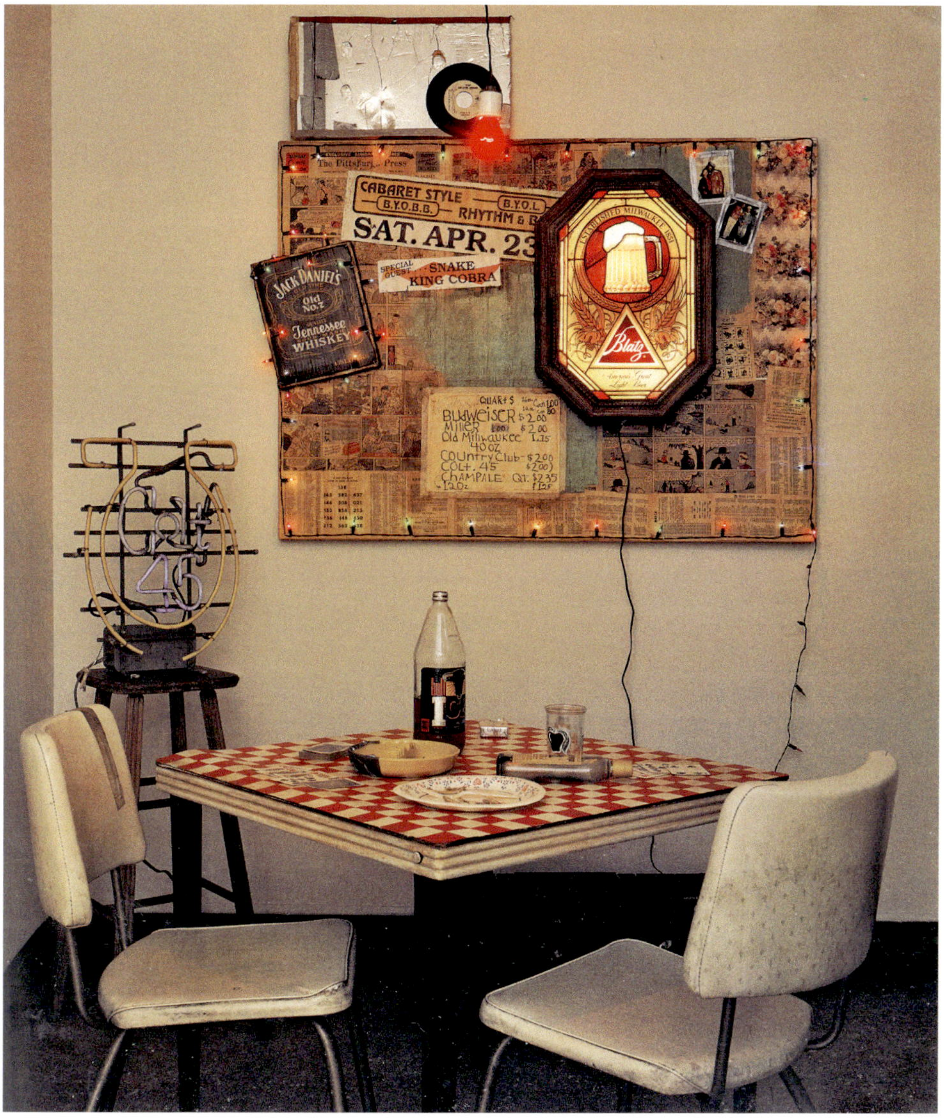

4.9 Renée Stout, *Wylie Avenue Juke* (installation view), included in the traveling exhibition *Dear Robert, I'll See You at the Crossroads*, 1995. From Marla C. Berns, *Dear Robert, I'll See You at the Crossroads*, 33.

the references to and implications of juju and conjuring in blues music, a layer of that sacred-secular dialectic may be rooted in the tension between old African-derived spiritual practices—like Vodou, Santería (or Lucumí), and Candomblé—and New World Christianity.

One element in Stout's installation was a bed with gossamer covering unkempt enough to suggest the aftermath of lovemaking and with a pair of bejeweled red slippers sitting in the middle. The title, *Man Trap* (figure 4.10), speaks to the men, like Johnson, who were lured to destruction by sexual liaisons, the kind often initiated during drinks and dancing at juke joints and roadhouses. The bedroom was one of the very few places black men could exert male power, but it held potentials for female power as well.

One might wonder if the sexual insinuations in blues lyrics and lore come from old intimations about the womb being a point of spiritual transition from that world to this and, by extension, an acknowledgment of the extra-ordinary potentials of women because this metaphorical "crossroads" is contained within, along with implied access to spiritual realms; this is the place where spirits are able to enter this world. Perhaps this is a foundational concept behind the force embodied in ideas of conjure women (like Laveau).

Stout's work evokes an era and a system active before the dominance of recorded music, radio, crossover, and white use of black expressive musical forms in the 1950s and thereafter by Elvis Presley and many others. She uses contemporary art practices to reference something deep inside the culture and entice identification by those folk who understand the history and references. "The whole lore behind Robert Johnson, the mythology behind Robert Johnson, was a framework for me to do a whole body of work. To examine the idea of what the crossroads means. And how it applied to Robert Johnson and how he got the power to access the power of the ancestors, whatever that power was he accessed at the crossroads to become the kind of bluesman that he was. That was the kind of story that needed a whole show to revolve around it."[37]

Present or implied in the work is the hum grown from the moan and those folkways at the root of black culture. Importantly, the work, as an installation, is a type of artistic *performance* and provides another layer of connection to the blues circumstances and transformational lore the artist is addressing.

Dear Robert is the kind of art that captures the spiritual weaponry folk turned to in negotiating a hostile environment to create hope of even

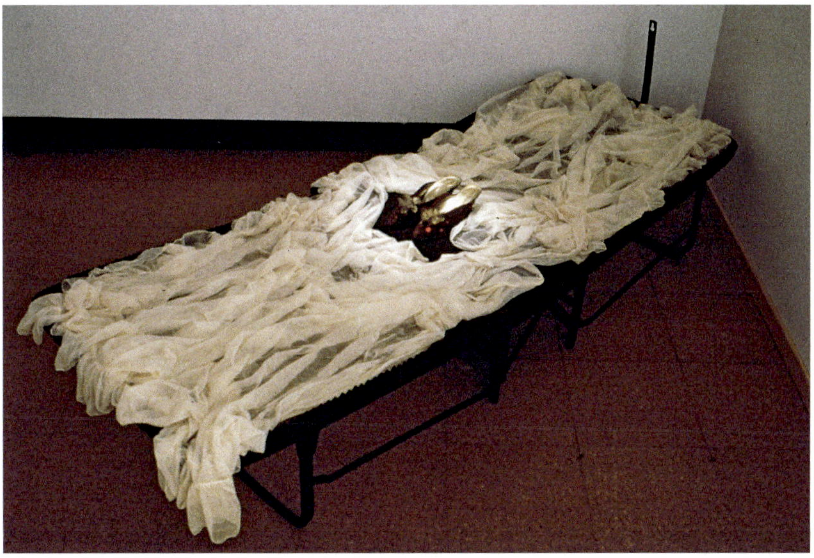

4.10 Renée Stout, *Man Trap* (installation view), included in the traveling exhibition *Dear Robert, I'll See You at the Crossroads*, 1994–95. From Marla C. Berns, *Dear Robert, I'll See You at the Crossroads*, 32.

small triumphs. Some found sanctuary in the church; others took the path of assuaging their harsh lives with nightlife and sensuous music. Stout's work succeeds as art, but it is African American in its evocations and cultural codes. For those inside the culture, deeper emotional invocations are produced, turning the work into more than a visual stimulus; rather, a verb actuating feelings, and perhaps memories, of sanctuarial experiences and warmth. Interestingly, Stout indicates that she discovered "the relationship between blues and conjure when I was first listening to blues. When I was younger, I didn't get the references, but as I got older . . . [I] started looking at African art and the New Orleans traditions and figuring out what roots were."[38]

Implicit in aesthetic renditions of or references to the blues is their playing out in social spaces. Blues players performed bittersweet chords for bittersweet experiences that were familiar. The songs might be cathartic and filled with irony, but they worked like cultural connective tissue linking folk into an organic, creative cultural entity. Audience tastes, sensibilities, and responses were considered in the concoction of performance styles. And the music acted as a healing agent.

Many African American artists embed signifiers of these social experiences and practices in their work to cue an audience in, and some, such as Stout and Romare Bearden, directly address blues culture and its surrounding folkways as artistic subject matter, transforming the subject itself into haute couture. Bearden's series of collages around conjure women used the title and coded elements to lead viewers more deeply into this world in imagery that was clearly modernist, abstract, and symbolic.

In 1954 Muddy Waters introduced the Willie Dixon song "I'm Your Hoochie Coochie Man," with lyrics clearly referring to the world of conjure and Hoodoo:

The gypsy woman told my mother
Before I was born
I got a boy child's comin'
He's gonna be a son of a gun
He gonna make pretty womens
Jump and shout
Then the world wanna know
What this all about

The second stanza contained familiar references to the system of conjuring and blues lore:

I got a black cat bone
I got a mojo too
I got the Johnny Concheroo
I'm gonna mess with you
I'm gonna make you girls
Lead me by my hand
Then the world will know
The hoochie coochie man[39]

Both stanzas and the title indicate the blues musicians' power with women, something that also created a reputation. That caused folk finding solace or inspiration in a gospel context, or those with middle-class aspirations, to warn against blues men. This hoochie coochie man with powers of transfiguration through music played on the indeterminacy found in the lore of Eshu. One of the praise stories about Eshu suggests he defies space and time. He "throws a stone today, and kills a bird yesterday."[40]

The other side of the implication is the power of women, particularly their ability to conjure. Muddy Waters released several songs in 1958 referring to these ideas. "She Moves Me" sings of being helpless with a particular woman:

She moves me, man
Honey, and I don't see how it's done . . .

She move a crazy man
Who say "now I'm not so dumb"
I take her to a funeral boy
The dead jumped up to run
She looked a deaf and dumb boy
Said "now I can speak"
She shook her ginger in a blind man's face
"Once was blind but now I see"

Waters released another song at the same time, "Louisiana Blues," which again normalizes the Hoodoo/conjure complex with the stanza:

I'm goin' down in New Orleans
Get me a mojo hand
I'm goin' down in New Orleans
Get me a mojo hand. . . .

Johnny Concheroo, mentioned in "Hoochie Coochie Man," refers to John the Conqueror Root, commonly associated with conjure. It is a reference to a trickster figure folk hero and is used in sexual spells and for good luck in gambling. Bearden introduced the "conjur woman" (Bearden's spelling) into his art in 1964 in a series titled *The Prevalence of Ritual*. He wrote, "A conjur woman was an important figure in a number of Southern Negro rural communities. She was called on to prepare love potions; to provide herbs to cure various illnesses; and to be consulted regarding vexing personal and family problems. Much of her knowledge had been passed on through the generations from an African past, although a great deal was learned from the American Indians. A conjur

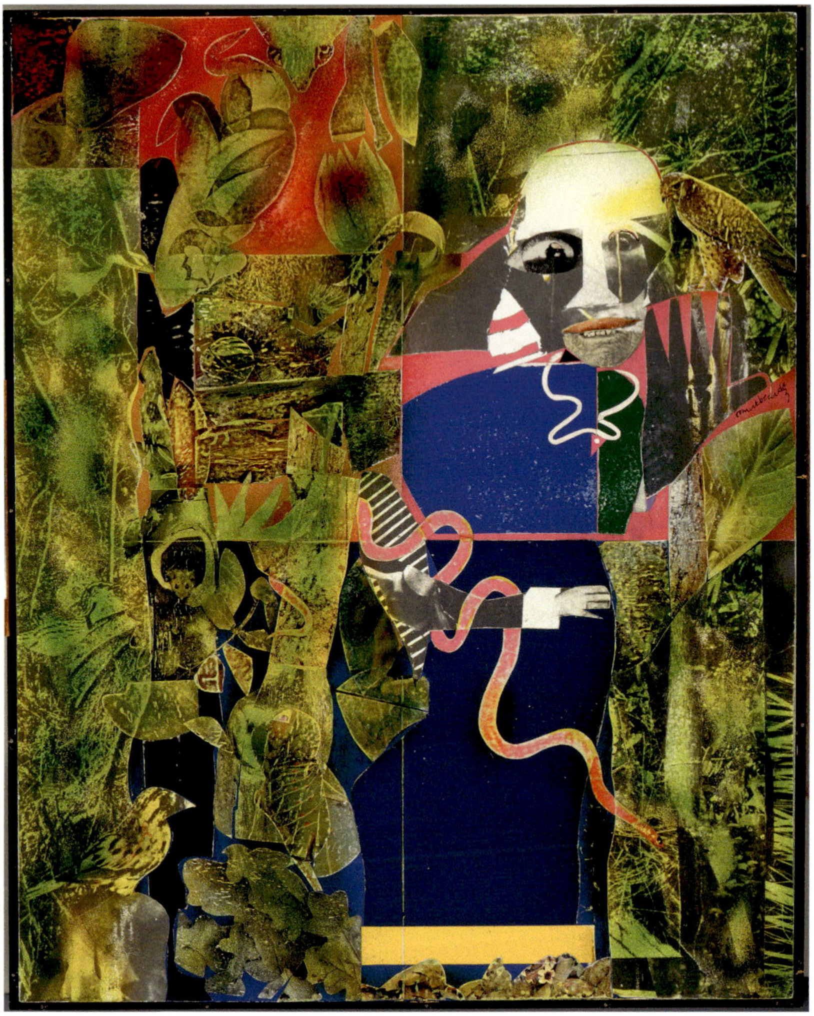

4.11 Romare Bearden, *Conjur Woman*, 1975. Collage with spray paint on paper, 46 × 36 in. Allen Memorial Art Museum, Oberlin College, Oberlin, OH. © 2023 Romare Bearden Foundation/Licensed by VAGA at Artists Rights Society (ARS), NY. Courtesy of Allen Memorial Art Museum, Oberlin College, R. T. Miller Jr. Fund.

woman was greatly feared and it was believed that she could change her appearance."[41]

The 1975 version of the conjure woman (figure 4.11) has her with a snake curled around her right arm, a hawk sitting on her left shoulder, and in the midst of vegetation and trees, observed by another bird in the lower left corner of the work. She has a collaged masklike face with a right eye opened wide, echoing the practice found in several West African cultures of bulging the eyes of a figure to indicate the inner pressure of an added spiritual presence or energy that might be associated with possession or being mounted by a spirit like an orisha. Among the Yoruba, and in African-derived New World religious practices, the equestrian metaphor of being mounted is more apt than the sense of demonic possession often layered atop such non-Christian practices in American popular culture. The believer and the spirit exchange divine energy and *ashé* through this process.

This metaphor also has the double entendre of a husband mounting his wife sexually—devotees of the orisha Shango (Xango) are often characterized as his wives and iconographically represented as kneeling women in supplication and offering—suggesting an intimate union that is more of a congress or partnership than being ridden by a commanding rider.[42] Spiritual trance is a willing partnership, and the spirit is invited and received rather than being a powerful intruder.

Given that Bearden's adulthood was concurrent with Robert Johnson and the full strength of blues culture, it seems appropriate to look at the threads in *Conjur Woman* that tie to Wifredo Lam's iconic 1943 painting *The Jungle* (figure 4.12). Acquired in 1945 by the Museum of Modern Art (MoMA) in New York, where Bearden conceivably would have become familiar with it—Nelson Stevens recalls seeing it in the lobby of MoMA in 1950 and reports that it was "the first thing you saw when you entered the Museum of Modern Art"—this painting references the same African-derived spiritual complex as the foundations of Hoodoo, in this case Santería (or Lucumí) from Cuba, for which Lam's godmother was a practitioner.[43] The surrealist and cubist figures emerge from a vegetative environment, as does Bearden's figure. The geometry and masklike faces resonate with each other in the paintings, but the subject shifts from the ideas of the spirit system and believers merging with spirits in Lam's work, to the practitioner manipulating the system in Bearden's work. The work also is a political commentary emerging from the ideas of the Negritude movement that grew out of France at that time.

In Lam's painting, the figures combining animal, human, and vegetative elements suggest humankind's oneness with nature. However, Robert Linsley writes, "Trodden down but still living the plant is a symbol of the patient defiance of the enslaved; but in the Césairean universe it also symbolizes the nature of African spirituality in tune with the 'rhythms of life.'"[44] Linsley indicates that there is no jungle in Cuba and "what we mostly see in this picture are stems of sugar cane."[45] Lam himself said,

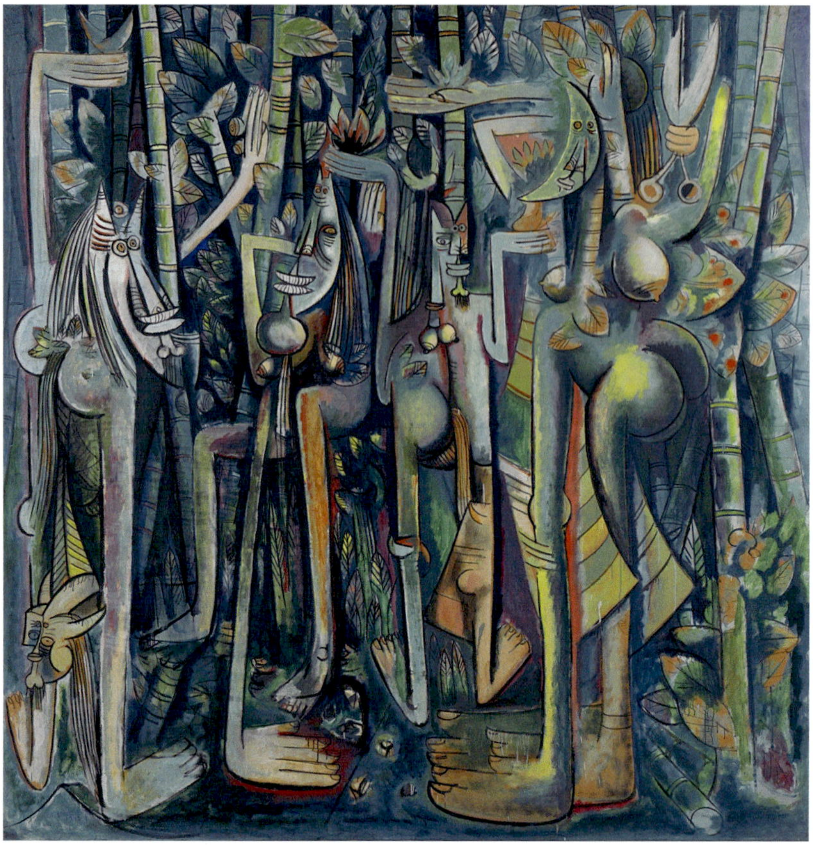

4.12 Wifredo Lam, *The Jungle*, 1943. Gouache and paper on canvas, 94¼ × 90½ in. Museum of Modern Art, New York. © 2025 Artists Rights Society (ARS), New York/ADAGP, Paris. Used by permission.

"The title itself has nothing to do with the real countryside of Cuba, where there is not jungle but woods, hills and open country, and the background of the picture is a sugar-cane plantation. My painting was intended to communicate a psychic state."[46]

Also, horse imagery suggests the concept of spirit possession represented with equestrian metaphors of believers being mounted, as mentioned above. Grafting the various imagery together creates a metaphoric intersection suggestive of the joining of the orisha with the devotee through possession. The palms-up gesture of several figures in the painting creates a sense of offering and surrender. Linsley argues that Lam became interested in Vodou in Haiti in 1944 during a visit by French surrealists André Breton and Pierre Mabille. In his art, "Lam's borrowings from Voodoo were extensive. . . . For example, Lam often makes hybrid human-horse figures, indicated either by equine heads, tails, or hooves. These allude to Voodoo terminology, in which the devotee is called a 'horse,' to be figuratively mounted by the Loa [spirit] in the act of possession."[47]

Lam also borrowed from Santería extensively in his artistic synthesis of African, Antillean, and European elements for his art. Later in his life, he borrowed also from the Afro-Cuban practice of Abakua, another African-derived cultural tradition.

John Yau, in his important essay about this work, suggests that Lam was recovering his heritage while participating in the surrealism movement, whose stated intention was, he indicates, "to overthrow the rational structures of Western Civilization."[48] Implied in Yau's article is that Africans and their New World hybridity are in conflict with Western hierarchies and ontologies.

Conjure and folk religious practices long have been tropes and signs for those black cultural forms rooted in African antecedents but also linked to slavery in the minds of aspirational black people and observational white people. Yvonne Chireau, in her book *Black Magic: Religion and the African American Conjuring Tradition*, writes that after the Civil War, "cultural reformers, including blacks and whites from the northern states, called for the repudiation of Conjure and other slave traditions, identifying them with degradation, ignorance, and the demoralizing experience of bondage."[49]

Despite these efforts, however, Chireau indicates, "When African Americans moved out of slavery and into the social order that freedom offered, they carried their spiritual traditions with them." These spiritual traditions "were ultimately present in almost every geographical location in which African Americans settled."[50] The suppression of these folk practices seemed rooted in the conflict between those in favor of mainstream Christian practices and the promise of social inclusion, and those in favor of the old ways that were found in the cultural sanctuarial spaces where conjure could be found.

The formerly enslaved Patsy Moses recalled:

> De conjure doctor, old Dr. Jones, walk 'bout in de black coat like a preacher, and wear sideburns, and use roots and sich for he medicine.

> He larnt 'bout dem in de piney woods from he old granny. He didn't cast spells like de voodoo doctor, but used roots for smallpox, and rind of bacon for mumps, and sheep-wool tea for whoopin' cough. And for snakebite he used alum and saltpeter and bluestone mix' with brandy or whiskey.
>
> He could break conjure spells with broth. He take he kettle and put in splinters of pine or hickory—jes' so dey has bark on dem'—covers dem with water, and puts in de conjure salt.[51]

Another former slave, Polly Shine, recalled, "When we got sick, we had the best of care. Maser would get us a Negro mama, and she doctored us from herbs she got out of the woods, for coughs and colds."[52]

Beverly Buchanan's 1992 mixed-media sculpture *Medicine Woman* (figure 4.13) draws from this same cultural history and complex. In one of Buchanan's short stories about the medicine woman, she wrote, "Stay away from white sassafras tea. It's dangerous, Emory said long distance from South Carolina. Red Roots are what you need for your medicine. I knew about red sassafras but white was a mystery. Mr. Mathis said his son could lower his blood sugar with yellow root tea."

Buchanan, writing about her *Medicine Woman*, said, "This sculpture has taken almost seven months to complete. But there did come that point—as I touched the floor—when I looked up and said, 'You no longer belong to me.'"[53] The work taps into black southern traditions drawn from Kongo roots with suggestions of bottle trees, and around her feet there is a box of the kinds of natural materials and bottles associated with natural healers and metaphorical associations. Buchanan was from North Carolina but also worked for a good part of her career in the Macon, Georgia, area.

It was common in nineteenth-century Central African Kongo culture to use allegorical materials for the notable nail figures and the larger category they belong to, called *nkisi* (see again figure 4.6). Often these allegorical materials were contained in wrapped bags attached to the figures as a part of *nkisi* complexes or objects.[54]

Theologian Theophus H. Smith suggests black culture itself is "coded discourse, figural transformations, and conjurational performance," and the Bible is used, in a sense, as "a magical formulary for African Americans: a book of ritual prescriptions for reenvisioning and, therein, transforming history and culture." Smith suggests conjure is a magical means of transforming reality, but it also involves healing. With the conjuror "we

4.13 Beverly Buchanan, *Medicine Woman/Evelyn/The Doctor*, 1992. Found object assemblage, 75 × 23¾ × 16½ in. Georgia Museum of Art, University of Georgia, Athens. Gift of the artist's estate.

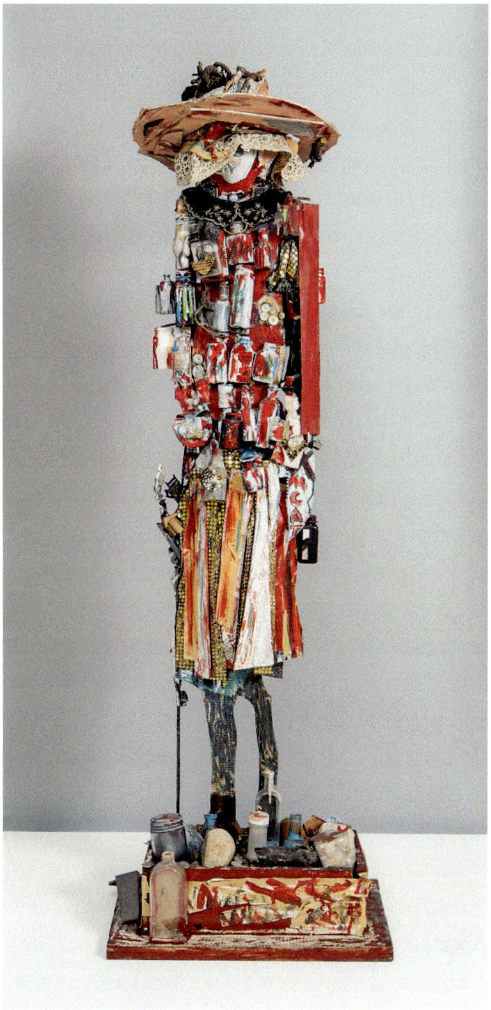

find not only a magician but also a kind of doctor. Such conjurors also claim the power to heal by means of their prescriptions—their pharmacopeia of herbs and roots, human artifacts, and similar materia medica."[55]

The magic of conjure might also be seen as "a primordial and enduring system of communication—as a form of 'language.' But it is obviously not simply speech or expression. Rather, magic is ritual speech and action intended to perform what it expresses." It creates a system of correspondences or signifiers such as might be found "in the philosophical-magical tradition of alchemy." Such correspondences "are a principal feature of contemporary sciences like chemistry" where we "construct a network of signs that enables us first to apprehend and then to transform reality."[56]

Smith helps us find, coded in Bearden's work, aspects of conjure. When we look at Bearden's *Mecklenburg* series, for example, we may similarly find encoded features like the "folk use of the Bible as a 'conjure book': as a kind of magical formulary for prescribing cures and curses, and for invoking extraordinary powers in order to re-envision, revise, and transform the conditions of human existence."[57] This view of conjure resonates with the earlier discussion of Yoruba notions of the language of divine intent embodied in speech; specifically *òrò*, and *ashé* as part of a cosmological system of transformative possibilities.

So why did Bearden reference this "invisible tradition" of conjuring and its associated expressions of ring shouts, "seeking" ceremonies, hoodoo practices, and the like? Rachael DeLue argues there is a "special relationship" between the conjure woman and "the very medium of collage," and in moving to collage in the early 1960s, not only was Bearden evoking his own experiences and memories, but "he understood the medium to have value beyond the artistic and also . . . he believed that as an object, a literal *thing*, a collage might do powerful, transformative work."[58] Collage emerged for Bearden as his major medium of expression during discussions of the Spiral group in 1963 as they sought creative efficacy in support of the civil rights efforts of the time. His compositional fragmentation and repeated emphasis on the eyes, both human and animal, in the *Prevalence of Ritual* series, which included his early conjure women, DeLue suggests, indicate an effort toward a new vision as well as increased visibility for African Americans. Collage, in a sense, suggests the aesthetic of secrecy mentioned above with accumulation and the layering of materials.

I would say the conjure woman and the system, or epistemological frame, in which she existed is at its root the sanctuarial space white people might only see with largely unintelligible fragmented vision. As DeLue says, she was "an idea, metaphor, or myth," and Bearden's use of her "called forth for him an alternate sphere, a rich and redolent zone of magic and the supernatural adjacent to but distinct from the everyday, what constituted a world apart from the prejudice, racism, and segregation regularly faced by African Americans in their normal existence," and this process "drew on African or African American culture for strength and solidarity as well as a way forward in the now."[59] In approximating a vision other than naturalized human vision, Bearden was using a medium to approximate metaphorically the transformative harnessing of the supernatural to interrupt and transform "the natural human-bound course of things."[60] The need for sanctuary would frame the desire for extra-ordinary solutions to the threat of the physical, racialized world in which African Americans lived. James Cone wrote that black people lived with an "existential tension" and a "general dissatisfaction with a cold and trouble-filled world." The blues is "a stubborn refusal to go beyond the existential problem and substitute otherworldly answers."[61] Yet blues references to the system of conjure opened up the transformative possibilities of spiritual power.

Hoodoo, conjure women, and blues music formed in a context that framed these practices as well as nurtured and sustained them. In 1963 Amiri Baraka labeled black folk as *Blues People*, and their cultural expression visualized might be seen as formulating a blues aesthetic or at least as creating coded touchstones of authenticity; signals of being an insider of the culture. The music functioned for people in their everyday lives and became the kind of music played at a fish fry, a family or community gathering telling tales or using metaphors understood by all. This blues aesthetic has become the root work for subsequent artists to return through reference, much like pilgrims to Marie Laveau's gravestone, to an authenticating battery to power their present work and light them as insiders back from the crossroads.

My wheel mule is cripple
My lead mule is blind
My wheel mule is cripple
My lead mule is blind
You know I ain't gonna buy my baby no more stockings
With the seam behind.

MUDDY WATERS, "My Captain" (1964)

CHAPTER 5

Gospel, *Tongues*, and Bearing Witness

> It was through [the old-time Negro preacher] that the people of diverse languages and customs who were brought here from diverse parts of Africa and thrown into slavery were given their first sense of unity and solidarity.
>
> JAMES WELDON JOHNSON, *GOD'S TROMBONES* (1927)

In 2005 Oprah Winfrey hosted a Legends Ball weekend at her Montecito, California, home to honor twenty-five legendary African American women.[1] At the Sunday event wrapping up the three-day weekend, BeBe Winans started singing the gospel song "Changed." He then passed the microphone to Shirley Caesar, then to Dionne Warwick, and on to Yolanda Adams, Chaka Khan, and Gladys Knight while the choir on the stage sang the chorus. Oprah said, "Jesus came!" The camera cut to Maria Shriver, who said, "They were passing the mike around, and I'm like, 'I hope they don't come near us!'" It was unscripted, completely improvised, and those who knew what was happening gave amens, moaned, clapped, stood and shouted, and sang along. Valerie Simpson took over, then passed it to Patti LaBelle! Black religiosity, ecstatic expressiveness, came out into the light as the very famous and nearly famous alike rode the spirit of the moment. Later, newswoman Diane Sawyer said, "For the rest of my life that may be the most transcendently spiritual moment I've ever been part of." What Sawyer experienced was "going to church." Black church.

§

Black people dealt with the dissatisfaction with their difficult existence in the United States in a couple of ways, including through blues expression and with spiritual practices. Church celebrations of survival and triumph were also such a ubiquitous experience for black people that signs and signifiers of that shared experience still evoke certain solidarity like that during Oprah Winfrey's event.

Chicago artist Archibald Motley Jr. created one of the more interesting visual explorations of such religiosity in 1929, around the time when the introduction of recordings began to take blues music out of the Deep South into the mainstream. After his successful 1928 solo exhibition in New York, where all of his notable portraits sold, Motley traveled to the South to visit relatives of his mother's brother in Arkansas near Pine Bluff. There Motley began to experiment with new subject matter as well as paint portraits of relatives and family friends. The painting of Mrs. Fowler, a family friend, is called *The Snuff Dipper* (figure 5.1) and follows Motley's almost ethnographic approach to black subjects. The title, like his *Octoroon* and *Mulatress* titles from a few years earlier, turns the subject into a representation of an archetype more than a unique individual and suggests an existential distance from her.

In 1928 Motley was lauded in the African American newspaper the *Chicago Bee* for his paintings of "octoroons, quadroons, mulattoes, and mammies."[2] The paintings were titled in this way rather than using the subject's name, turning them as a series into an ethnographic inquiry of a sort. Mrs. Fowler's visage, complete with a toothpick coming from the right side of her mouth, is transformed into an ethnic type as well. The subject appears in front of a simple, flat background wearing simple clothing painted without much attention to its detail or textural illusion, as had been common in many of Motley's earlier portraits. The title adds character allusions to the subject and penetrates a bit of the mystery behind the unsmiling pose that reveals little of her personality.

However, the taciturn facial expression is, in a sense, a cultural gesture echoing the composed facial expression often prescribed for public postures and formalized in the archetypical faces found in sculpture from many West African carvings prior to this period. Even the most natural of African sculptures, the Ife heads of the Yoruba (ca. eleventh–fifteenth century), present a controlled visage with emotionless eyes. Most African American photo portraiture up to this period, beyond the technical considerations of better film speeds that became available to photographers in subsequent decades, show people in control of their facial expressions.

Four years after Motley's painting, P. H. Polk of Tuskegee, Alabama, produced *Pipe Smoker* (1932; figure 5.2), a similar image of an elderly black

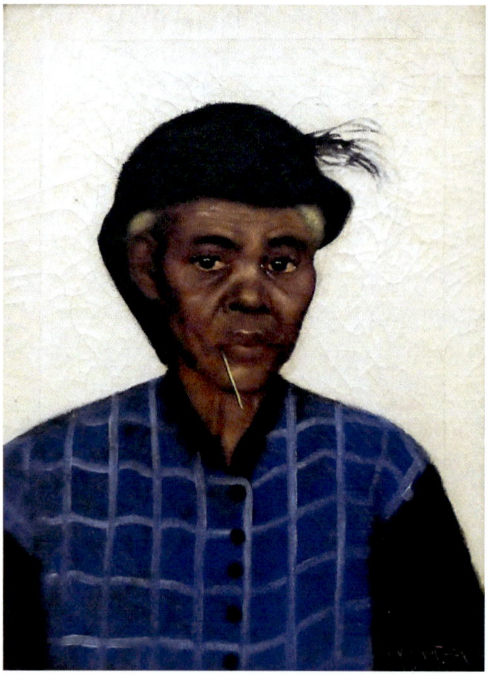

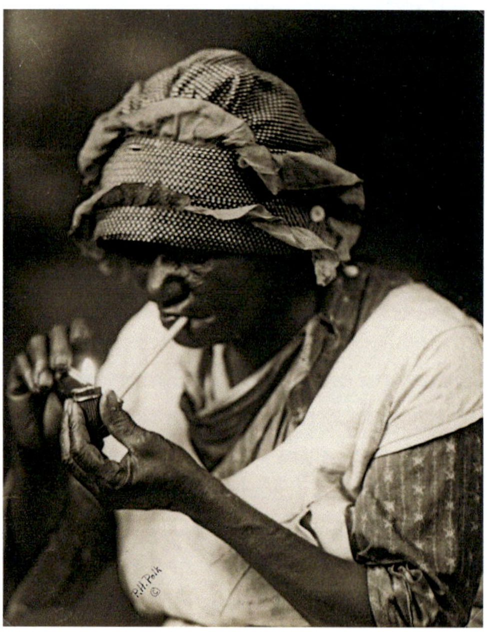

5.1 (*top*) Archibald Motley Jr., *The Snuff Dipper*, 1928. Oil on canvas, 22 × 16 in. In this portrait of an African American woman with a toothpick in her mouth, the woman's face is realistically detailed and shaded, while her clothing and her background are simpler and flatter. The painting illustrates the artist's almost ethnographic approach to black subjects, as well as similarities between early twentieth-century African American portraiture, which featured subjects controlling their facial expressions, and a much older tradition of West African carvings.

5.2 (*bottom*) Prentice H. Polk, *The Pipe Smoker*, from the Nexus Press Portfolio, 1932 (printed 1981). Gelatin silver print, 10 × 8 in. (sheet); $9\frac{5}{8} \times 7\frac{9}{16}$ in. (image). An elderly black woman, her eyes hidden from the gaze of the camera beneath the brim of her bonnet, holds a match to her tobacco pipe. Her expression is stoic and dignified, fixed solely on the ritual act of lighting her pipe, hinting at a depth of wisdom and character turned inward, protectively masked from the eyes of outsiders. This image expresses the act of public masking, not just as a political tactic of racialized subjects but also as a cultural artifact of Yoruba traditions of decorum. Jesse Metcalf Fund. 84.223.2. Courtesy of RISD Museum, Rhode Island School of Design, Providence.

rural woman lighting tobacco who, while not acknowledging the viewer or the camera, maintains a controlled, dignified facial expression. Both images provide a sense of a strong, confident personality while maintaining the public mask attributed to the need for protection and public privacy in a hostile environment but also carry the echo of the cultural admonitions for decorum often found at the root of Yoruba *gẹlẹdẹ* masquerade traditions, which offer sideways critiques, for example, of Western visitors for their public displays of affection. Masking in public was not just a response to racialized social conditions but also a cultural artifact.

Alain Locke wrote an essay, "Enter the New Negro," for the March 1925 issue of *Survey Graphic* magazine, which he also edited. In announcing a new urban, confident, and more geographically diverse black population, Locke noted, "For generations in the mind of America, the Negro has been more of a formula than a human being" and needed to be liberated from "unjust stereotypes." He argued that the day "of 'aunties,' 'uncles' and 'mammies' is equally gone. Uncle Tom and Sambo have passed on" and that, with the growth of class differentiation, "if it ever was warrantable to regard and treat the Negro en masse, it is becoming with every day less possible, more unjust and more ridiculous."[3]

Like W. E. B. Du Bois in his 1903 book *The Souls of Black Folk*, Locke looked at black vernacular ways and music as a trope for black culture, a sign of authenticity. "Recall how suddenly the Negro spirituals revealed themselves; suppressed for generations under the stereotypes of Wesleyan hymn harmony, secretive, half ashamed, until the courage of being natural brought them out—and behold, there was folk-music."[4] Motley, like Du Bois and Locke, was not a part of black vernacular cultural experience—all had middle-class backgrounds and aspirations—but he turned toward its observation and interpretation in his late-modernist style of genre scenes.

Amy Mooney, in her 2004 exploration of Motley and his work, offers that Motley was meticulous with the setting and details of paintings so that they were "replete with meaning." Mooney argues that "through careful examination of skin tone, conscious labeling, and direct references to class hierarchies, Motley explored the shifting definitions of racial identity."[5] While many of his contemporaries in the New Negro era sought to humanize and personalize subjects to counter the objectifying typecasting of a great deal of American visual representation of African Americans, Motley seemed to deftly critique the racialized classifications while exploring the diversity of class, heritage, skin tone, gestures, and living circumstances of black people. Though class and color were separating factors among black experiences and attitudes at the time, in the end racial categorization placed virtually all black people within what operated like a caste.

Tongues (Holy Rollers), another painting from his Arkansas journey, continued Motley's turn toward his mature style, when he focused mainly on genre scenes of black social settings (figure 5.3).[6] At what apparently is an evening revival service, the preacher sways to his right with arms held high above his head at the pulpit with members of the congregation under his sway, so to speak. A woman seemingly filled with the spirit mirrors the preacher as she faces the viewer, mouth open in spiritual ecstasy and exaltation, and sways to her right. It is a moment filled with sound as the musicians play, people clap and shout, a woman to the left of the stage uses a tambourine, and most mouths are open in voice.

Mooney points to the pulled-back curtains framing the scene as a revival of a much older technique from European painting, establishing the tableau as a stage of sorts to bring the viewer into the composition. Motley used this tactic in his 1927 interior genre scene *Stomp* (figure 5.4). Also, consistent with Motley's career-long awareness of the "symbolic quality of light," he "illuminated the church interior with three electric lights" as "an appropriate reference to the Trinity."[7] A musical band rather than the old rhythms of the broom and the body animates Motley's *Stomp* scene. Like *Tongues* it nonetheless contains a mix of vernacular expressionism that was far removed from the kind of Catholic services experienced by his family yet consistent with the everyday lives of working-class black folk that seemed to fascinate him.

Note as well that *Tongues* does not depict a mournful rendition of "Amazing Grace," or Negro spirituals like "Go Down Moses" or "Steal Away to Jesus" that might be found in the work, for example, of the Fisk Jubilee Singers, who traveled the country beginning in 1871 performing these songs (figure 5.5). This is a moment that seems lifted from James Weldon Johnson's 1927 classic *God's Trombones: Seven Negro Sermons in Verse*. Johnson wrote in the preface, "I have witnessed congregations moved to ecstasy by the rhythmic intoning of sheer incoherencies. . . . [The preacher] often possessed a voice that was a marvelous instrument, a voice he could modulate from a sepulchral whisper to a crashing thunder clap."[8]

Johnson wrote about the emotional intensity aroused when adept preachers amped up the rhetoric: "The change in the congregation was instantaneous. An electric current ran through the crowd. It was in a moment alive and quivering; and all the while the preacher held it in the

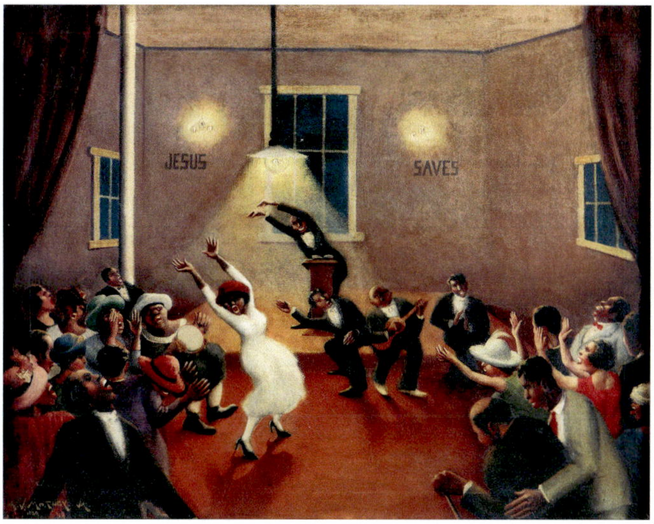

5.3 Archibald Motley Jr., *Tongues (Holy Rollers)*, 1929. Oil on canvas, 29¼ × 36⅛ in. Collection of Archie Motley and Valerie Gerrard Browne. © Valerie Gerrard Browne/Chicago History Museum/Bridgeman Images. Used by permission.

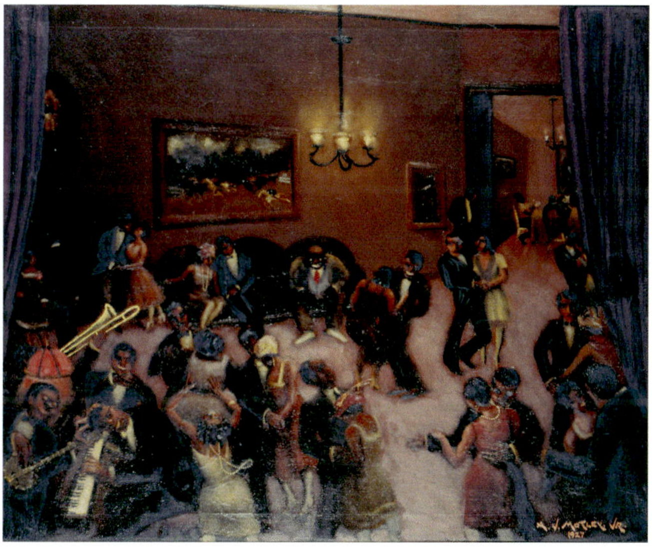

5.4 Archibald Motley Jr., *Stomp*, 1927. Oil on canvas, 11¾ × 14½ in. Private collection/© Chicago History Museum/© Estate of Archibald John Motley Jr. All rights reserved 2024/ Bridgeman Images.

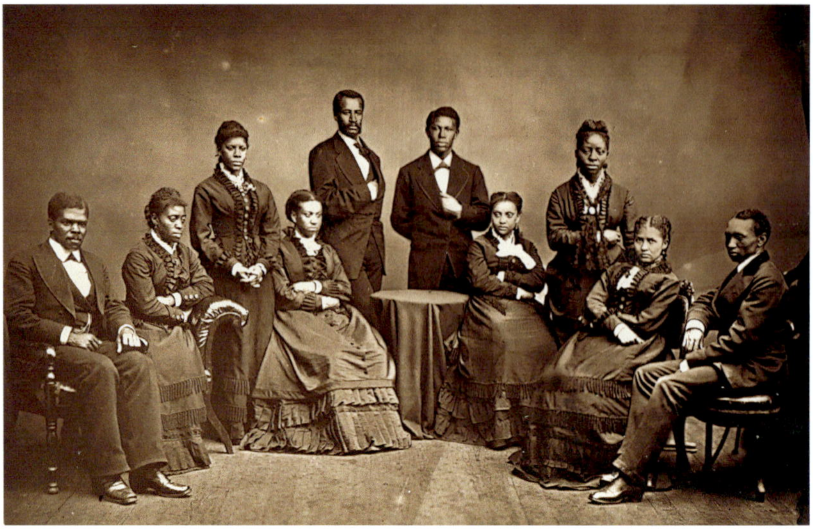

5.5 Fisk Jubilee Singers in 1875. This photo was published in London in *The Wesleyan-Methodist Magazine* in 1898. From George Lester, "Fisk University," 39.

palm of his hand."[9] Motley's preacher appears to be in orchestral mode, conducting the crowd. His raised hands are palms down as opposed to the palms-up gesture of the woman in white. Everyone seems to be leaning in the direction of his gesture, and many of the women in the audience also have their hands raised. There is a shout going on! As Zora Neale Hurston explained, "Broadly speaking, shouting is an emotional explosion, responsive to rhythm. It is called forth by (1) sung rhythm; (2) spoken rhythm; (3) humming rhythm; (4) the foot-patting or hand-clapping that imitates very closely the tom-tom."[10]

Hurston suggests that shouting is infectious and common in the collective privacy of vernacular spaces like the one Motley has pictured. She says, "Shouting is a community thing. It thrives in concert. It is the first shout that is difficult for the preacher to arouse. After that one they are likely to sweep like fire over the church. This is easily understood, for the rhythm is increasing with each shouter who communicates his fervor to someone else."[11]

Importantly, Hurston, who like Motley was a cultural observer within her own community, indicates that within the communal experience, individuality and creativity flourished. "It is absolutely individualistic. While there are general types of shouting, the shouter may mix the different styles to his liking, or he may express himself in some fashion never seen before."[12]

Hurston was able to witness shouting as an insider, but white people were not usually as welcome. Lydia Parrish, who collected shout songs from the Sea Islands off the coast of Georgia in the early 1940s, reported that her informants were self-conscious about performing in front of her, and it was "years before I was permitted to see the St. Simon's Negroes indulge in this innocent performance. Why they should have been so secretive about such a pastime I cannot understand."[13] Art Rosenbaum in 1998 described the elements of the ring shout he observed that were consistent with nineteenth-century accounts:

> [Lawrence] McKiver, as lead singer or "songster," began or "set" a song. At his side sat a "sticker" or "stick man," beating a broomstick on the floor in rhythm. Behind them a group of other singers, or "basers," answered McKiver's lines in call-and-response fashion, at the same time setting up counter-rhythms to the stick beat with clapping hands and patting feet. Then the "shouters," women dressed in the long dresses and head rags of their grandmothers' day, began to move in a counter-clockwise circle, with a compelling hitching shuffle, often stooping or extending their arms in gestures pantomiming the content of the song being sung.[14]

To the untutored observer, the movements looked like dancing, but Rosenbaum indicated that "nonagenarian Deacon James Cook later explained the difference: 'Back in the days of my coming on in the shout, if you cross your feet you were dancing, but if you solid, move on the square, you were shouting.'"[15] Importantly here, *shouting* initially referred to the movements, not the vocalizations. As the pioneering African American linguist Lorenzo Dow Turner (1890–1972) indicated, the word is a Gullah dialect survival of "the Afro-Arabic *saut*, sometimes pronounced 'shout,' meaning a fervent dance around the Kabaa in Mecca." Early practitioners might have used the concept of shout as a way to praise God, "reinforced by the English word 'shout'" in the Bible.[16]

Shouting also differs from spirituals, hymns, and jubilee and gospel songs, especially from the "sorrow songs" like those Du Bois wrote about in *The Souls of Black Folk*. The practice is group affirming, upbeat, and the content of the songs is positive rather than lamenting one's circumstances. Shouting functioned outside the organized church structure and often was practiced surreptitiously in "praise houses" in the woods, or after church services, when the benches were moved away to create an open space. Deacon Cook said that the shout is seasonal because "shouting ain't no easy job. The tradition of shouting is when it was cold weather."[17] Parrish observed that "the hold of shouting is tenacious, and it is practiced during the Christmas holidays to this day. All the country Negroes enjoy it immensely."[18]

The floor in Motley's *Tongues* painting (figure 5.3) is clear of pews or benches, and the male just in front of the preacher in the center of the painting is expressing a gesture known as *kneebone*, a bent-knee accompaniment to a song of prayer. The shouter Lawrence McKiver, also quoted by Rosenbaum, explained while discussing a song called "Kneebone Bend":

> That's the oldest slave song that ever was sung by black people when they first come over from Africa over here. See, the song would say "kneebone in the wilderness," you see, they didn't know where they was—so that was going to a place they . . . didn't know nothing about, understand? So they would sing this song, "kneebone in the wilderness, kneebone in the valley," they was praying at the time, that's why they say "kneebone bend," they was bending down, they was praying. . . . That's the way my mama told it to me, and aunts. I had some old ancestors that put out these songs, you know.[19]

Writing about the song "Knee-bone Bend," Parrish says, "In the shout song, Knee-Bone, curious twists and exotic tones are employed—including the musical, yet nasal 'ha-nnn'—that must be heard to be appreciated. None of our musical symbols is capable of suggesting the strange turns used in this as well as others of the more primitive Afro-American chants."[20]

The song is repetitive and was used both for shouting and also for rowing boats. Interestingly, Parrish says that "the other two rhythms, the hands and heels," were not used for the rowing because they would have "thrown the rowers off their beat." The lyrics of the song are given:

> Knee-bone when I call you
> H-a-nnn knee bone
> Knee-bone when I call you
> H-a-nnn Lord knee-bone bend
> Bend my knee-bone to the ground
> H-a-nnn knee-bone

Bend my knee-bone to the ground
H-a-nnn knee-bone bend
Knee-bone Zachaniah
H-a-nnn knee bone bend.[21]

We can excavate from Parrish's observations the tonal qualities, mentioned earlier, found in African languages and musical expression. She also notes the complicated, multilevel rhythmic quality to this deep vernacular form. While Motley's painting is not showing the ring shout, we can discern some of these elements of shouting embedded in the image. At the heart of shouting is spiritual ecstasy and related practices and indicative gestures. The painting is not a documentary object, but it is evocative and full of cultural signs and signifiers. Many postures, expressions, and gestures found in its images represent prayerful and spiritual engagement.

For example, in many West and Central African masking traditions half-closed eyes are indicative of an inner, otherworldly focus due to the presence of spirit within. Likewise, bulging or overly wide-open eyes suggest the energy of a spiritual visitor (figure 5.6). A number of the faces in *Tongues* echo this signification, though Motley would have had no knowledge of this. The work of Motley and Hurston extended beyond the ethnographic or anthropological observations found at this time in the work of the celebrated French ethnographer Marcel Griaule among the Dogon, for example. Their research more authentically included a sense of bearing witness to vernacular practices at the root of their own culture.[22]

Regarding vernacular cultural studies, we may postulate an element of conjure encoded in Motley's painting. Applying the ideas of Theophus Smith, we can see in artistic works features similar to those attributed in the preceding chapter to the collages of Romare Bearden. To repeat, such features involve "a folk use of the Bible as a 'conjure book': as a kind of magical formulary for prescribing cures and curses, and for invoking extraordinary powers in order to re-envision, revise, and transform the conditions of human existence."[23] Similarly, blues music and the gospel experience are secular and sacred stances for dealing with the existential difficulties black people faced, as discussed in the previous chapter, in a world of vexations. Both offered a means of alchemy for the transcendence or catharsis of harsh times and circumstances, performatively "making a way out of no way."

To this we can add Beverly Robinson's ideas about African Americans ritualizing spaces and her notion that "preachers ritualized the pulpit in

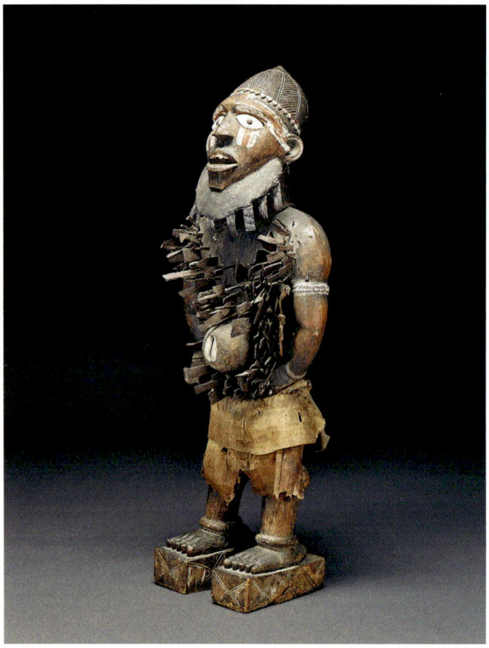

5.6 BaKongo *nkisi nkondi* (standing power figure) with overly wide eyes. These figures are seen as vessels for inhabitation by a *simbi* (spirit) that animates them. Democratic Republic of the Congo, Chiloango River region, Yombe peoples, late nineteenth to early twentieth century. Wood, iron, raffia, ceramic, pigment, kaolin, red camwood, resin, dirt, leaves, animal skin, and cowrie shell, 43¾ × 15½ × 11 in. Dallas Museum of Art. Foundation for the Arts Collection. Gift of McDermott Foundation. Image courtesy of Dallas Museum of Art. 1996.184.fa.

a tradition that was common to the deep structure of their heritage." She writes that early preachers were able, "like the traditional griot, to translate text into something understandable, particularly when most of the text was too cryptic to follow." Also, Robinson argues, the preacher's storytelling was "not a passive event; it is actively conjured. . . . The story teaches how to deal with existing forces by creating a mode which demonstrates . . . potency in relationship to what might have been considered overwhelming odds."[24]

Formulations of transformation are mimetic practices in African and African diasporal cultures from West and Central Africa and are a part of the African cultural syntax, the language of living despite a shifting mix of expressive elements in varied settings. Smith indicates that there is a "multicultural character of African American culture itself, which is not monocultural in terms either of Afro- or Euro-American referents."[25]

Richard Powell suggests that Motley's painted church, though it might be modeled on an actual structure in Arkansas, is reminiscent of the storefront churches that began to proliferate in Chicago as more and more migrants from the South arrived.[26] Southern migrants became cultural suitcases packed with their folkways, music, and religious expressiveness that found new, evolved expression in Chicago and elsewhere. The rustic attire and brogan-type boots of the tambourine player on the left suggest a rural setting, while the more formal attire of the band members might intimate a more urban setting. The variety of attire, the various skin tones, the plainness of the windows (instead of stained glass, or a blank wall instead of a large cross), and the pulled-back curtains imply that Motley threw a wide net in capturing black spiritual practice and cultural gestures as well as artistic conventions in composing this image.

Motley's curious relationship with black folk culture seems to be embodied by his resorting to what has been interpreted as a doppelgänger in his genre paintings through a recurring figure balding on top and often facing away from the viewer or with his head down. Motley himself was not bald until much later in life, so this figure made an interesting choice. Powell wrote that he is a physical antithesis, but Motley's conceptual doppelgänger often performs as a symbolic witness.[27] What might have been his first appearance came in *Stomp*. Powell observes that this fat man became a surrogate "for the real-life voyeurs of Bronzeville, whether Caucasians, African Americans, sly gawkers, art gallery visitors, or, like Motley, a symbolic observer from within the raucous interior."[28] Rather than engaging in the cabaret pleasures of the setting, this observer gorges himself gratifyingly with seeing. Still, I find most useful an interpretation of this figure as primarily Motley himself, an idea amplified by the belief that all art is on some level autobiographical.

Motley, with his contradictions—living in two (or more) worlds, excavating subtle elements of black urban life while perpetuating some of its problematic assumptions—might be seen as a trickster figure. He moved across racialized neighborhood boundaries, vastly different worlds—Motley lived in a predominantly white neighborhood and occupied a different class background than many of his subjects. His wife was a Chicagoan of German descent. He visited Bronzeville as a fascinated, invited observer. His literal and virtual oscillations between these worlds mimicked the attributes and movement of Eshu. Yet, like the character Claire in Nella Larson's 1929 novel *Passing*, Motley seemed drawn with relentless fascination to Bronzeville's cultural play and nightlife.[29] Claire kept returning to the black community in the story at great risk to her established status as passing for white and to her marriage to a white man with stated disdain for Negroes.

Motley's doppelgänger made what appears to be his second appearance in *Tongues*, after having emerged two years earlier in *Stomp*. He is in the lower right of the picture frame, leaning on a cane and being helped by a younger man. As he leans left into the scene, this bald figure is the only person who is uninvolved with the emotional and ecstatic exuberance all around. Anthropologically he might be described as a participant observer. Like Motley, he is there documenting an Other performing culture. Yet he is a witness more than an intruder.

We find him again in two 1934 paintings, *Barbecue* and *Black Belt*. The bald man is in the front of the street scene in *Black Belt* (figure 5.7), but he is turned toward the viewer, hands in his pockets, and is not engaged with anyone else in the scene. His sleeves are rolled up as if he is working, but he stands motionless while all around him people are engaged with each other or animated with gestures, gazes, or being rendered with diagonal lines or smiles.

Barbecue (figure 5.8) at first seems to be an indoor scene, but two buildings in the background, the one on the left with escaping chimney smoke, where the meat apparently is being cooked, indicate an outdoor scene. The bald man sits at a table to the lower right eating what must be a rib or chicken wing (symbolically engorging the setting?), again with eyes downward, and engaging no one despite sitting next to a woman dressed in bright blue. The mix of cloth-covered tables and outdoor buildings with two tuxedo-wearing waiters moving between them, as well as a vanishing horizon line, turns the setting into a sort of mise-en-scène, a staged virtual setting. Yet it is rife with keenly observed cultural details of dress, skin color, hairstyles, gestures, and various class and labor roles and acts. Again our observer has his sleeves rolled up, unlike his surrounding companions. His pleasure and work are seeing.

If we return to *Tongues*, the bald man does not have his sleeves rolled up, but this might be, if we follow the diagonal of his body and left arm in the painting, his come-to-Jesus moment. The arms of the preacher, the raised arms of the woman in white, and the right hand of the bent-knee singer all point to "Jesus" on the wall in the upper left of the painting. Has the bald man gotten the faith, a commitment to black life in all its levels and complexity?

Whether intentional or not, *Tongues* taps into several fundamental elements of the American black experience and its aspirations, ideas of freedom, and expressive or symbolic forms. Religious music functioned, as did the religion, as a cultural verb. James Cone says it affirmed universality because the "essence of black religion was the emphasis on the *somebodiness* of black slaves."[30] Also, Cone continues, "They shouted and they prayed; they preached and they sang, because they had found some-

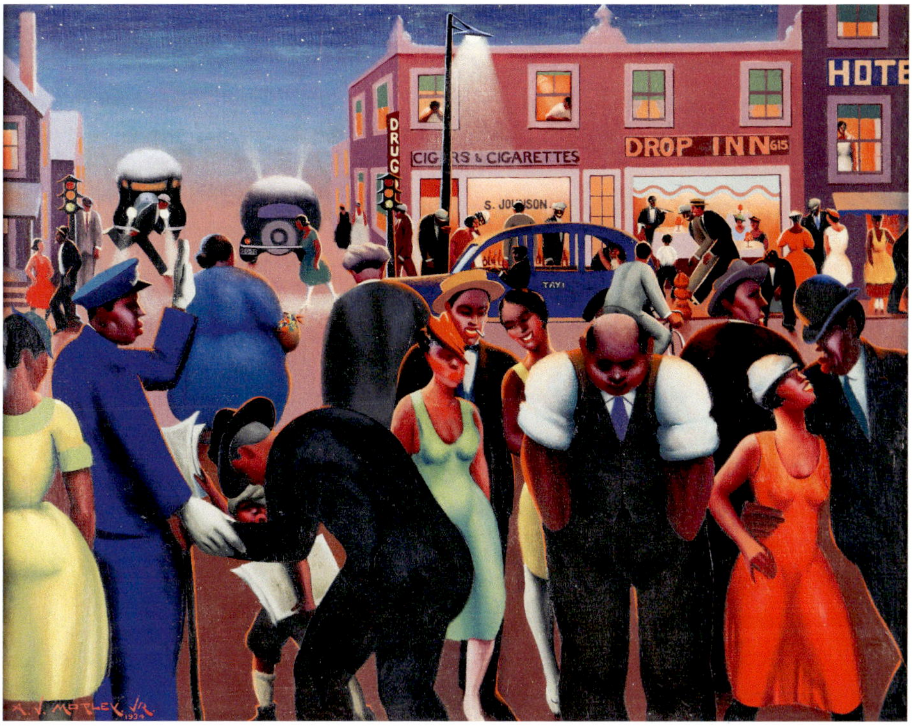

5.7 Archibald Motley Jr., *Black Belt*, 1934. Oil on canvas, 33 × 40½ in. Gift of Harmon Foundation. Hampton University Museum, Hampton, VA © Chicago History Museum/© Estate of Archibald John Motley Jr. All rights reserved 2023/Bridgeman Images.

5.8 Archibald Motley Jr., *Barbecue*, 1934. Oil on canvas, 39 × 44 in. This depiction of a large outdoor gathering of African American men and women dressed in fashionable attire, socializing and eating barbecue, is an abstract gradient of colors. Motley has drawn himself into the painting, which suggests that the artist developed his style by inserting himself into these gatherings and observing the cultural details of dress, skin color, hairstyles, gestures, and various class and labor roles and acts.

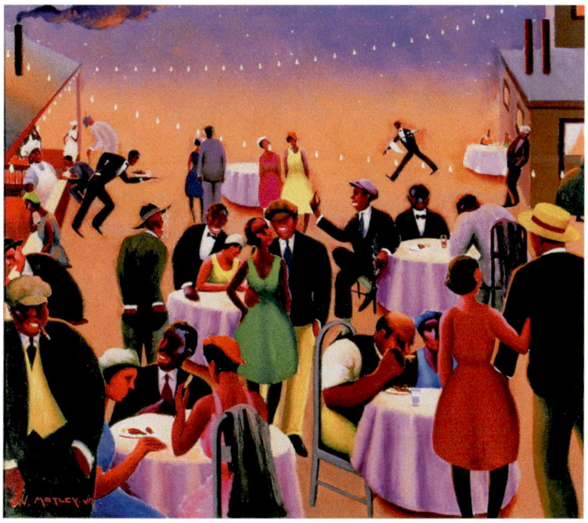

thing. They encountered a new reality; a new God not enshrined in white churches and religious gatherings."[31]

Black religiosity continued to perform as a signifier for African American artists. In chapter 1 we see how Hale Woodruff's woodblock print *By Parties Unknown* (figure 1.6) used the church as a social and political referent for black communal life. But implied also was the role of the preacher as an activist leading freedom movements and struggles. The dumping of a lynch victim's body on the steps of a church indicated a repudiation of that activism.

Additionally, black religion served as an agency for liberation and change. Cone says that the "theme of liberation that ran through slave religion explains why slave holders did not allow black slaves to worship openly and sing their songs unless authorized white people were present to proctor the meeting."[32] Remember, black people preferred their own worship and churches away from white people and often abandoned white churches immediately on emancipation.

Charles White's epic 1952 image *Preacher* (figure 5.9) used foreshortening techniques from below the preacher's hands to create a heroic image of the preacher more as an allegorical figure than a specific personality. In a culture with an emphasis on spiritual transformation and power, liberation struggles often were linked to obeah men or women (in the case of Denmark Vesey and Jamaican maroon leader Nanny), spiritual visions (Nat Turner), church leadership (Martin Luther King Jr. and the Southern Christian Leadership Conference [SCLC]), extra-Christian activism (Elijah Muhammad and the Nation of Islam, Malcolm X), and even the hell-and-brimstone fury of abolitionist John Brown.[33]

The emotional oratory of Baptist services, including speaking in tongues (glossolalia), often associated with Pentecostal denominations, suggests the incantatory use of the Bible as a conjure book and its use in oratory rituals (Smith), and Dwight Andrews's epigraph in chapter 2 about the sung word being more powerful than the spoken word. At the center of these associations, we often find the minister, preacher, or charismatic/prophetic leader. Like Motley's preacher, White's preacher is orchestrating with his hands, at once holding down a congregant with his right-hand gesture, while making a point pushing us forward, conceptually if not physically. Many photos of Martin Luther King Jr. are from a similar angle, with his right hand conducting his message in verisimilitude with Motley's and White's preachers in a life-imitating-art moment captured on film (figures 5.9, 5.10, and 5.11).

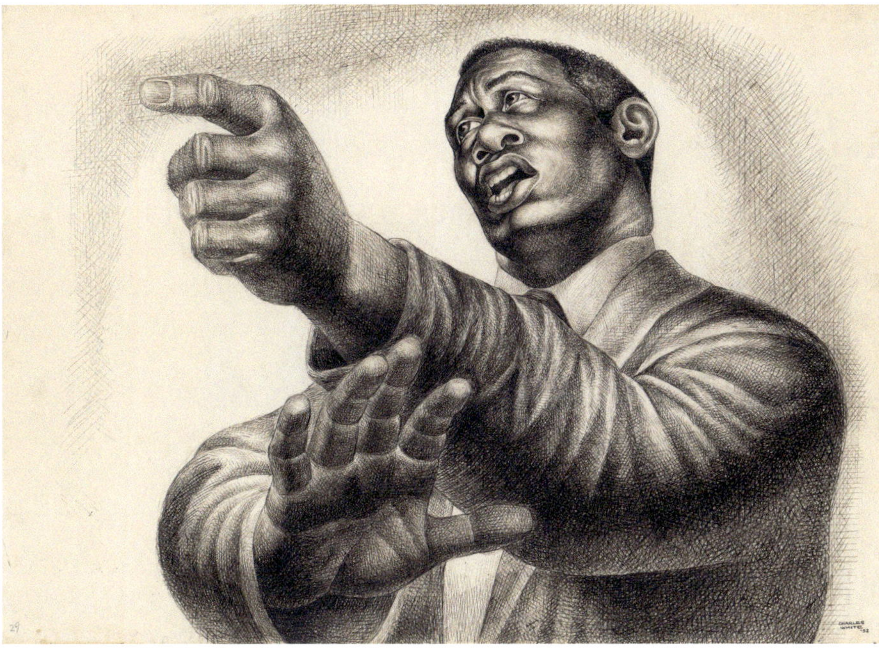

5.9 Charles White, *Preacher*, 1952. Pen and ink and graphite pencil on board, $22\frac{13}{16} \times 29\frac{15}{16}$ in. (sheet). Image: 22. Accession number 52.25. Whitney Museum of American Art, New York. © 1952 Charles White Archives. Courtesy of Charles White Archives. Digital image © Whitney Museum of American Art/Licensed by Scala/Art Resource, NY.

Importantly, black churches like the one reimagined by Archibald Motley in *Tongues* offered places where folk could express old religious and spiritual tendencies unfettered by the white gaze or the anticipation of it. Full-throated expression and the implications of the magical reality of a spiritual universe that include the potentials of conjure, being filled with the spirit, and ecstatic worship offered hope and catharsis in a mirrored reflection of the way blues music worked to relieve people from life's harsh realities and disappointments. Reading Motley's painting culturally through the black interior instead of, or in addition to, its formal relationship to European modernism offers richer textural possibilities than otherwise might be the case.

The preacher served as the ritual master of this universe; the provocateur of the process, the biblical conjuror, and the doorway to spiritual access and, therefore, healing and liberation. The church was a place behind

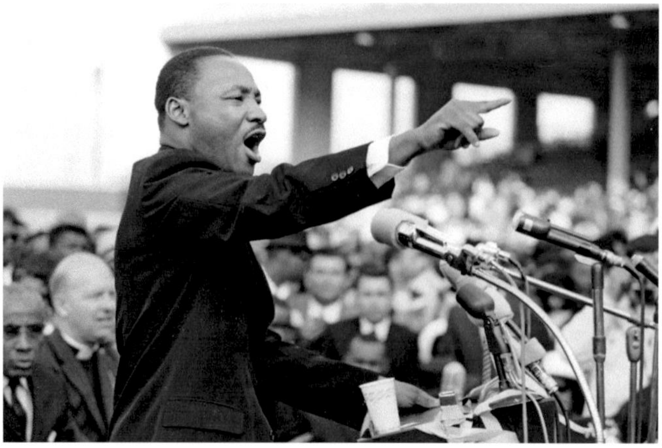

5.10 Dr. Martin Luther King Jr. in 1963, speaking at a civil rights rally in Los Angeles. He points with the index finger of his right hand, a gesture commonly used by prophetic leaders of black liberation movements. King's gesture links him to other black liberation leaders, including Denmark Vesey, Nat Turner, and Malcolm X. © Julian Wasser, photographer.

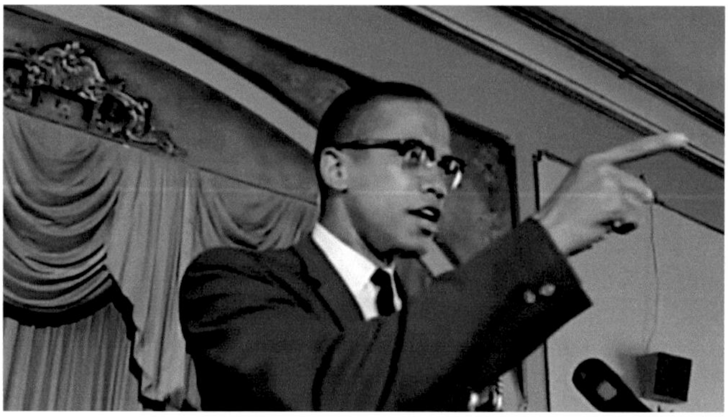

5.11 Malcolm X is captured here pointing with his right hand in an often-photographed gesture. This still image is from a filmed 1962 speech in which he condemns police brutality and a police raid in Los Angeles that killed Nation of Islam member Ronald Stokes. He emphasizes his point with an outstretched right hand and pointed index finger, pushing the audience forward conceptually.

the mask, behind the veil, and a cultural and emotional charm to hang around one's neck, per se, when traveling back out into the racialized world. And people often sang:

> Oh Freedom! Oh Freedom!
> Oh Freedom, I love thee!
> And before I'll be a slave,
> I'll be buried in my grave,
> And go home to my Lord and be free.
>
> "OH, FREEDOM," African American spiritual, quoted in James Cone, *The Spirituals and the Blues* (1972)

CHAPTER 6

Undone

Bottle Trees, Charms, and Flashing Spirits

> My mother valued her mother's spiritual intelligence and thus trained me to accept knowledge acquired through psychic and spiritual experiences as a credible epistemological source.
>
> DIANNE STEWART, *THREE EYES FOR THE JOURNEY* (2005)

> I'm interested in incorporating very ancient religions into contemporary imagery and ideas, keeping the ancient ideas alive so that they can serve a very useful purpose in everyday life.
>
> ALISON SAAR, QUOTED IN MICHAEL D. HARRIS, "ALISON SAAR: THE NATURE OF US" (2017)

As I entered the Otis Art Institute gallery in Los Angeles in 2013, a gauzy material hung in front of me, forcing my gaze upward. It was the garment hanging from a seated female figure in a chair on the wall about sixteen feet in the air. It was Alison Saar's sculpture *Undone* (figure 6.1), a striking work filled with airy space and earthy implications. As I approached the work, it became apparent that beneath the gauzy garment was something that at first looked like the female figure's entrails. But they turned out to be the branches of a bottle tree dangling from an exaggerated umbilical cord/branch hanging beneath the seated woman. This offered an invitation for a cultural reading of the work.

Bottle trees, according to oral and written histories as early as 1776, come from Kongo practices and have been found in the Caribbean and across the Deep South from Texas to South Carolina.[1] Eudora Welty

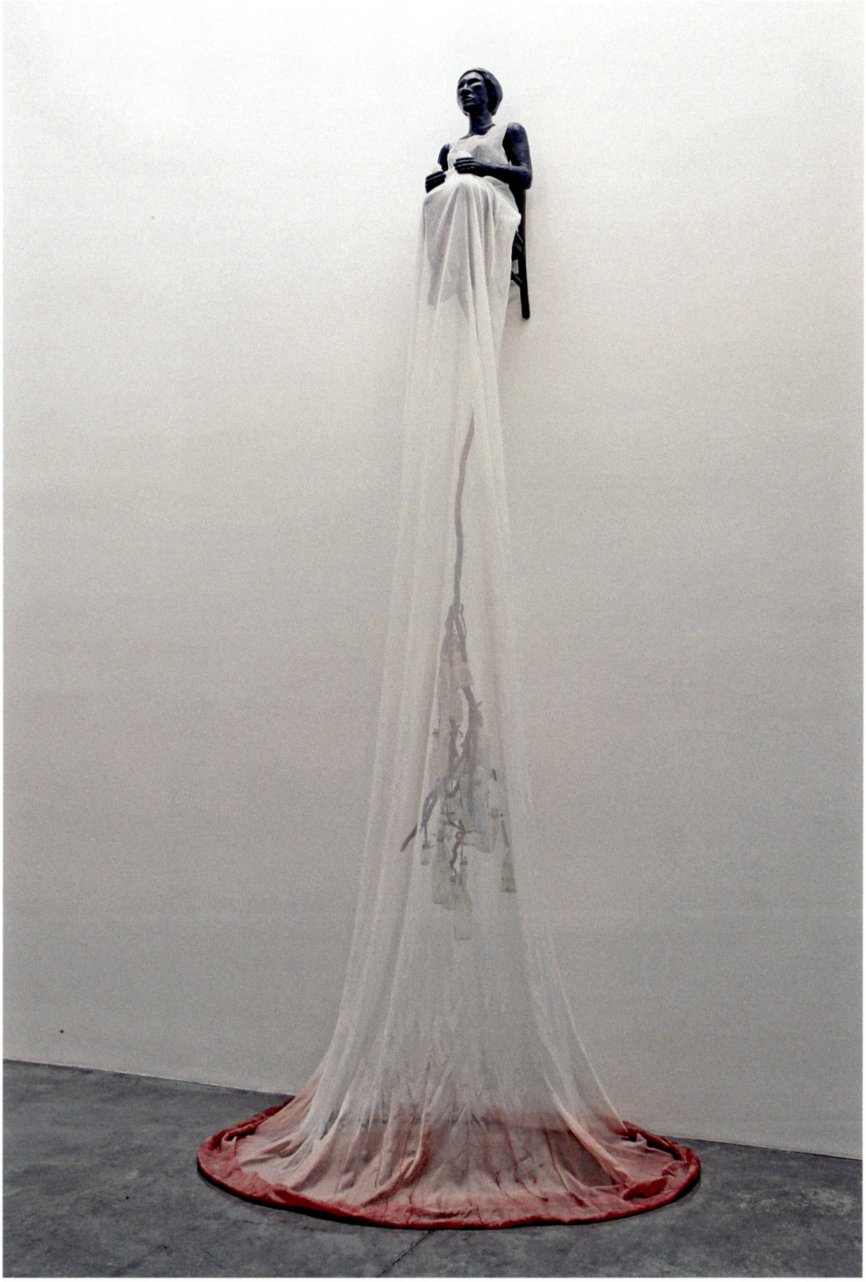

6.1 Alison Saar, *Undone*, 2012. Fiberglass, cotton dress, and found chair and objects, 180 × 60 × 60 in. © Alison Saar. Courtesy of L.A. Louver, Venice, CA.

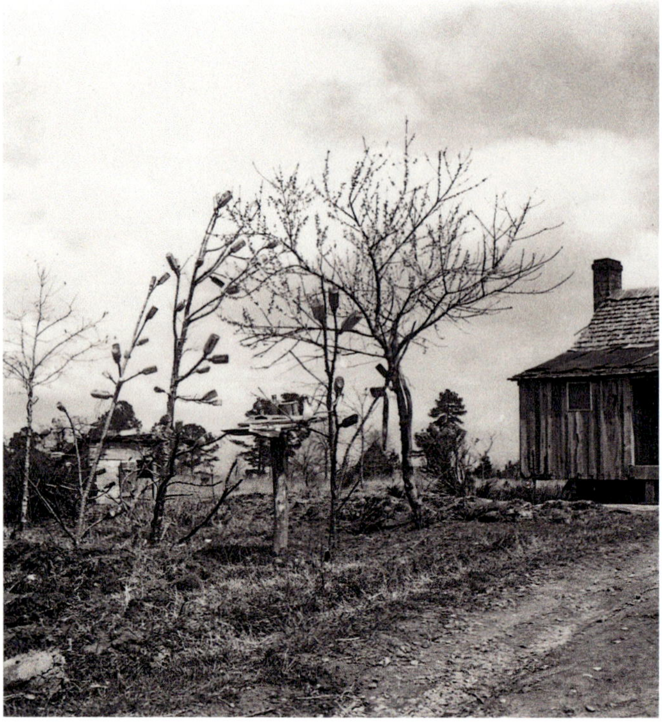

6.2 Bottle trees photographed by Eudora Welty, 1930s or 1940s Mississippi. While Welty was working for the Works Progress Administration she photographed this home in rural Mississippi. Bottle trees like the three in the foreground of this photo, with empty glass bottles (often multicolored) attached to the branches of trees, began to be recorded in the Caribbean and across the Deep South in the eighteenth century. They have their origin in Kongo practices. One common interpretation of their use is to protect from evil spirits by trapping them inside the bottles to be destroyed by sunlight. From Eudora Welty, *One Time, One Place*, 45.

photographed some in Mississippi during her time working for the Works Progress Administration in the 1930s and 1940s (figure 6.2). One of the common interpretations of their usage is to protect from evil spirits, who are attracted by the colors and flash of the bottles and become trapped inside, to be destroyed by the morning sunlight. The sound of the wind blowing across the bottles is said to be the sound of the spirits trapped inside.

Often attached to crepe myrtle trees, the bottles are the remnants of a spiritual tradition that recognizes human life to be a part of a continuum connected to and affected by the unseen world. In Kongo culture, added objects, accumulations, charms, and grave adornments contribute to an aesthetic that differs from the gestural and symbolic markers in Yoruba traditions. It is not as dependent on color, inscribed lines, well-defined shapes, iconography, or marks. Nor do we find equivalence to the Yoruba orisha in the organization of the Kongo spiritual system. Its creolization in the New World through Vodou, Candomblé, and Hoodoo examples adds twists that we see in blues music, southern grave decoration, memory jars, and incantatory practitioners such as the obeah man and the conjure woman (like famed New Orleans Hoodoo priestess Marie Laveau).

The glass of bottles glitters, and in Kongo traditions, as Robert Farris Thompson has written, the "intimation of glory in glittering objects and the embedding of spirit therein become a spiritual fundament in the making of African-American charms."[2] Thompson continues, saying that taking mirrors of glass from the home of a dead person in Kongo and in coastal Georgia, and using them embedded in the headstone or on the grave, "holds the spirit at a safe distance from the living."[3]

However, the umbilical matter hanging below the chair in the work *Undone* (figure 6.3) suggests "a reversal," according to Saar: "a reversal [from] the bottle trees luring spirits into those bottles as a means of protection so they won't go elsewhere." In *Undone*, "her ideas and her dreams and her own spirits . . . are trapped in these bottles. They can be dreams and aspirations and ideas and things like that. Things that we have that aren't realized, or they're never realized, is what's in question here."[4] Saar suggests that certain women's dreams and aspirations might be "either unborn or they're aborted," and she is depicting it "as a physical birth or a miscarriage." The work is talking "about ideas as opposed to babies."[5] She adds, in her description of the work, that the bottles are "full of fermenting or festering dreams and ideas."[6]

Bottle tree references have appeared in Saar's work before, several times suggesting that hair for many black women embodied a cultural discourse. She says that *Undone* is most related to her 1999 work *Compton Nocturne* (figure 6.4). Saar says, "It's a figure kind of playing off the idea of the bottle tree. These are sort of her personal ideas and spirits and paths and memories that are sort of trapped in the bottles. Out of her hair this time instead of out of her uterus."[7]

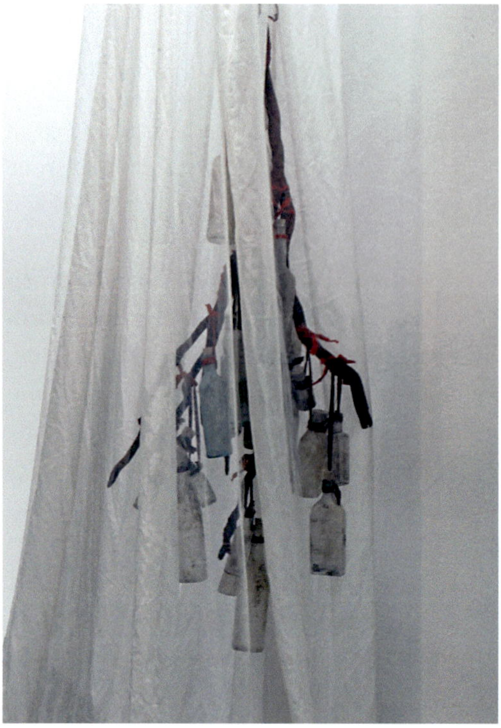

6.3 Alison Saar, *Undone* (detail 1), 2012. © Alison Saar. Courtesy of L.A. Louver, Venice, CA.

Compton Nocturne uses a reclining nude female with a richly textured body covered with repoussé metal pieces colored by an oxidized patina, along with a bottle tree coiffure. Many of the various-sized bottles in the branches/hair appear to have an opaque white interior. With its full figure, the nudity of this work suggests symbolic, ritual nudity instead of the sexualized nakedness one might find in Édouard Manet's *Olympia* (1863) and other reclining nudes in Western art traditions. A January 1999 review in the *Los Angeles Times* paternalistically places the work in an art historical circle, stating, "Its form melds narrative traditions associated with the American South into Modern images as familiar as Rousseau's 'Sleeping Gypsy,' Matisse's 'Blue Nude' and any number of German Expressionist examples—all of which owe debts to precedents in African art."[8]

A year earlier, *Delta Doo* (figure 6.5) employed the artist's signature stylized head and face with hair forming a bottle tree. The title uses *doo* as a double entendre suggesting both a manipulated hairdoo and the system of Hoodoo. The head is not obviously gendered (with lip cosmetics) as it appears in her 2002 print version of the same title (figure 6.6). In the print,

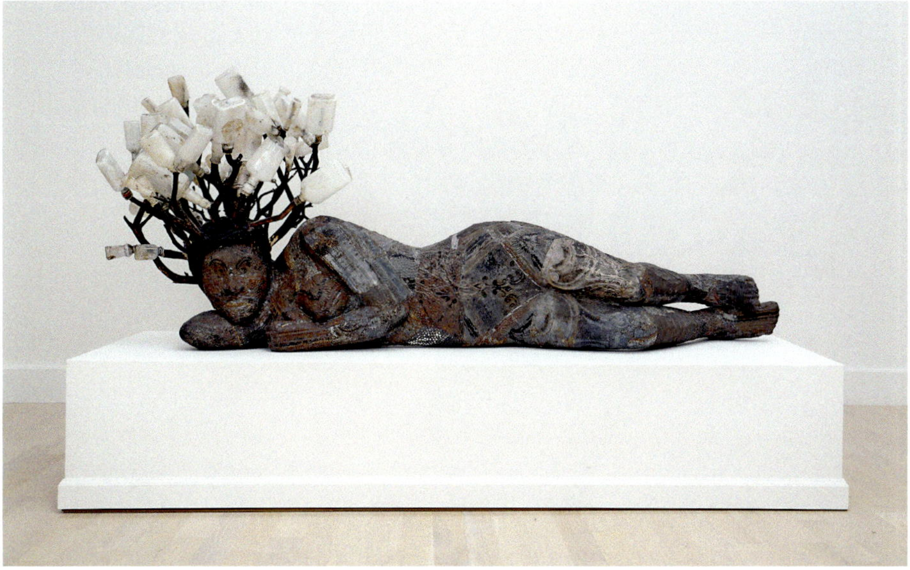

6.4 Alison Saar, *Compton Nocturne*, 1999. Wood, tin, bottles, paint, and tar, 33 × 80 × 28 in. Weatherspoon Art Museum. © Alison Saar. Artwork courtesy of L.A. Louver, Venice, CA. Photo courtesy of Weatherspoon Art Museum, University of North Carolina at Greensboro.

the bottles are varied colors of green and blue glass, and the woman's hair appears more as hair branches and/or upraised dreadlocks.

Dreadlocks add additional layers of significance to the work. They apparently appear as the hairstyle of Greek kouros figures from three thousand years ago, but for the African diaspora, we find the Jamaican Rastafarian movement drawing from the Old Testament book of Numbers, chapter 6, for a mandate.[9] Shamans in various cultures, thought to speak to spirits or deities, wear locks, and Yoruba priests of Olokun, god of the sea, wear them. They are found among priests of the Akan of Ghana, a strong source group for Jamaica during the slave trade. Saar's body of work and her stated intentions make the excavation of cultural material plausible and necessary.

Saar consistently has done sculptural and print work exploring the roles, spiritual energy, and plight of women of color. She has, through imagery, linked women to power, mystic traditions, feminist issues, and motherhood. Hair can be an important concern among women, and her work emerges from personal experiences and considerations around it:

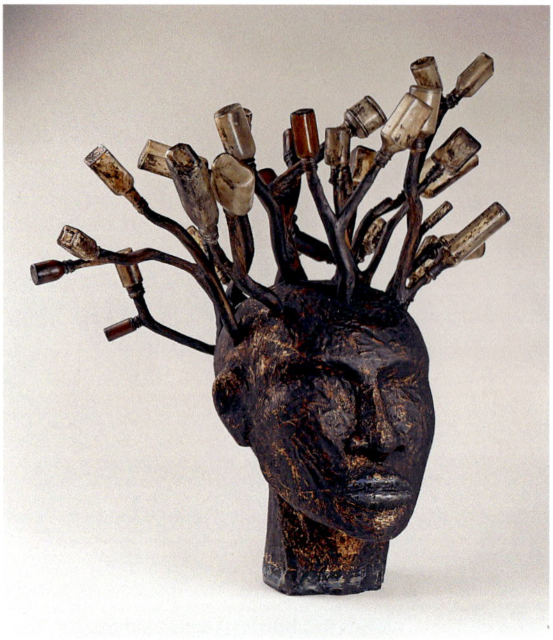

6.5 Alison Saar, *Delta Doo*, 1998. Copper and mixed media on wood, and bottles, 31 × 28½ × 21 in. © Alison Saar. Courtesy of L.A. Louver, Venice, CA.

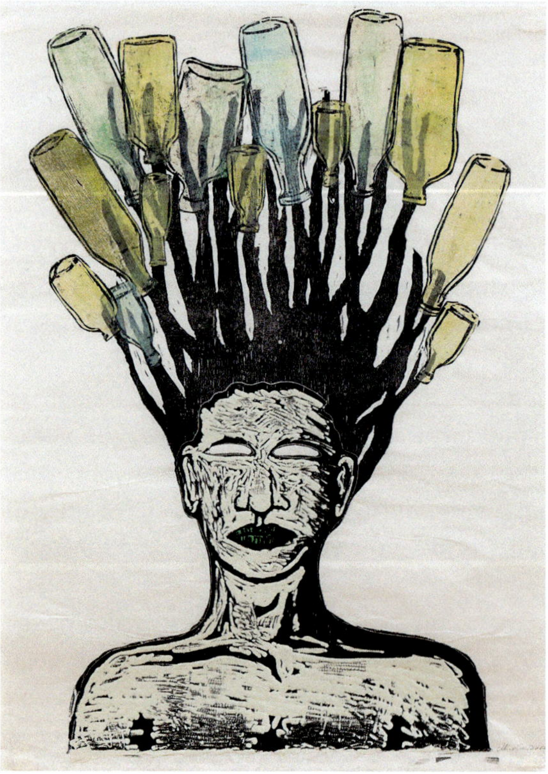

6.6 Alison Saar, *Delta Doo*, 2002. Monoprint/woodcut and Chine collé, 33⅞ × 24⅜ in. © Alison Saar. Courtesy of L.A. Louver, Venice, CA.

> It comes out of personal connections with my family's history and going to the beauty parlors and all that routine. So much effort goes into maintaining or redirecting a black woman's hair. Whether it's about straightening it, or whether it's about letting it go natural.
>
> Also, a part of my fascination with it is that, because I'm so fair, my hair is the only thing that [does not belie] my African American heritage. That was also a part of my fascination with it. Yes, all the drama about black women's hair.[10]

Several African American female artists, including Lorna Simpson (see *You're Fine*, 1988) and Renée Stout, also have created images and sculptures that, like *Compton Nocturne*, resist the masculinist tradition of the reclining nude and subvert its assumption of the consumption of the female body by the male gaze of the viewer. Saar and Stout both used signifiers of spiritual and cultural systems and practices in their works to turn potentially sensuous nudity into a ritual form resisting the colonizing male gaze. Ritual nakedness is symbolic of the removal of secrets and agendas, and examples abound in African art, including the male and female Ogboni or Oshugbo figures in Yoruba art representing the secret society of ruling elders. Stout's 1988 *Fetish No. 2* (figure 6.7) is a life-size nude self-portrait turned into a Kongo-inspired *nkisi nkondi* figure.[11]

The sculpture's approximation of a ritual object, including cowrie shell eyes and a monkey hair headdress, repositions the colonizing male gaze to that of a virtual nongendered ritual audience member. Haitian Vodou priest André Pierre told Thompson that "shells symbolize the existence of spirit in the sea" and the shell "encloses elements of water, earth, and wind. It is a world in miniature."[12] The shells create the same blank, spiritually transfixed eyes we see in Saar's print. The headdress further disrupts the discourse about women's hair.

The elevated woman in *Undone* (figure 6.1) sits on what implies a birthing chair, though that specific link was not the artist's intention. Birthing chairs (see figure 6.8), also known as parturition chairs, were used for centuries until the nineteenth century, usually for home birth or at a birthing center. They allowed women to be in a squatting position during final labor and had an opening to help the mother push the baby out more forcefully. A woodcut of a birthing chair was published in 1554 in a book written by Zurich doctor and obstetrician Jacob Rueff.[13] There is evidence of a version of the chair or a stool for this practice going back to Egyptian papyri and the Old Testament.

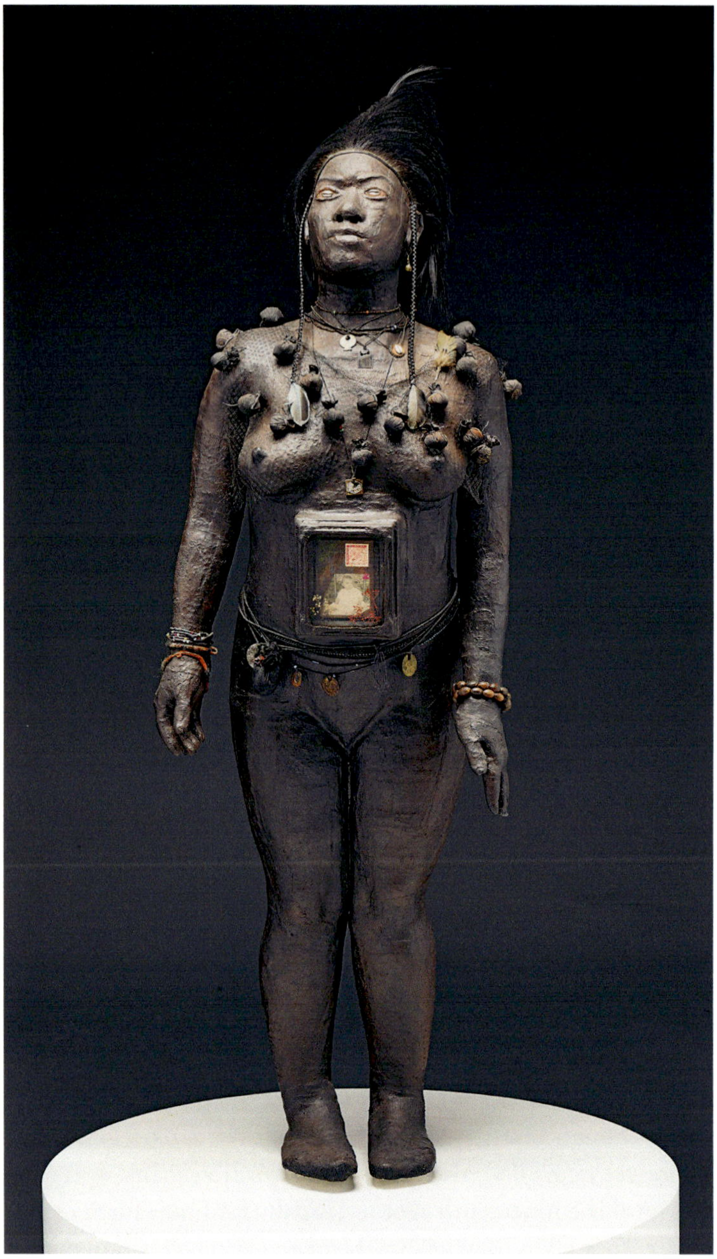

6.7 Renée Stout, *Fetish No. 2*, 1988. Mixed media (plaster body cast), 64 in. high. Dallas Museum of Art, Metropolitan Life Foundation Purchase Grant. 1989.27. © Renée Stout, Washington, DC. Courtesy of Dallas Museum of Art.

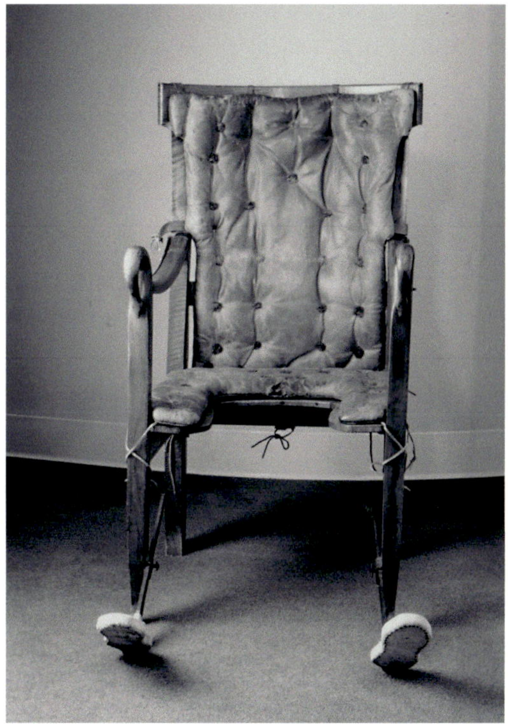

6.8 Birthing chair, advocated by Hendrik van Deventer (1651–1724), called the "Father of Modern Midwifery." Bavaria, ca. 1750. Kansas University Medical Center, Ralph Major Photograph Collection: Eighteenth Century. Courtesy of Clendening History of Medicine Library, University of Kansas Medical Center, Kansas City.

The umbilical bottle tree branch of *Undone* pulls from Kongo ideas and cultural remnants transposed into African American settings, but we might also explore Yoruba ideas of the womb as a spiritual portal giving women intimate contact with spiritual powers; an access unavailable to men. The womb is the threshold for spirits to enter this realm from the other. These assumptions are embedded in the existence and function of carved *ère-ìbejì* figures associated with twin birth and the accompanying high infant mortality among the Yoruba, inspiring the concepts and practices around the carvings.[14] The value of children is embodied in the Yoruba saying, *Ọmọ l'ere aye* (Children are the wealth of life). Children, already living as their essence in the spiritual realm, enter this world through the womb. Deceased twins are said to have returned to their playmates from before birth in the spiritual realm. The *ère-ìbejì* is used to persuade the surviving twin to remain by replacing the departed one, or to ritually implore future twins to remain in the physical realm.

Combining Yoruba and Kongo imagery and ideas proved useful for Saar. Figure 6.9, for instance, incorporates a male *nkisi*-like figure bristling with nails standing atop what appears to be an auto battery. His right hand extends in an ambiguous gesture that might be offering or receiving. The nails, not found in Yoruba sculpture, evoke Kongo practices, but the pile of metal at its feet, the battery, and the whiplike metal in his left hand suggest the Yoruba orisha Ogun who is associated with metal, the road of travel, aggression, war, and technology. The figure appears to be accepting an offering in readiness to act on one's behalf. Seemingly inert physically, the figure, being met at a crossroads, is rooted in metaphysical power. As annotated by the museum curator, Richard B. Woodward, it was originally conceived by Saar as part of a tableau titled *Crossroads* and recreated at the Virginia Museum of Fine Arts in 1993. In the context of Saar's other works this piece represented "the products of man," as the artist remarked for the installation; products that "can be used for good (tools) or evil (weapons). Opposite this figure there stood a sculpture of a woman with long roots extending from her legs downward to denote nature" (see figure 6.10).[15] Interestingly, that juxtaposition recapitulates long-held notions of nature as female and culture as masculine.

Birth has a metaphysical aspect that my daughter described as something unexplainable and unconscious that happens when the child transitions out of the womb at a particular moment; a moment that might be like the lights flickering in rational consciousness. She described the experience as "inter-dimensional" and said that the minute of birth seems impossible and that something "beyond the mechanics of the birth process" occurs.[16] Perhaps this is what inspired Saar to lift the figure in *Undone* figuratively, literally, and metaphorically above the mundane realm of midwifery, birthing chairs, and such (figure 6.11). It all takes place beneath a dress become a veil, a folk reference famously used in W. E. B. Du Bois's 1903 book, *The Souls of Black Folk*. Along with the book's other meaning of "double consciousness" as introduced in chapters 1 and 2 of this book, the veil also serves as a metaphor for spiritual insight: seeing into two worlds.

The face of the figure in *Undone* is a dark, almost cobalt, blue, perhaps echoing Henri Matisse's *Blue Nude*, mentioned in the Christopher Knight review above, perhaps implying the long presence of indigo in African and African American histories. Indigo is the dye of choice in the traditional Yoruba practice of resist-dye *adire* cloth, often associated with female orisha like Oshun (a riverine goddess) and Olokun (god of the sea), and made by women.[17] Saar, in a telephone conversation, indicated

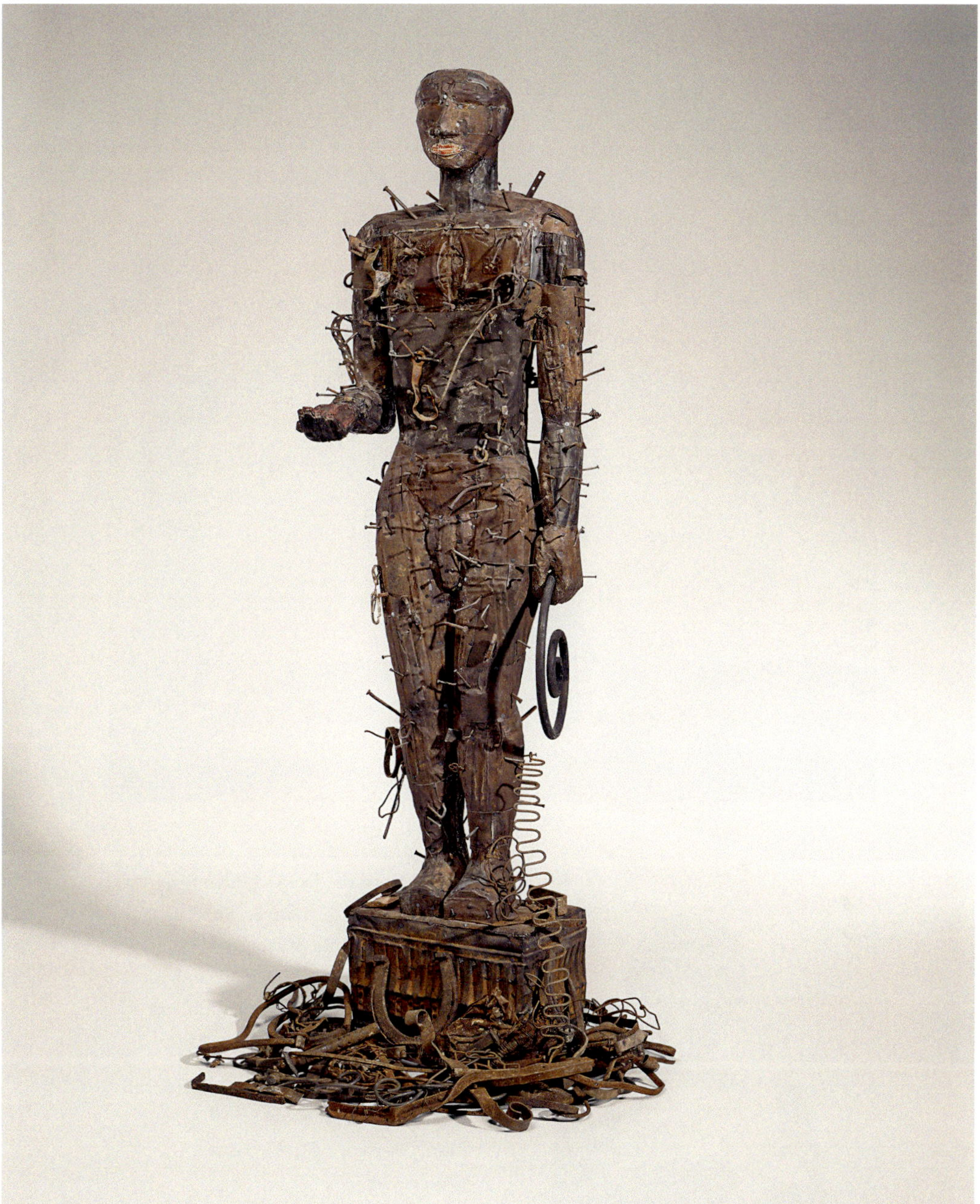

6.9 Alison Saar, *Untitled*, 1989, from the *Crossroads* installation. Wood, copper, flowers, and tin, 70 × 20 × 28 in. © Alison Saar. Courtesy of L.A. Louver, Venice, CA, and Virginia Museum of Fine Arts, Richmond. Photo: Katherine Wetzel © Virginia Museum of Fine Arts, Sydney and Frances Lewis Endowment Fund, 92.233A-QQQ.

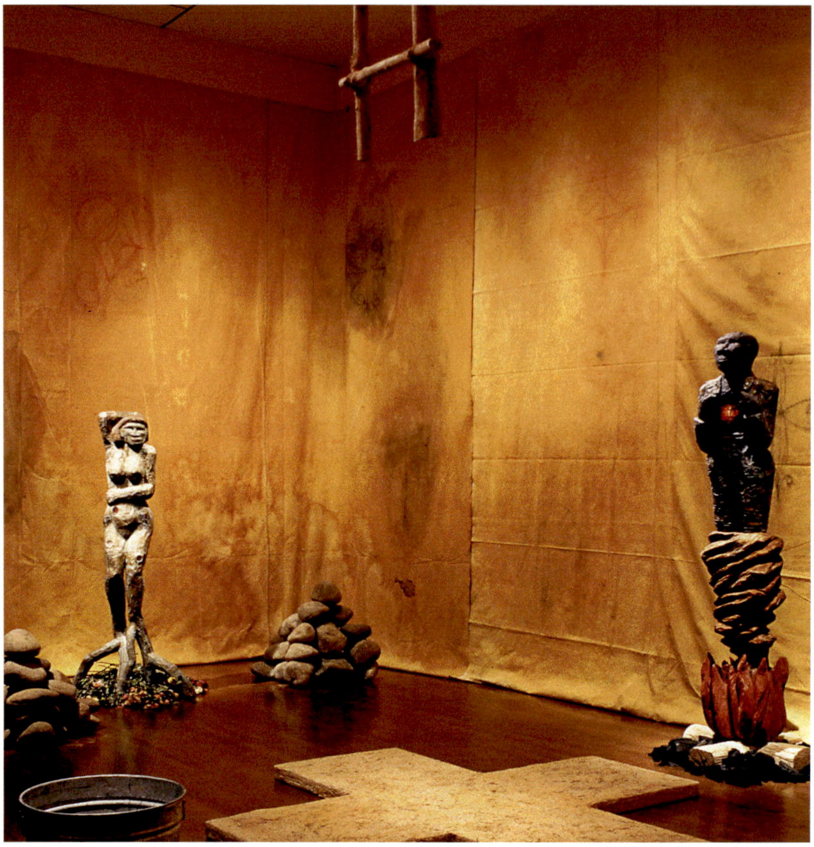

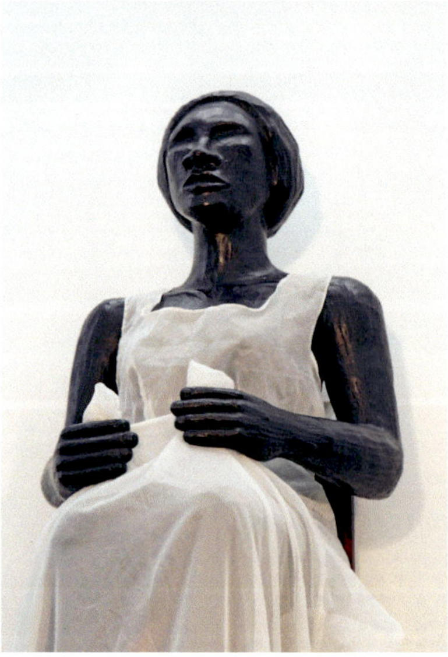

6.10 (*above*) Alison Saar, *Crossroads*, 1993. Mixed media. © Alison Saar. Courtesy of L.A. Louver, Venice, CA, and Virginia Museum of Fine Arts Photo Archives, Richmond. Installation photo: Ann Hutchison © Virginia Museum of Fine Arts.

6.11 (*left*) Alison Saar, *Undone* (detail 2), 2012, seen from below. © Alison Saar. Courtesy of L.A. Louver, Venice, CA.

that her use of the color implies, also, the transfigural aspects of the indigo process, which involves an almost alchemical appearance of color from a colorless fluid.

The very bottom of the gauzy gown sits on the floor and suggests the blood of childbirth (figure 6.12). Blood appears to have soaked the hem of the garment and seeped upward in a wonderfully executed illusion. The application of a dash of color adds an aesthetic jolt to the work that is largely deep blue, white, and dark brown (the chair). In this interpretive analysis of Saar's work, I wish to suggest water and blood to be the fluids of ritual and transformation. Blood is the carrier of life and energy, and many cultures use it in sacrifices for that reason. Christians use the Eucharist idea of bread and wine at the Last Supper of Christ as the foundation of Communion to ritually consume the blood and body of Christ.

Crossing water, like a river, symbolically conveys the idea of moving into another realm, like the Christian idea of crossing the River Jordan that has long had a presence in American spirituals. It meant going to the Promised Land, whether a place of freedom for the enslaved or a spiritual freedom place from the sorrows of this life. During the birth process, when a woman's water breaks, it marks the beginning of the child's crossing over into the physical world. The slave song about crossing water, "Michael Row the Boat Ashore," has among its improvised lyrics:

> Jordan's river is deep and wide, hallelujah
> Meet my mother on the other side, hallelujah.
> Jordan's river is chilly and cold, hallelujah.
> Chills the body, but not the soul, hallelujah.[18]

Cosmograms

> The altar becomes perceptible as a realm of grace.
>
> ROBERT FARRIS THOMPSON, *FACE OF THE GODS* (1993)

The umbilical bottle tree branch in *Undone* works as a virtual crossroads, cosmogram, and *nkisi* object, all of which can act as altars. Crossroads and crossings and bottle trees mark spiritual intersections/passages and literally or figuratively act as cosmograms, which themselves can act as altars,

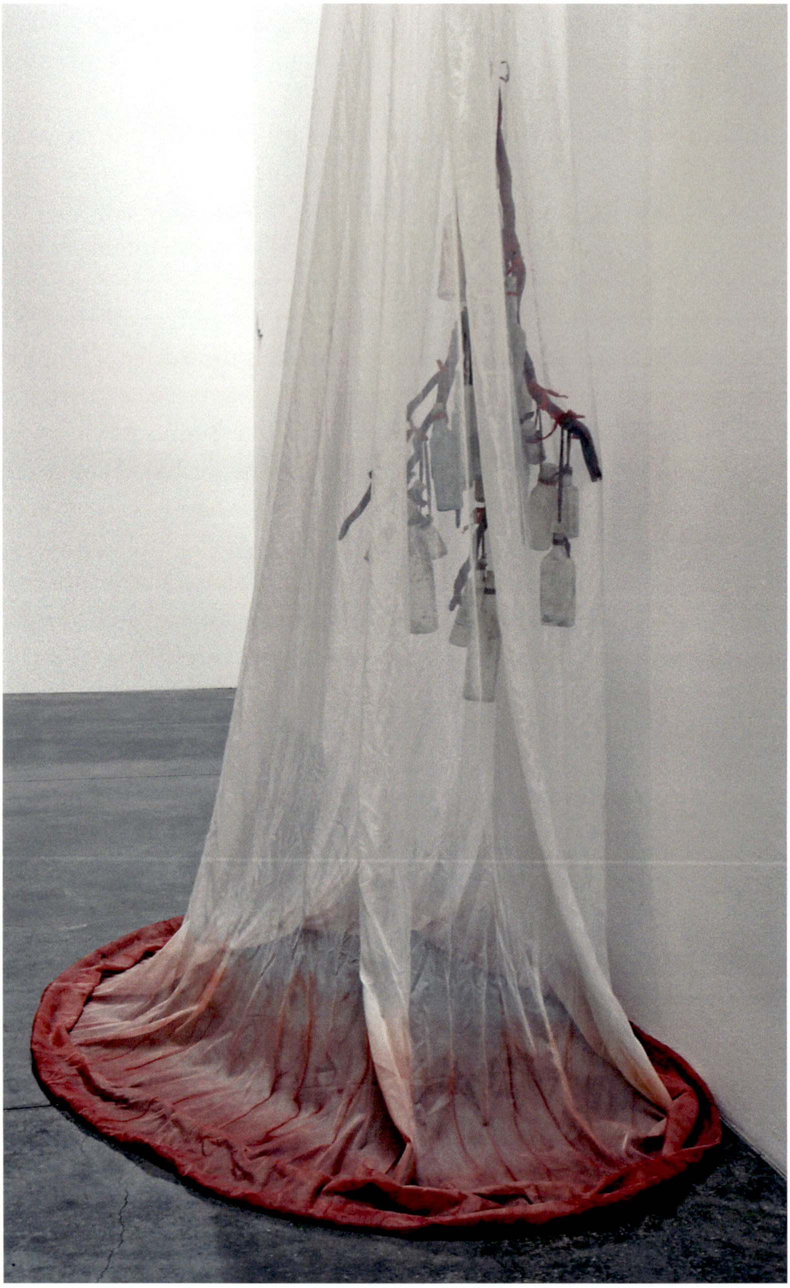

6.12 Alison Saar, *Undone* (detail 3), 2012. © Alison Saar. Courtesy of L.A. Louver, Venice, CA.

meeting places for encountering spirit. They mark or signify "where one might go to offer sacrifice or prayer to the ancestors." Bottle trees seem to embody Thompson's contention that "crossroads or forks in a path are viewed in many Bantu cultures of the Kongo-Angola region as virtual cosmograms *trouvés*. . . . A forked stick further miniaturized the concept, providing a scale model of the line that divides the living from the ancestral realm."[19]

The crossroads acted as a virtual surrogate for the cosmogram. As Thompson states, "It was where one went to ask favors of the cosmos."[20] Protection and healing are a great part of such cosmogram-related requests rendered at crossroads; requests miniaturized in another way with *veve*, the elaborate ground emblazonings—symbolic drawings or designs used in Haitian Vodou ceremonies, and usually articulated with a temporary powdered material like cornmeal.

Among the alternate terms for the cosmogram is the *dikenga* circle: "It is a core symbol in Bakongo religion that depicts the physical world . . . the spiritual world . . . the Kalûnga line that runs between the two worlds, the sacred river that forms a circle through the two worlds, the four moments of the sun [summer, spring, winter, fall], and the four elements [earth, air, fire, water]."[21]

The Kongo cosmogram has at its center a cross with circles on each end signifying what Thompson has called "the Four Moments of the Sun,"[22] that is, the East as birth, North as the high noon of life, West as death, and South as midnight in the underworld.[23] Wyatt MacGaffey wrote that "the land of the dead is another world, mirroring the land of the living and reached by entering or crossing bodies of water," and that the masters or priests (*ngangas*) of *nkisi* charms acquire their special powers by rituals of initiation "during which they are believed to make such journeys."[24] The cosmogram featured below (figure 6.13), for example, depicts the journey from childhood through adulthood and elderhood to death as the path to ancestorhood.

Blues and crossroads references, as mentioned in chapter 4, signify this system of belief with the spiritual realm as contiguous with the earthly one, and communication with spirit entities as a pre- and postlife continuity. The cosmogram centered by a cross graphically explicates and evokes the continuities of this spiritual ontology with permeable boundaries between the seen and unseen worlds. In the Kongo world of *minkisi* (sing. *nkisi*) the grave operated as a crossroads. Thompson indicates that a *dikenga* is "the master symbol of inclusive consciousness," and the tomb

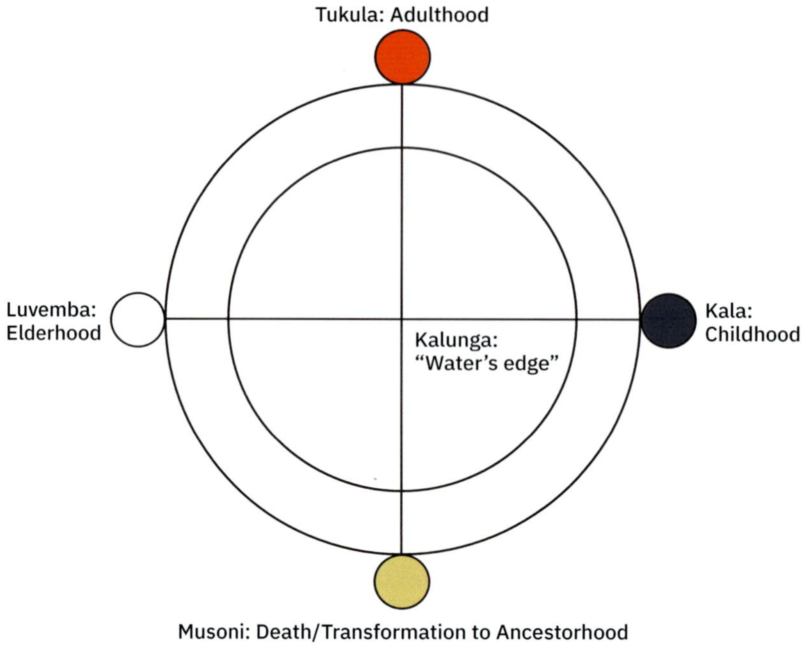

6.13 *Dikenga* cosmogram. Created by Michael D. Harris.

is "an *nkisi* (charm) for moral intimidation and spiritual transcendence." Spirits can be enclosed "within an appropriate container with spirit-embedding earths, along with spirit-admonishing elements, that tell the spirit through shapes, puns, and gestures, what to do or not do for the owner of the charm."[25]

Charms, ground emblazons, *minkisi*, crossroads, even a person or ritual expert filled with spirit, become altars in Kongo spiritual expression. Thompson argues that the "primary altar is the tomb" and that *minkisi* become "extensions of the tomb" in an elaborate system that maintains active connections between the realms of the living and the spirit world where the dead reside.[26]

And it is here that we find Marie Laveau in New Orleans being asked to help or heal people nearly two centuries after her death. Also, this unveils another layer of meaning in Renée Stout's 1990 work *Headstone for Marie Laveau* (figure 6.14). The work, adorned with charms and *nkisi* (or juju) bags, and with active elements seeming to be growing out of its top, is itself a charm and a cosmogram.

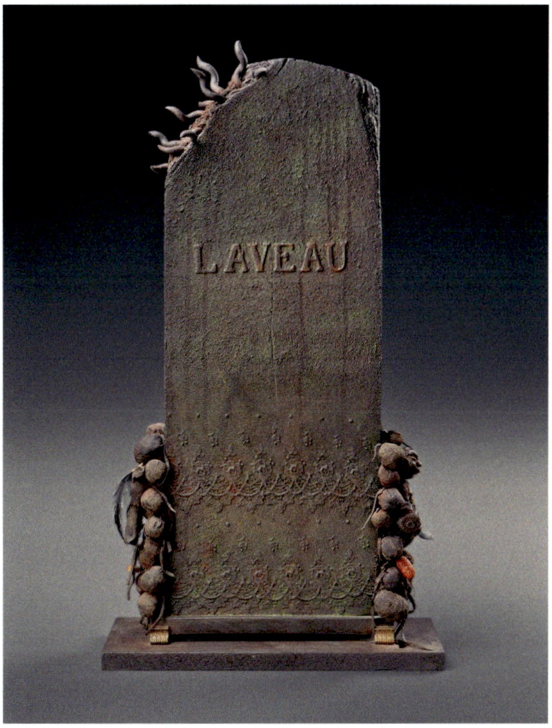

6.14 Renée Stout, *Headstone for Marie Laveau*, 1990. Wood and mixed media, 29 × 15½ × 5¼ in. Museum of Fine Arts, Houston. Gift of Barrett Collection, Dallas, 2003.97. © Renée Stout. Used by permission of the artist. Courtesy of Museum of Fine Arts, Houston.

To turn back to *Undone*: MacGaffey has researched field notebooks from the late nineteenth century when Belgian colonials investigated the practices around *nkisi* objects and collected many of the ones found today in the Royal Museum for Central Africa in Tervuren, Belgium, just outside Brussels.[27] In one, an account described aspects of the cosmological system and how the spirits (*bisimbi*) relate to *minkisi*. In this citation, the use of blood adds another ritual connection to Saar's work:

> [The ghost] then revealed his name to the man in his sleep, saying: I am one who formerly lived on earth and have died the second death; take me and keep me to be your *nkisi*. . . .

> . . . They take earth from the grave and rub it on the statue. Then they return to the grave and sacrifice a chicken and drip [the blood] on the *nkisi*.[28]

Ras Michael Brown defines the Kongo spirit entities called *simbi* ("cymbee") as he documents their presence in Lowcountry South Carolina in the antebellum period. They emerge from the Central African cultural roots of many people in that region. *Simbi*, or *cymbee*, were associated with water springs, and Brown says that they

> were the Lowcountry manifestations of Kongo nature spirits known as the simbi, entities once central to Kongo perceptions of the spiritual landscape. The simbi served as guardians of the natural environment and of the people who lived in their domains and functioned as the chief intermediaries between the physical "land of the living" and the spiritual "land of the dead."
>
> . . . They were markers of beginnings and of the deep past. They exemplified the original inhabitants of a territory, and the relationships these spirits had with people imparted a status of primacy to anchor communities of the living in a country.[29]

Thompson reveals that *simbi* are manifested in unusual rock or wood formations, or through special pools, and these places may serve as natural altars. This is the "Kongo topology of the spirit, as initiatory places wherein to meditate and communicate with the dead." He says also that "persons in ecstasy invoke before such presences."[30] Lowcountry shouting, with folk being filled ecstatically with the spirit, would then be linked to these ideas. Such a cultural reading offers additional significance to Archibald Motley's painting *Tongues* (figure 5.3), discussed in chapter 5.

Brown says, "We can determine that a large majority of those taken to South Carolina came from communities whose cultural and linguistic roots reached back to their distant Niger-Congo ancestors." In addition to the linguistic connections, Brown writes, "The Niger-Congo ancestors devised conceptual frameworks that remained central to the cultures of their descendants as these subsequent generations diverged into distinct and far-flung societies throughout Central, Eastern, and South Africa. Foremost among these were ideas about interacting with the spirits of the land of the dead, which included nature spirits and ancestors, and with the natural environment of the land of the living. . . . For those carried across the Atlantic, ideas of this kind proved invaluable in reconstituting the communities and reestablishing connections to the invisible, spiritual domain necessary for daily life."[31]

African migrations and diaspora in Africa, Brown is arguing, maintained some fundamental linguistic and cultural continuities that manifested in the ideas and practices associated with *simbi* among the majority of captives brought to Charleston by the middle of the eighteenth century. The Vili (Mubiri) merchants of Kongo were involved in the trade, drawn in by its profitability and their disconnection from the Catholic ruling elite. The Vili were a part of the society but seen as a separate group with a reputation for their "trading acumen." They had a certain level of autonomy because people perceived them "as purveyors of spiritual power, which afforded them influence and protection."[32] Therefore, many captives taken to the Lowcountry, if not Kongo, "had at least minimal contact with the Kongo cultural realm before their departure from West-Central Africa."[33] It is not far-fetched to define Lowcountry cultural practices as reimagining Kongo systems.

The two works by Alison Saar and Renée Stout, *Undone* and *Fetish No. 2*, take on the characteristics of charms and cultural cosmograms (and imply *simbi*) with their astute deployment of African American and African objects in contemporary artistic statements. In this, they tap into fundamental notions of how displaced Africans enacted processes to root themselves in the new soil, the new landscapes, in which they found themselves. Brown argues, "People of African descent also accepted that the physical landscape had sacred dimensions that had to be engaged for both the spiritual development of individuals and the well being of communities."[34]

Displaced from ancestral depth in African settings, people used familiar elements to re-create the principles of their living. Brown indicates that this allowed them to ground themselves in new settings "in ways absolutely necessary to reestablishing connections between the land of the living and the land of the dead, bring children into this new world, grow food for their families, resist the ravages of disease," deal with the "countless assaults on their humanity inherent in the experiences of captivity and enslavement," and resist the claims to power by their oppressors. *Simbi* represented an ancestral link and a means to forge new communities for the living.[35] Their use in new settings amounts to an African syntax governing a new lexicon or vocabulary.

In discussing the importance of the ancestor in black creative work, Toni Morrison insists that "it was the absence of an ancestor that was frightening, that was threatening, and it caused huge destruction" in the work. She suggests that it would be interesting to examine black literature "on what the writer does with the presence of an ancestor."[36] Morrison echoes Alain Locke's 1925 call for black artists to tap into their African heritage in his important essay "The Legacy of the Ancestral Arts."[37] Locating these ancestral and cultural references in the works of Stout and Saar—an echo of the foundational practices organized around *simbi* in the Carolinas—suggests and articulates a similar process of stabilizing one's individual identity within a larger relocated and shifting communal environment. They exert what Okwui Enwezor, in discussing the work of Cuban expatriate artist Maria Magdalena Campos-Pons, calls "the diasporic imagination."[38]

Enwezor writes of the challenges of "how to build a cultural identity in the traumatic site of the New World and how to negotiate and bridge the gap between the subjugated memory of African cultures and a dominant European model shaped by slavery." Africans and their descendants also negotiated the incongruences of shifting from "a racialized self to a cultural self, a change of both cultural content and context."[39] They used charms, rituals, African spirits, and religious formulae to jury-rig a new eschatology and epistemological frame and relationship to their new lands. Artists use this new cultural topology and experiences within it to ground their work; to root it beneath the superficial substrata of art worlds, art histories, styles, and popular culture.

Body Work

Alison Saar, in her art, often works with female nudes in recognition of the female body as a site of identity formation and self-empowerment through resistance to masculine control and definition. She addresses personal female issues, her own experiences with her children, and larger metaphorical concerns. *Rise Sally Rise* (2003; figure 6.15) was partly inspired by the children's song "Little Sally Walker."[40] Here is a Phyllis Kind Gallery exhibition description from 2003: "It is about transitions, her daughter moving into adolescence. . . . Rise Sally Rise, depicts an adolescent girl sitting in a child's chair too small for her developing body. The chair hangs on the wall in limbo and her long tangled hair cascades towards the floor entangled with bottles."[41]

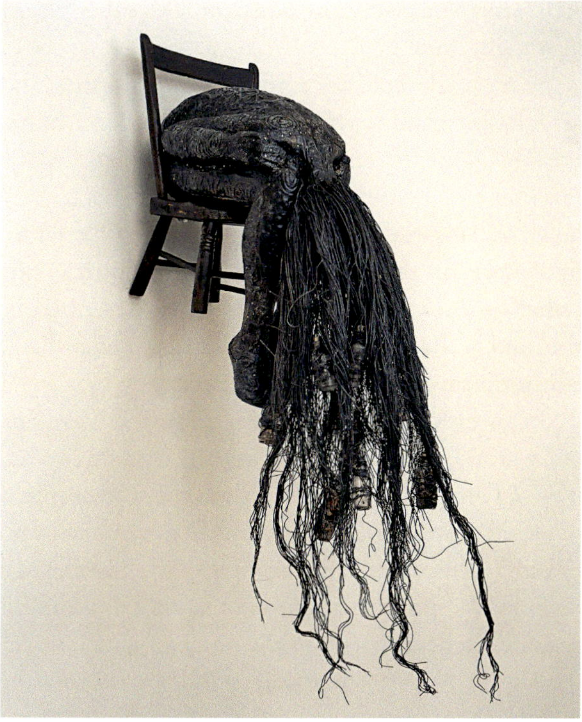

6.15 Alison Saar, *Rise Sally Rise*, 2003. Linoleum print, 11 × 8½ in. (sheet); 9³⁄₁₆ × 7 in. (image). © Alison Saar. Courtesy of L.A. Louver, Venice, CA.

With the elevated chair described as representing a limbo between worlds, we find another aspect of *Undone*: the idea of childbirth as the traversing of two worlds within the female body. In another conversation Saar mentioned her daughter, Maddy, as the model of a daughter moving between childhood and the growing sass of adolescence. "I had done a piece called 'Rise, Sally, Rise' and—hmm, my daughter Maddy must have been about ten at that time and just starting to get sassy—and I was like, you know, on a residency for two months, and I was getting these photos of her in . . . booty-shorts, and going into motherly shock."[42]

Threading folklore, African fragments, female identity, and mother-daughter relationships through her work is all a part of what Alison Saar intends. As she indicated, "It was really poignant to me, this idea that a work of art could, somehow, turn a page, or shed a light, or lead back to a source. And that's one of the things that's exciting about being an artist; that your work threads people to other places, and not necessarily in straight lines."[43]

Saar's work oscillates among various spiritual and corporeal concerns, associations, and representations of women. In *Snake Man* (1994; figure 6.16), she explores what appears to be a nexus rather than a crossroads. His eyes have no pupils, indicating a trance state, a consciousness focused on an otherworldly inner awareness. It could refer to a ritual performance by a powerful person when an invited spirit is present; what has been called *possession* but more accurately is described as the spirit mounting the head of the believer in an equestrian metaphor. The snake in this print is an emblem of metaphysical mastery.

In an African ethical/cultural realm, the snake can become an indicator of *simbi* and *nkisi*. Brown tells us that there are two orders of *nkisi*: *nkisi* and *nkisi si*. Citing documents as early as the seventeenth century, Brown writes of sacred groves (*chibila*) maintained as centers for honoring ancestors, including "sacred trees, shrines, priests, and consecrated objects"; sacred spaces included "'a spring or a lagoon or swamp or well of some kind containing or connected with perhaps the home of its snake,' the snakes representing the nkisi si."[44] This association adds to a scene of transgressive sexuality the undertones of spiritual trance and transfixation. As in blues culture, we find the tension between the secular and the sacred energizing the same space.

While Alison Saar expresses her interests and experiences as a woman through her work, the specificity of her cultural heritage also is embedded in the expression. Sometimes the histories and old cultural references discussed here are intentionally evoked by artists, but often they are deeply embedded within Africana cultures and are evoked through the cultural experience of the artist unconsciously. In the sense of phenomenology, the specificity of their West or Central African cultural fragments often is embedded in the expression of creativity in the diaspora. With Saar, her work contains allusions to the metaphysical imperatives of women as the conduit for spiritual entrée into the world through birth, but also as manipulators of the unseen; the intuitive and relational aspects of being are given emphasis.

Both Saar and Stout root their work in Kongo traditions and their reemployment in Hoodoo or Haitian Vodou. Yet Yoruba ideas, symbols, and references make cameo appearances in their work as well. In that sense, some of their works simulate charms and cosmograms for those knowing the systems from which they draw references. Embedded within them through signifiers are notions of altars and crossroads, places where

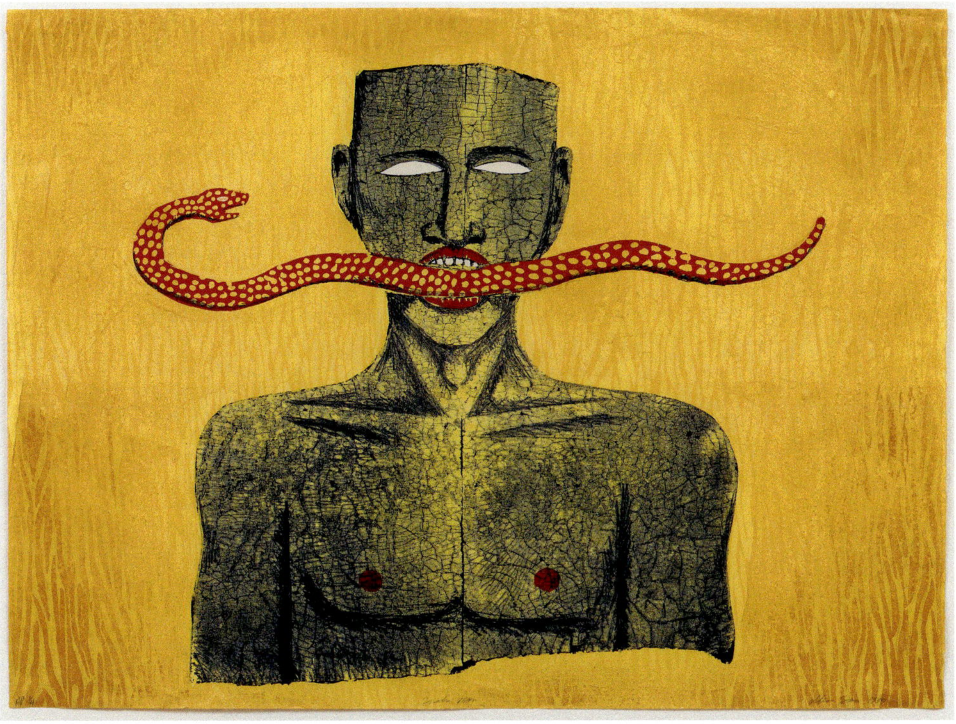

6.16 Alison Saar, *Snake Man*, 1994. Lithograph and woodcut, 27 15/16 × 37 1/8 in. Edition AP 1 of 4. Signed and dated in pencil (lower right); titled in pencil (lower center). Collection: Ruth Chandler Williamson Gallery, Scripps College, Claremont, CA. © Alison Saar. Courtesy of L.A. Louver, Venice, CA.

people encounter the spiritual and communicate with the other side. Both imply the female body as an important part of this spiritual topography.

With *Undone*, Alison Saar has expressed the universal within the specifics of African diaspora culture. The work is art, crossroads, nexus, charm, shrine or altar, and a statement that birth invites spirits into a cultural environment that will inform their journey through the four moments of the sun. For the uninitiated, it might do artistic, aesthetic work only. These are not liturgical or ritual objects, but as art, we can excavate the cultural ideas mentioned here as a part of the frame within which the work sits. And struts. It speaks of art and personal histories and the lives of women, but also it whispers of sanctuaries and secrets and collective privacy to those who know.

CHAPTER 7

Talking in Tongues

Revisiting/Reflecting Kara Walker

> Racism is a visceral experience . . . that . . . dislodges brains, blocks airways, rips muscle, extracts organs, cracks bones, breaks teeth. You must never look away from this. You must always remember that the sociology, the history, the economics, the graphs, the charts, the regressions all land, with great violence, upon the body.
>
> TA-NEHISI COATES, *BETWEEN THE WORLD AND ME* (2015)

Kara Walker's work is inventive, aggressive, ironic, humorous, loud, repeatedly surprising, painful, satirical, accusatory, sexual without being sensual, and matter-of-factly violent. Like Romare Bearden's collages, she has stamped a medium and technique with her individual voice so powerfully that creative ventures into the realm of silhouettes by others now seem derivative. I find that it is useful to come back to the work several times to sift through the rubble left by her explosion onto the art scene.

When artists speak in cultural tongues through their work, they speak to the choir per se, invigorating them and lifting the spiritual excitement of the experience. However, the unconverted also are targeted; those visitors in the audience who have not committed to the visual, cultural, or theoretical orthodoxy practiced by the artist.

Kara Walker is an African American artist, but is she performing African American art? When I viewed one of her tableaux at Harvard during a 1998 conference built around her work, a horse on its back, head in a howl reminiscent of the one in Pablo Picasso's *Guernica*, being ridden sexually by a young black girl, I was convinced that it was not. Her work at first glance does not speak from within Africana sanctuarial spaces, nor does it offer cultural cues or references to black audiences. However, I am now convinced that Walker's work expands the category to include a provocative genre extending beyond the social criticism of artist Charles White (1918–1979), and she signifies in ways more wickedly ironic than artist Robert H. Colescott (1925–2009), all the while defending her humanity and challenging the art world. Just one corner of figure 7.1, for example, features a bent-over boy playing a musical instrument with fluid (blood?) dripping from his mouth while a woman turns a windup gear attached to his back. Here we see artistic commentary on history and culture that induces the viewer to decipher the scene and remotely witness the victim's experience.

Resistance to slavery, segregation or apartheid, and racialized injustice has persisted throughout the slave period and its aftermath in the African diaspora. In Kara Walker's case, I wish to argue that her work can be interpreted as mounting creative resistance to racist histories and structures through a "signifying" performance with foundations within the black interior. Signifying denotes a universal rhetorical strategy, particularly evident in African diaspora communities, for indirectly, ironically, or playfully commenting on meanings or situations.[1] Walker's artwork also creates a nexus for collision and conflict among artistic intention, activism, and interpretation. To this she recently added, with her large installation *A Subtlety or the Marvelous Sugar Baby* (figure 7.2), diachronic and synchronic questions about capitalism as the initial force behind slavery, colonialism, and the construction of race.

A Subtlety, which tongue-in-cheek is anything but subtle, used the black female body stereotyped as a huge mammy sphinx with protruding breasts, big lips, a bandana, and large haunches raising upward to reveal a ten-foot vulva from behind as a means of making a statement about the role of sugar in the slave trade and the subsequent exploitation and stereotyping of the black female. Sexualizing the asexual mammy stereotype turned the statement into a spectacle, leading to lines of people waiting to get inside to see the work, and a host of ironies and contradictions among viewers, the work, and the remarkable acceptance and celebration of the critique within the New York art and cultural scene.[2]

Walker's chaotic gallery tableaux might be seen as talking in tongues; an emotional eruption within the staid orthodoxy of the art world. The

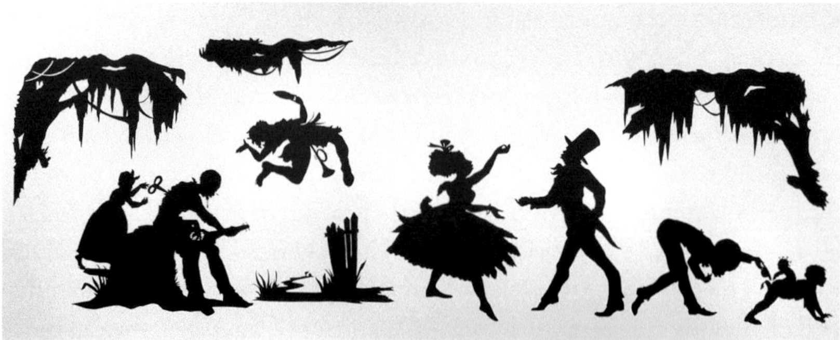

7.1 Kara Walker, *Presenting Negro Scenes Drawn upon My Passage Through the South and Reconfigured for the Benefit of Enlightened Audiences Wherever Such May Be Found, by Myself, Missus K. E. B. Walker, Colored* (detail), 1997. Cut paper and adhesive on wall, 12 × 85 ft. This work—playing on *Gone with the Wind* as well as Georgia's Cyclorama, which depicts the Battle of Atlanta—helped launch Walker's career as an artist. Artwork © Kara Walker, courtesy of Sikkema Jenkins and Co., New York. Digital file from the exhibition *Color Bind: The MCA Collection in Black and White*, Museum of Contemporary Art Chicago, 2012–13. Collection Museum of Contemporary Art Chicago, Gift of Susan and Lewis Manilow, 1999.52. Photo: Nathan Keay, © MCA Chicago. Used by permission.

metaphor seemingly at work here is known as *glossolalia* and commonly is associated with practices found within Pentecostal denominations of Christianity.[3] Rather than comparing Walker's chaotic, sexually charged tableaux to the underworld fantasies of Hieronymus Bosch, it seems to be interesting to locate her expression within a spiritual practice often associated with African American emotive religiosity. It must be stated that this reading of Walker's work is at odds with her stated intentions, and she has told me so.

Walker's work is both personal and socially conscious, juxtaposing her own experiences, historical nuances and details, with issues about race and gender in present-day society. Walker's artwork, using simple forms with details found only on the image edges, is able remarkably to convey or allude to layers of significance, multiple histories, and personal experiences. The imagery and contextual frame of her work give voice to things you cannot say in public. Yet, at this historical moment with its creeping popular cultural excesses, loudly speaking the unspeakable may be the only way to be heard above the cacophony. Another commentator observes, "Her panoramic vignettes appear whimsical at first glance, but upon inspection are gruesome and unbearable to take in."[4]

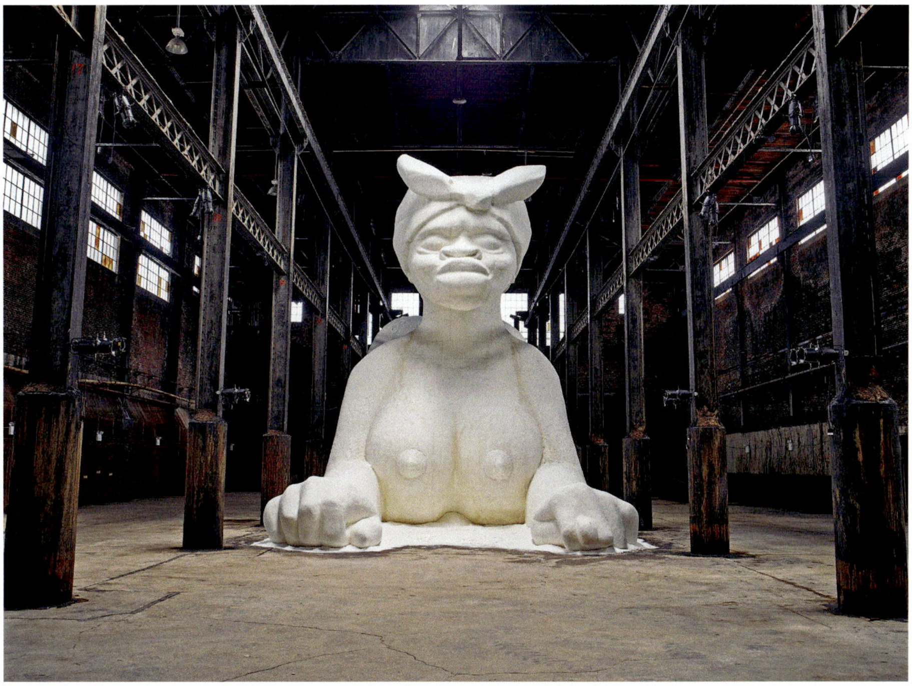

7.2 Kara Walker, *A Subtlety or the Marvelous Sugar Baby: An Homage to the Unpaid and Overworked Artisans Who Have Refined Our Sweet Tastes from the Cane Fields to the Kitchens of the New World on the Occasion of the Demolition of the Domino Sugar Refining Plant*, 2014. Polystyrene foam, sugar, approx. 35½ × 26 × 75½ ft. Installation view: Domino Sugar Refinery, a project of Creative Time, Brooklyn, NY, 2014. Photo: Jason Wyche. © Kara Walker, courtesy of Sikkema Jenkins and Co., New York.

Contextual Madness

Racial definitions became a necessity during the sixteenth and seventeenth centuries in the colonial United States because of the enormous profitability of the chattel enslavement of Africans in the Americas. Interracial interaction threatened the integrity of the slave system and led to formal legal boundaries and definitions.[5] John Hope Franklin suggests that sexual liaisons and interracial marriages seem to have been a central concern. He wrote, "Although Virginians greatly appreciated the importance of enslaved labor in the development of the colony, they soon became apprehensive about such large numbers of blacks living among whites. Already whites and blacks were mixing, and a mulatto population was emerging."[6]

Moses Williams (1777–ca. 1825) was the son of a mixed-race couple, Scarborough and Lucy, who were acquired between 1769 and 1775 by American artist Charles Willson Peale while working in Maryland, it is believed, in payment for a portrait commissioned by a local plantation owner just before moving his household to Philadelphia.[7] Art scholar Gwendolyn DuBois Shaw has written:

> Williams was born and raised within his master's Philadelphia household, and . . . after his manumission, he worked as a silhouette maker in Peale's Museum. . . .
>
> Raised alongside the numerous Peale children, who by necessity were trained to be useful members of the museum's staff, Williams was instructed in taxidermy, animal husbandry, object display, and eventually the use of a silhouette-making machine, the physiognotrace.[8]

In a convincing argument, Shaw suggests that the silhouette of Williams (figure 7.3) was a self-portrait and that his artistic practice was a means of freeing him from slavery and a mode of agency transforming, to some degree, his social status. Williams bought himself out of slavery a year early. Shaw quotes Rembrandt Peale, who reported that Moses Williams "soon acquired such dexterity and accuracy, that the machine was confided to his custody with the privilege of retaining the fee for drawing and cutting. This soon became so profitable, that my father insisted upon giving him his freedom one-year in advance. In a few years he amassed a fund sufficient to buy a two story brick house, and actually married my father's white cook, who during his bondage, would not permit him to eat at the same table with her."[9]

In arguing that the image of Williams is a self-portrait, Shaw supposes that the image was manipulated to reduce indicators of his race, though the rounded nose and full lips remain. She suggests that "Moses Williams purposely created an image in which his own features would connote tropes of whiteness rather than blackness."[10] Williams's profession, the engine of his freedom and redefinition, is a part of the image itself as text. However, before manumission Williams, unlike most of the Peale children, was not taught the higher art of painting and color, and "when [his] career failed he lost the primary thing that had represented his freedom and independence."[11]

Shaw, using Henry Louis Gates's book *The Signifying Monkey* as a reference, suggests that renaming and revising are a form of signifying. In

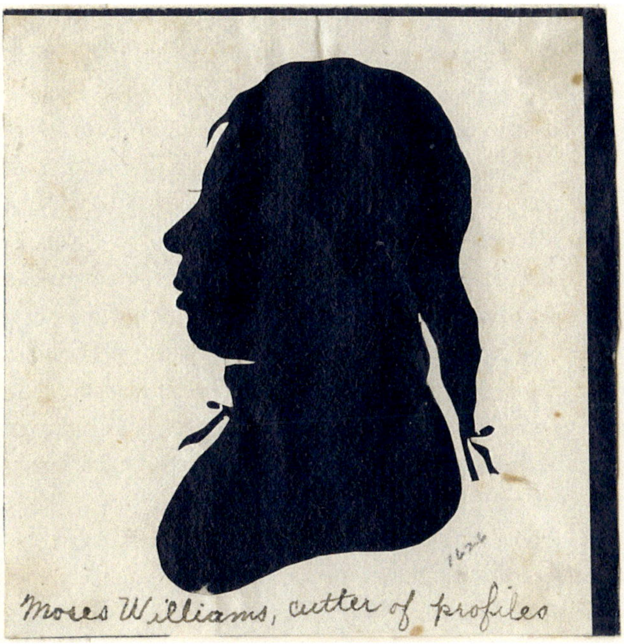

7.3 Silhouette of Moses Williams, one of the earliest African American artists to work in this format, 1803. Williams was an enslaved man apprenticed with the Charles Willson Peale family. Source: Library Company of Philadelphia, https://www.flickr.com/photos/library-company-of-philadelphia/2919836425/.

Moses Williams's case his parents, in tandem with a 1786 Pennsylvania law requiring the manumission of all enslaved persons at the age of twenty-eight, changed their surname to Williams from Peale; the slaveholder's name being a mark of possession.[12] Renaming, for the formerly enslaved, represented an act of agency; a power to transform their status and stature. Slaves often used the name Moses to indicate a status in the land of Pharaoh but also a return to one's actual heritage in freedom. Hand alterations to the machined silhouette image, and the use of his name and profession, signified Williams's free status and agency. Shaw writes, "Rather than letting the traced image remain as the machine—a machine that, it is important to remember, was invented by one of his owner's cronies—rather than letting the traced image remain as the machine had recorded it, he went back into it and revised it with his scissors. As they cut into the paper, Williams wrote his own story upon the one produced by the mechanical conception of his enslavers. Through this act he achieved agency over a small part of his representation within the public sphere."[13]

Similarly, in her repertory Kara Walker is using this anachronistic format—the silhouette—to attack the context of its use, to signify, and to gain agency over her ancestors' history. The system of slavery led to the definition of race in the terms we understand today. Both the North and the South were complicit in the slave system, so Walker's use of a slave context as an analogous critique of the entire American racial landscape and its reflection in the art world is on point. Coupled with primitivist notions about non-European people (which often were grafted on preexisting mythologies and definitions about forest creatures such as the satyr and minotaur, as well as denigrating ideas about people from lower classes), a system of confining and demeaning definitions and meanings formed to explain and contain plantation life.[14] Yet white males sexually exploited black women with impunity. While E. Franklin Frazier argued that "mulattoes or mixed-bloods constituted 37 percent of the free Negro population" of the United States in 1850, census figures from the time indicate only about 10 percent of the enslaved population was classified as mulatto.[15]

This is the context that Kara Walker somehow is able to exaggerate, and she uses the plantation as the frame for a nexus of sex and race and violence. It is from this trance of rape, exploitation, violence, greed, and spiritual bankruptcy that Walker conjures up her glossolalia of almost unintelligible speech. Is it babbling insanity or the spiritual logic of speaking in tongues across realms? Because she is creating images, this work in tone has the character of automatic writing and resembles surrealist ideas expressing the subconscious through drawing, and her use of cut imagery hints at decoupage. At the same time, Walker intentionally uses exaggeration in ways that seem to signify about black complicity in racial discourse.

To cut to the chase, race (and racism) functioned effectively in the construction and maintenance of the hugely profitable slave system. It had real-world benefits for those at the top of the system, much as the drug trade functions today. However, as the system began to be outlawed in the mid-nineteenth century, racism no longer had a functional raison d'être. It had its uses in the conceptual illusions of white supremacy, but the motivations of its construction actually no longer existed. Racists in the second decade of the new century are, in my mind, mental primitives clinging to seventeenth- and eighteenth-century ideas in the twenty-first century.

Walker has suggested that race does not belong in late twentieth-century and twenty-first-century discourse, and its presence is bizarre, its history perverse and violent, and in many ways sexual tension, jealousies, rivalries, excesses, and absurdities were central players within actual racial histories in the United States. Her 2007 work *Authenticating the Artifact* (figure 7.4) creatively builds on her earlier silhouettes with the addition of color, and the quilt-like patterns reinforce the primacy of the sexual victimization of black women in the antebellum period. Additionally, she has inverted her practice of using a black silhouette on white space to tell her tales with the use in this work of white figures on a darker background. This is, at once, an artful play with negative and positive space, and a hint of invisibility for the racialized figure. We are shocked to find the lovely young woman within the image to be gently fingering a decapitated male head while behind her his hanging entrails drip down into the scene from out of the frame as though they are artifacts from his lynching and disemboweling from a tree also out of the frame.

In figure 7.6 Walker employs a visual strategy that perhaps purposefully echoes Aaron Douglas's 1934 mural, *An Idyll of the Deep South*, from his *Aspects of Negro Life* series (figure 7.5); albeit in a way far more graphically violent. In Douglas's mural, concentric circles organize and anchor the center of the composition and focus attention on a group of musicians playing in front of a dancing couple; all are framed by trees barely entering the top edge of the image. Workers, seemingly barefoot, work the soil on the right, and one of their members has paused to experience the music. A star on the far left sends a sharp, narrow beam through the composition, giving inspiration to a kneeling figure whose eyes gaze upward at the star, whose light rips across his face. If a viewer is careless, the feet of a lynched male among the tree leaves can go unnoticed. As our eyes follow the lynch rope down into the painting, a kneeling figure, back to the viewer, seems stricken by grief at the murder. The victim's body is presented as a matter of course in southern life; at once an ironic twist to the title and a powerful commentary about the random violence that was so often an everyday presence in Negro life.

Arguably a related work by Walker, *Bureau of Refugees: Mulatto Hung by a Grapevine near Road Side Between Tuscaloosa and Greensboro* (figure 7.6), is more abstract in form and returns to Walker's practice of placing silhouetted figures on a white background, though this time they are red and green twisted around a black vine; a wonderfully sly (even if unintentional) use of the Black Power palette of red, black, and green. The title refers to a recurrent theme in her work: interracial sex. Mulatto children were the outcome of sexual liaisons that were seldom acceptable

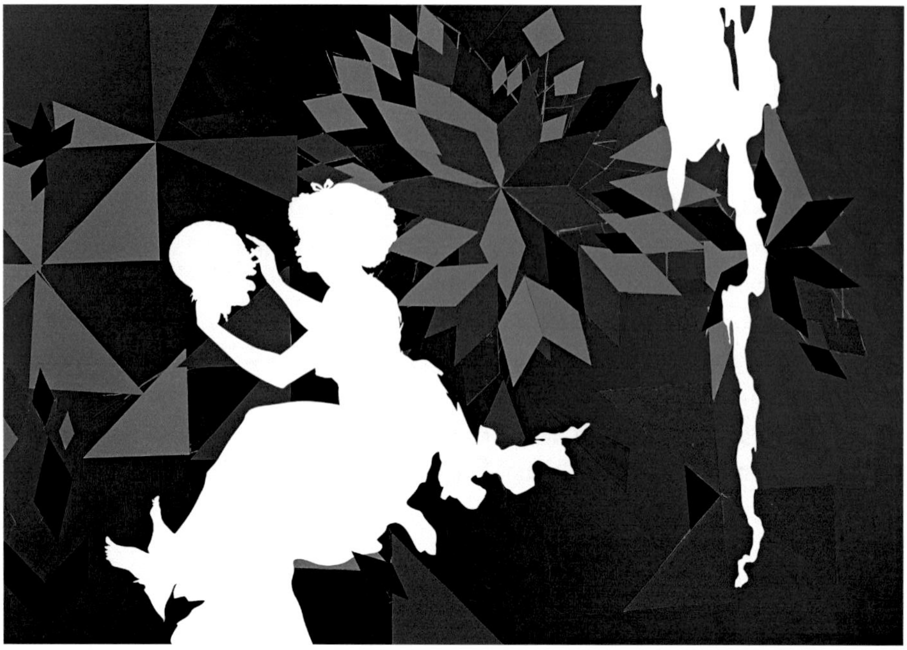

7.4 Kara Walker, *Authenticating the Artifact*, 2007. Mixed media, cut paper, and acrylic on gessoed panel, 60⅛ × 84 × 2 in. © Kara Walker, courtesy of Sikkema Jenkins and Co., New York.

in the antebellum period and often remained illegal in many southern states a century after Emancipation. There is the terrorism of lynching, an interesting play on the colloquial notion of mixed-race women as "redbones" and insinuations that the entire South is complicit in this violent drama. What is different are the subtle suggestions of a temporal move into the post–Civil War period of the Freedmen's Bureau through the civil rights era a century later. The Greensboro sit-ins of February 1960 were a significant action in the movement, and Tuscaloosa is on the western side of Birmingham. The area between the two cities involves half of Alabama, Georgia, South Carolina, and half of North Carolina.

The colorful image in *Bureau*, enhanced by the use of complementary colors red and green playing off one another, has the random liquid quality of a Rorschach stain. I read this as having psychological implications, possibly invoking a sense of racist violence as a psychodrama. Sex and violence provide the equivalent nightmarish excess of a Bosch painting. Also applicable to viewers of Walker's works is the logic of author Toni

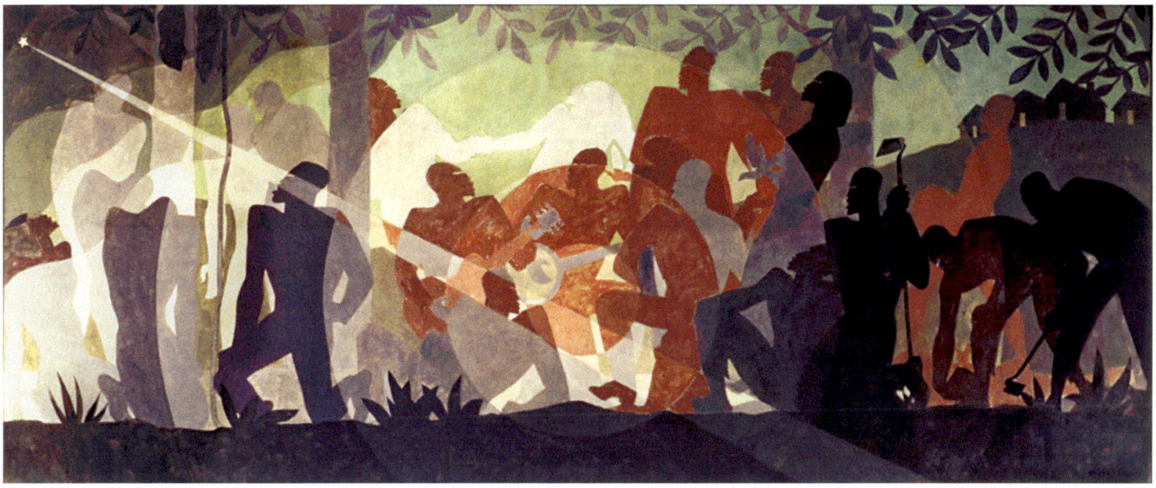

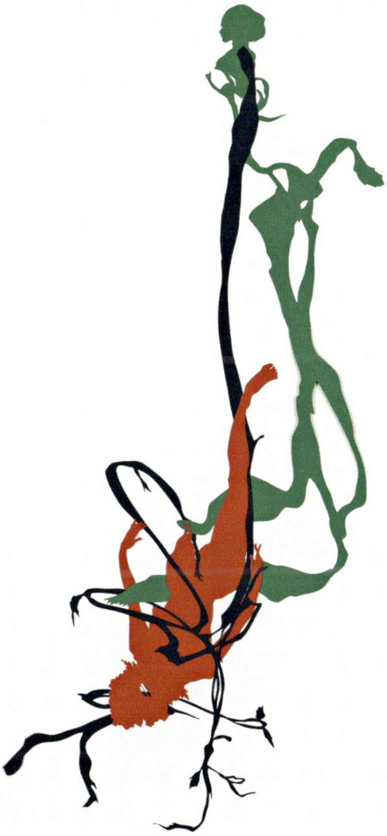

7.5 (*above*) Aaron Douglas, *An Idyll of the Deep South*, from the series *Aspects of Negro Life*, 1934. Oil on canvas, 57¾ × 138¼ in. New York Public Library Digital Collections, Schomburg Center for Research in Black Culture, Art and Artifacts Division, https://digitalcollections.nypl.org/items/634c04bc-fed3-b0e8-e040-e00a18063c1a.

7.6 (*right*) Kara Walker, *Bureau of Refugees: Mulatto Hung by a Grapevine near Road Side Between Tuscaloosa and Greensboro*, 2007. Cut paper on paper, 30¾ × 20½ in. © Kara Walker, courtesy of Sikkema Jenkins and Co., New York.

Morrison's suggestion in her book of essays *Playing in the Dark* that the fabrication of a black or "Africanist" persona in the United States should be studied for its implications regarding the fabricator. Here we may extrapolate from Morrison's literary perspective to its larger significance for social relations:

> Regardless of the race of the author, the readers of virtually all of American fiction have been positioned as white. . . . What does positing one's writerly self, in the wholly racialized society that is the United States, as unraced and all others as raced entail? What happens to the writerly imagination of a black author who is at some level always conscious of representing one's own race to . . . a race of readers that understands itself to be "universal" or race-free?

Reflecting further, Morrison observed the following form of race-related reflexivity.

> As a writer reading, I came to realize the obvious: the subject of the dream is the dreamer. The fabrication of an Africanist persona is reflexive; an extraordinary meditation on the self; a powerful exploration of the fears and desires that reside in the writerly conscious.[16]

Similarly, Walker's Rorschach blot is the stain of racism on the soul; it is the mark of Cain and America's original sin. Removed from the rational setting of capitalist profiteering, race is rooted in irrational, subconscious realms, and Walker's glossolalia, her painful speaking in tongues, evokes a trance state located within that consciousness. Perhaps she has implied that one must descend into the inferno to locate and justify the violent and persistent history of race in America. She has cast the plantation as an asylum where one can assess and analyze the insanity of racism and white supremacy.

As *New York Times* critic Holland Cotter wrote of Walker in 2007, "And then there is the theme: race. It dominates everything, yet within it, Ms. Walker finds a chaos of contradictory ideas and emotions. She is single-minded in seeing racism as a reality, but of many minds about exactly how that reality plays out in the present and the past. For her the reliable old dualities—white versus black, strong versus weak, victim versus predator—are volatile and shifting. And she uses her art—mocking, shaming, startlingly poignant, excruciatingly personal—to keep them this way."[17]

7.7 Carte de visite of Gordon, an enslaved man bearing the marks of a whip on his back, reproduced by Mathew Brady, 1863. Albumen photograph on card mount; mount 3⅞16 × 2⅜16 in. National Portrait Gallery, Smithsonian Institution, NPG.2002.89. Licensed under CC0 1.0.

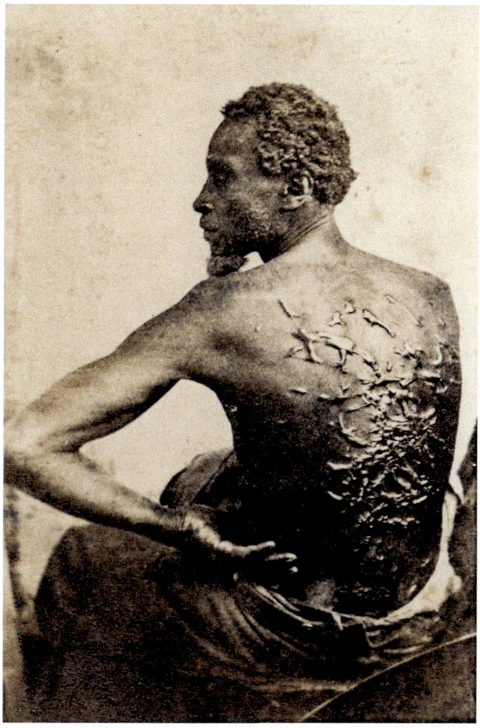

Walker is not speaking from the sanctuarial social spaces of the Africana experience, but she is addressing the persistent raison d'être for the existence of such spaces. However, this reading of her work suggests satirical aspects that echo black signifying practices—indirect and ironic, even if playful and disturbing, as introduced in the discussion of figures 7.1 and 7.2. Here we add that the subject matter's excesses tap into prayer-meeting moments of speaking in tongues, much in the same way John Coltrane's late work employing three saxophones and two drummers created abstract, arrhythmic sounds that make sense when framed as echoing a Pentecostal service where many people are speaking in tongues from the Holy Spirit. In any case, we are taken beyond the familiarity of experience into realms that exceed the rhythms and reason of the everyday world.

In some ways Walker's work implicates her own disfigurement by the products and residue of this environment, as suggested above by Morrison's idea of fabricated reflexivity. Also reflexive was the title of Walker's 2007 exhibition at the Walker Art Center in Minneapolis (not related to Kara Walker): *Kara Walker: My Complement, My Enemy, My Oppressor,*

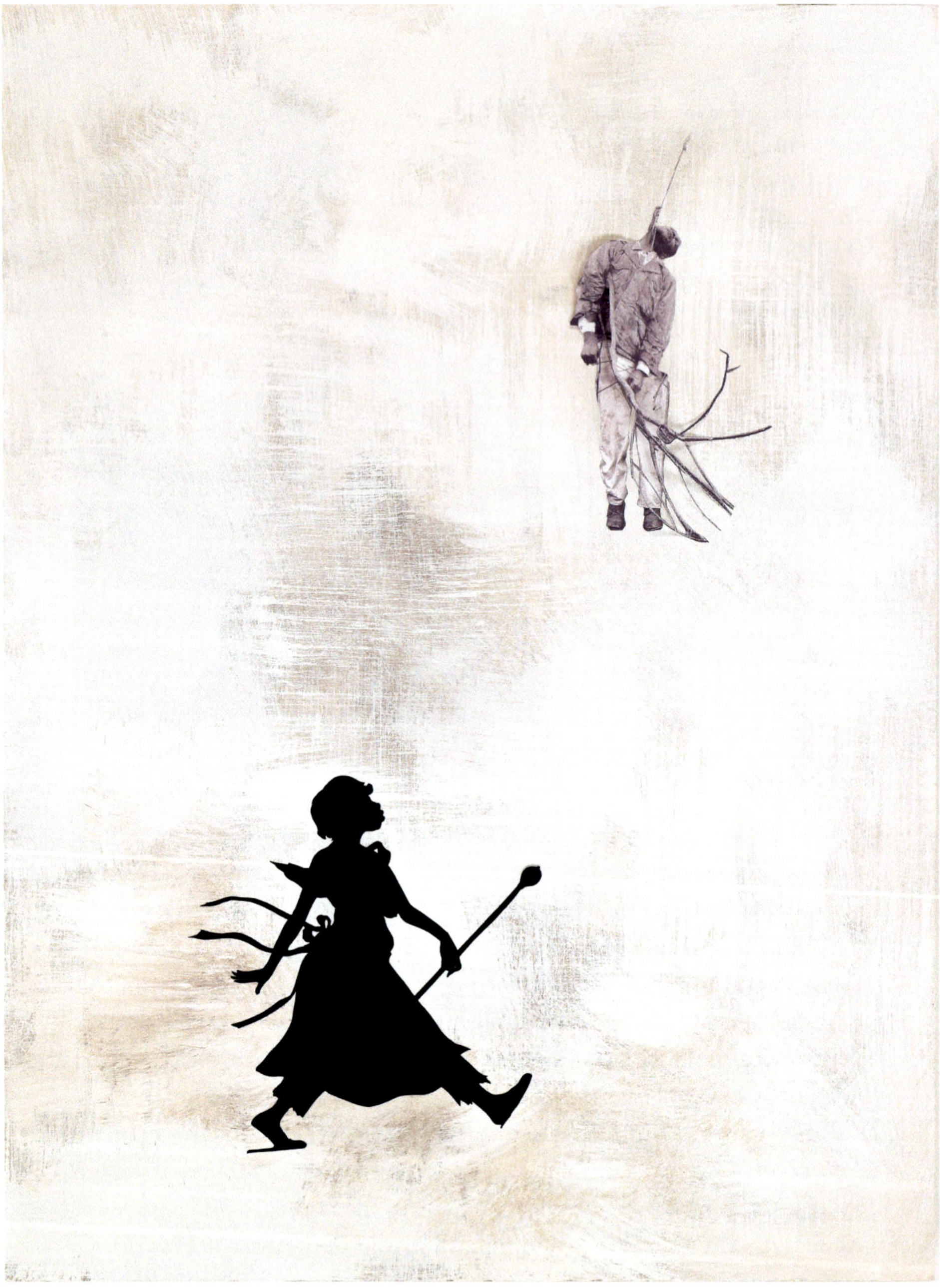

7.8 Kara Walker, *Somebody Call an Ambivalence*, 2007. Paper collage and gouache on wood panel, 24 × 17 × 1¼ in. © Kara Walker, courtesy of Sikkema Jenkins and Co., New York.

My Love. Painfully for black people, the exhibition explored the complicated antagonism toward and identification with white people that many black people feel. Conversely, it also mirrored the hatred and fascination many white people then and now have felt for black people. Titles that feature the word *Negress*, in addition to untitled works and stereotypical figures in silhouette form, all serve to emphasize the impersonal namelessness imposed on folk in racist discourse. The empowerment of self-naming remains unachieved in these works. By contrast, the formerly enslaved Isabella Dumont as a free woman became Sojourner Truth by renaming herself. In addition, she marketed or "branded" herself with a photograph that appeared on a *carte de visite* in the 1860s with the caption, "I sell the shadow to support the substance."[18] She sold her identity or image to sustain its source, a practice counteracting the depiction of nameless subjects in Walker's art.

Walker's work is artistic genius, as many admirers and scholars have attested, but it is rude, blurting out the unspeakable and the unspoken.[19] Within Walker's work is the unspeakable question of whether there is, in fact, an element of desire, of insane, illicit pleasure within or beneath the angry dynamic. The work is challenging, confrontational, creative, and disturbing. But, to employ the well-used idea of W. E. B. Du Bois, it has a double consciousness, a double edge, and it is full of double entendre.

It is a questionable assumption to define artwork done by a black person as African American art. Walker's work, however, roots itself within the idiom culturally by reference, perspective, and practice despite challenging conventional African American sensibilities. She is not alluding to expression within sanctuarial spaces, but her visual practice itself takes on the character of the expression often found in some of the expressive spiritual forms within. Sophisticated irony and satirical exaggeration can risk being missed by those it targets because, relative to racial stereotypes and archetypes, the imagery can reflect and iterate in some ways what is normalized in their system of belief. Years ago, a female friend told me of seeing porcelain pickaninny figures in an antique shop and being taken aback when an elderly southern white woman looked at them saying that they were "cute."

For some, Walker's rapturous acceptance by the art world and mainstream media and institutions despite her rude criticism of racial histories and hierarchies and her sexually charged imagery seems to confirm this sinister shadow cast by her work. Walker's task is a difficult one, but one she seems to successfully complete by challenging and critiquing both victim and victimizer as having something similar to an enabling relationship. It seems that solutions and accusations are not the objective, but daring self-examination might be a part of the goal.

Walker expresses the rage of the black experience and the psychic injuries seldom visualized but commonly present among sensitive people. Her audience is not primarily a black one, but like so many before her, she seems to be speaking to power from a public space. There are some things about her speech that are uncomfortably private. Yet the private pain that Walker makes public comes from her experience of moving to Georgia when she was a teenager and finding herself within the unabashed racial structures, assumptions, exploitations, and social constructions of the American South. In a shamanic sense, she visually takes us on a journey through chaos, disfigurement, and discord toward a re-membering of her/our fragmented (dismembered) psyche. Her journey through the deluge and racial apocalypse is also our journey to wholeness and healing and potential transformation.

An Unauthorized Reading

As quoted in chapter 2, Guthrie Ramsey argues that "cultural forms such as tales, stories, and music (especially the performative aspects of such) function as reservoirs in which cultural memories reside. These memories allow social identities to be knowable, teachable, and learnable."[20] No different from music, ethnic identity is expressed when it is "performed."[21] When artists draw imagery and codify references from their cultural reservoirs and musical or religious performances, viewers rooted in these spaces can identify with the work as speaking to or for them.

In this light, I attempt here to reinterpret my previous reading of Walker's work in terms of religious possession, talking in tongues; a means to transmit deeper, superlogical information in the ritualized settings of worship or private prayer. This can be a means to vitalize the spirit, to transcend trouble, and to speak of things not easily worded.

Admittedly, Walker's work adds a sinister twist to this notion because of the hellish subject matter and surreal events depicted. And, again, she adds the risk of iterating white supremacist structures by producing scene after scene of black victimization and powerless complaint. She also complicates racial discourse by implicating black people as contributors to its persistence, an approach that is particularly uncomfortable for older generations raised during the civil rights and Black Power eras and ideas, but the implication is empowering because it precludes, interrupts, and limits notions of victimization or essentialist condemnations by white people. Walker is not speaking in the cultural tongues of black sanctuaries, but rather she has emerged from those places questioning the quarantines that necessitate them. She risks, in the sense of the primordial Yoruba concept of too powerful divine utterance or *òrò* expressed in chapter 1, speaking into existence the very thing she wishes to eliminate. The work imposes a namelessness on its subjects, and despite the physiognomic particulars of white people and black people captured in the imagery, Walker's silhouettes essentialize the subjects rather than producing the individuality of Moses Williams's self-portrait.

The images in Walker's work do not necessarily evoke the common references of shared black cultural experience, but they do speak to the nightmarish *racial* experiences many African Americans have known and continue to know in America. They perform as an irritant to a society that wishes to obfuscate the racist nature of conservative politics and the social and institutional structures that consistently produce similar outcomes for African Americans to those that were experienced by their parents and grandparents in terms of educational opportunity, health care and wage disparities, the injustices of the criminal justice system, and the consistent resistance to even modest attempts to redress a persistent history of discrimination and inequality.[22]

Walker's work *The Treasure Hunters* (figure 7.9) from 2007 floats silhouettes above a ground of quilt-like patterns and jumbled newspaper clippings. This background space suggests the vernacular practice of having complicated jumbles of newspaper clippings and graphic drawings pasted to the walls of meager dwellings to slow down malicious spirits at night to prevent them from harming the inhabitants. Asymmetrically patterned quilts often could be found atop beds in those same homes. These elements quietly root the work in black vernacular practices—they are the cultural ground on which this story stands—which might have been common during the antebellum and postbellum periods Walker's imagery evokes.

An artist's primary obligation is to develop mastery and to do their work despite the social obligations often projected onto them by others (as I have done here with Walker, to some extent). Still, just as many blues musicians practiced and modified an expressive form that, through

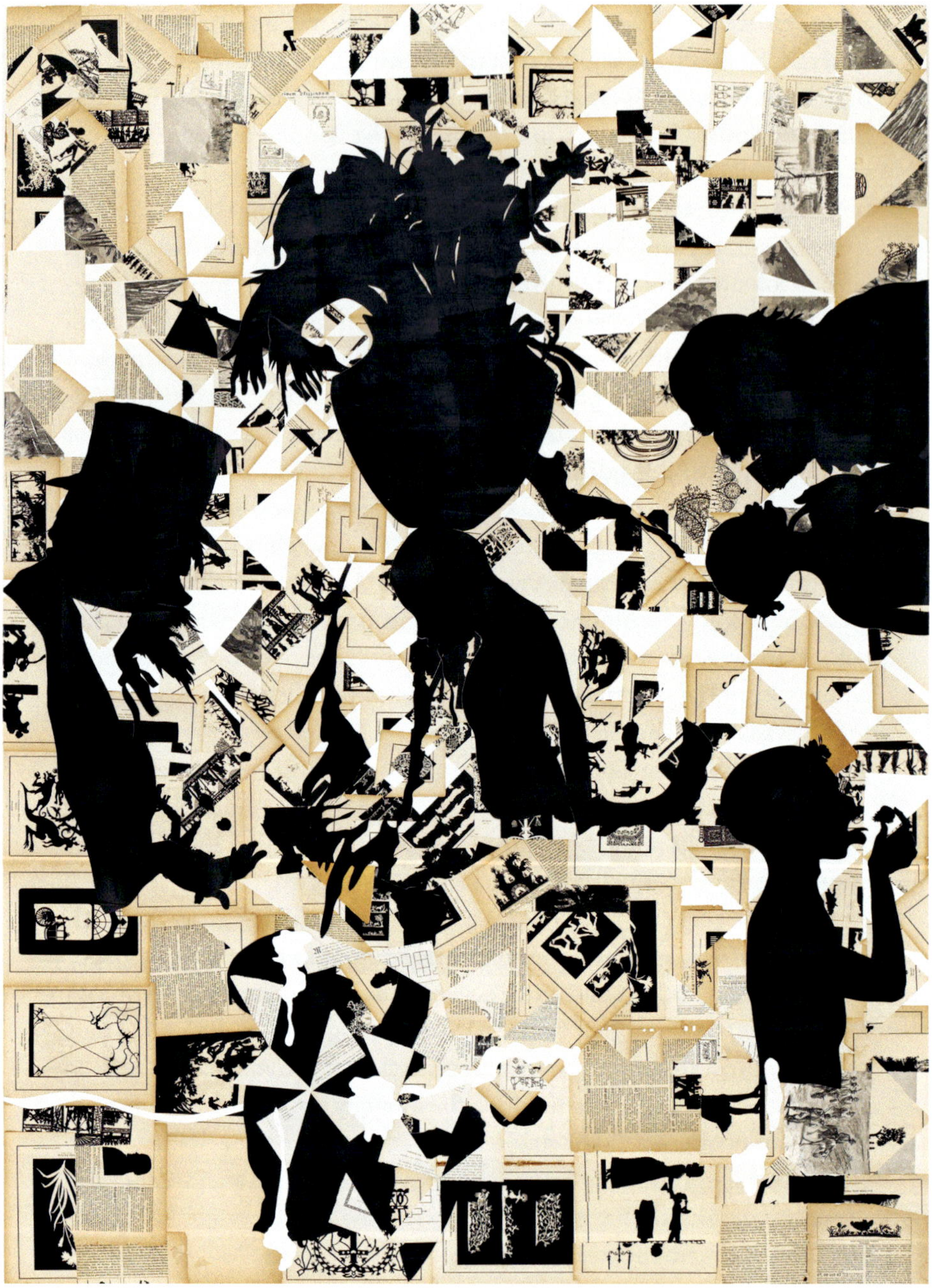

7.9 Kara Walker, *The Treasure Hunters*, 2007. Mixed media, newsprint, cut paper on gessoed panel, 84 × 60 in. © Kara Walker, courtesy of Sikkema Jenkins and Co., New York.

call-and-response, had a dialogue with its audience, many visual artists have done work that has acknowledged their communal audience. Kara Walker has collaged elements of ecstatic black religious experience with the shamanistic dismemberment and potential re-membering of the black body as a critique, exaggeration, regurgitation, and exposure of the experience of enslavement and the persistence of racism, as being one of sex and violence and as a ritual plea for her own healing. I have not always agreed with what she has done, but as I understand it more, I recognize how she is talking that talk; talking in tongues while signifyin' and while confessing her own pain. Walker has offered us a vicarious transfiguration on one side and a withering reminder that "postrace" and "postblack" are still aspirations rather than realities. What she has done is, to quote friend and scholar Moyo Okediji, "slippery and beyond historicized imagination."[23] And somehow I am left wondering whether, like the viewing of a Rorschach image and in view of Toni Morrison's insight into race and reflexivity, my musings on her are more about me the viewer than about the viewed.

Coda

In a press release for her fall 2017 exhibition at the Sikkema Jenkins and Co. Gallery in New York, Kara Walker wrote, "I don't really feel the need to write a statement about a painting show. I know what you all expect from me and I have complied up to a point. But frankly, I am tired, tired of standing up, being counted, tired of 'having a voice' or worse 'being a role model.' Tired, true, of being a featured member of my racial group and/or my gender niche."[24]

CONCLUSION

Bebop Ghosts and Freedom Songs

> [Jazz] is the truth of a desire for a refined and impassioned portrait of the presence and the power and the possibilities of the human spirit.
>
> STANLEY CROUCH, "PREMATURE AUTOPSIES" (1989)

> There are moments in Black music where the voice without words is used not to imitate instruments but to demonstrate a human expression more direct than any instrument can rival, reflecting the cries, squeals, moans, and sighs of people caught in various stages between ecstasy and agony.
>
> CLYDE TAYLOR, "'SALT PEANUTS'" (1982)

Culture uncovers the human spirit from beneath the conditions of the flesh. Racism is one of a number of violent domineering systems that attempt to slaughter that spirit. People sing and dance and carve out their communal selves, free to serve the wind and light. The Yoruba think of *ashé*—that spiritual force within their creative voicings—as the divine spark clothed by expressivity for human fashioning. This is what art does. For people in the African diaspora—for people performing spirituals and blues, gospel and jazz, be-bop and reggae, samba and mambo, rap and hip-hop, and future musics yet unnamed—we find ghosts, freedom songs, rituals of spirit, and the color of worlds seeded by remembered and lost ancestors. It is in culture where we find self-conscious life and the fight to stay alive. Alongside the relentless micro-aggressions and murderous macro-violence of racism, culture is safe within sanctuarial spaces, literal and figurative, and is played and practiced and voiced and savored and carried in pockets as codes of membership.

When people seek to be free, or feel free, they explore ideas and possibilities detached from the mundane and the corporeal. It is in this rare moment when that "desire for a refined and impassioned portrait of . . . power and the possibilities of the human spirit" becomes airborne.

Individuality is strongly associated with art in the modern and postmodern world, as well as the constructed narratives of Western civilization, though Tim Wise suggests this to be largely illusion. "There is no such thing as an individual human being abstracted from their social context," he insists.[1] It is necessary to frame creative individuality within the contexts that allow and foster it. Art is not disconnected from human endeavor; it does not live as a thing alone. The musical expression often called jazz operates with assumptions of freedom and creativity and often is described as an example, metaphor, or simulacrum for abstract painting (and the reverse as well). Improvisational and expressive freedom seems often to be accompanied by assumptions of having formed within, or being inspired by, the African American experience and is a part of the cultural reformulations in the African diaspora that have foundations in African cultures.

How do we reconcile improvisational freedom with culture? The consistent refrain I have encountered with several artists involves the argument that one's cultural foundation informs the voicing and vision of musicians and artists; therefore, no conscious effort is necessary to express it authentically from inside the culture. In a 2003 discussion with James Phillips, Jeff Donaldson, and Murry DePillars, all members of AfriCOBRA (figure C.1), it was argued that Robert Farris Thompson's 1983 classic book *Flash of the Spirit*, articulated the translation of Africana sonic, visual, and gestural patterns into organizing principles merging African expressivity with New World and European elements to create what he called the black Atlantic visual tradition.[2]

In an interview, abstract painter Oliver Lee Jackson described how free expression is rooted in culture this way: "We have a particular sensibility. It's clear as a bell. It's so clear that everybody recognizes it. Everything that you make that comes out of you, you are recognized. . . . That's speaking with your voice. That's not asking anybody. Blues. Spirituals. I mean, it goes on and on. So, that's the saving grace, that you have enough confidence, under this kind of pressure that tells you what you should be doing that you decide. You have to trust your sensibility. Ain't nothing written down."[3] Jackson uses this understanding to see himself and appreciate exploratory musicians as having the freedom to express whatever their

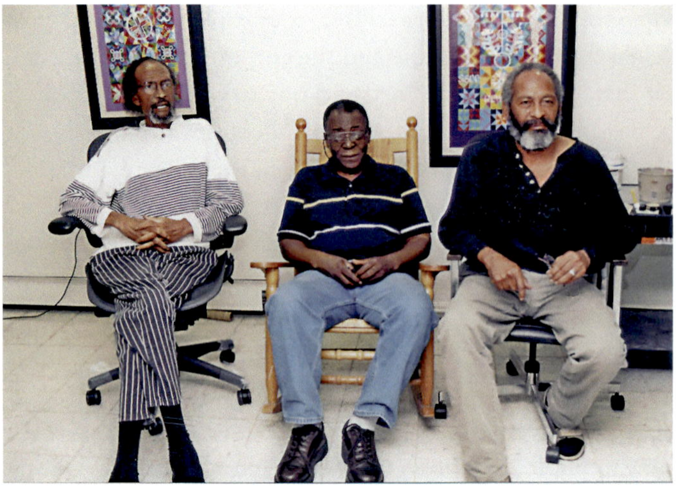

C.1 Jeff Donaldson, Murry DePillars, and James Phillips at Donaldson's home, 2003. Photograph by Michael D. Harris.

sensibilities are, with the sense that, on a deep spiritual level, that voice being expressed is emerging from a particular sensibility; an epistemological frame, a way of being in the world (see figure C.2).

Artist and photographer Adger Cowans expresses a similar outlook. He says, "What's coming through me. Just like a singer has a voice and they sing, and you're touched by the feeling of that voice, or not. And the more people that are touched by that feeling, the closer they are to what I call 'raw spirit' or direct spirit. . . . Just like jazz players. They give you that feeling that's happening right then."[4] Cowans emphasizes the spiritual process in finding one's voice, perhaps the way, in some spiritual traditions, your unique voice is to be found when meditating and chanting. That voicing is founded within a particular sensibility or tradition, needing no emphasis to express itself. Within this freedom of expression through the personal voice and imagination, Jackson feels that the culture then can surprise and innovate. He says that no one could anticipate bebop or hip-hop. Many resisted exploratory forms of music until they learned to hear them. "When I heard that, I was quite young. And all the hip dudes older than me were listening to Lester Young. I wanted to be like them. And that shit was gobbledygook to me. But I had to be cool. Then one day, my ears opened up. That sh*t was moving!"[5]

Here we return to Paul Carter Harrison's interpretation of this aesthetic freedom, explored in the introductory chapter and defined as *experiential*

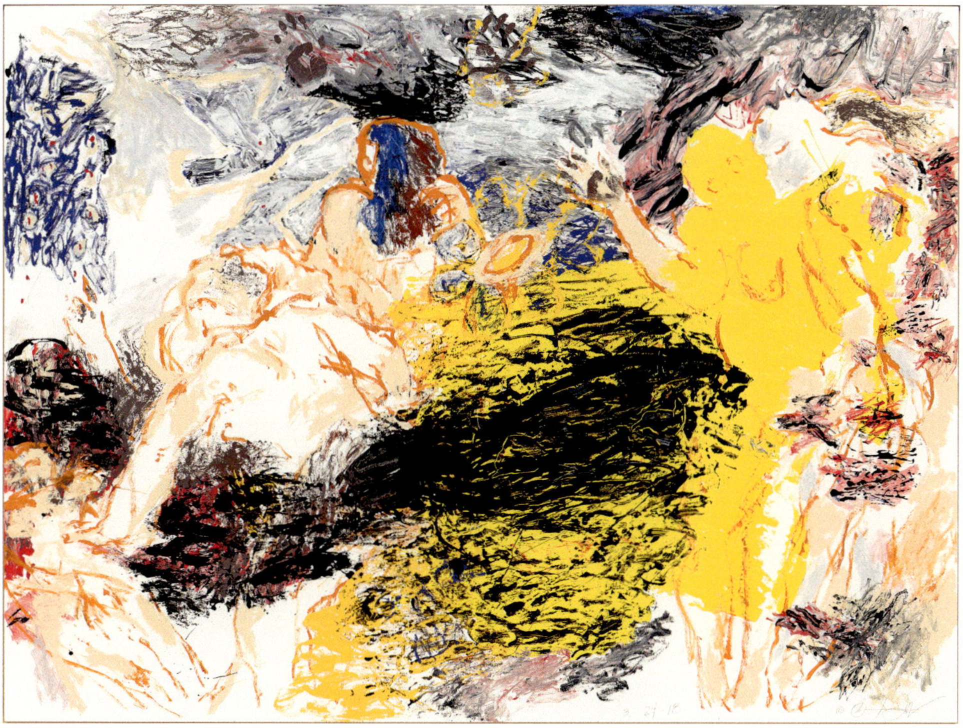

C.2 Oliver Lee Jackson, *No. 5*, 2018 (3.24.18). Oil-based paints on panel, 72 × 96 in. This work emerges from figures and embodies Jackson's intention that figure and background are on the same level. Photo: National Gallery of Art, Washington, DC. © Oliver Lee Jackson.

phenomenology: "These are not necessarily conscious decisions. This is really, in your cultural experience, how you perceive relationships (unless it has been tutored out of you). It's not *doing* aesthetics; aesthetics emerge from your perception of reality."[6] In our context here, the response to differing experiences is interpreted through the cultural syntax of African cultural foundations and their rootedness in a spiritualized or inflected reality, whether consciously or not. Tuning in to this may take the viewer or listener to a free, spiritual place evoking a higher experience. Culture is not just social action but is a basis for expressive freedom and for exploration of human possibilities.

While being interviewed by Carrie Mae Weems, Kenya-born artist Wangechi Mutu said, "I never imagined that making art would be of any use to anyone, including myself, if it wasn't speaking about something that grounded me, if it wasn't about the story that was coming out of my relationship to my family, to my land, to the people I love, to the people I don't love anymore, or to the people I want to love. Art-making was never just about being expressive. For me, it is very much about the utterance of humanity."[7]

While considering what elements and tendencies might inhabit an Africana art aesthetic, Robert Farris Thompson suggests that the art emerges from life and lived experiences, as reiterated by Mutu, the idea that culture is the matrix humans form to organize and codify their relationships to themselves, each other, nature, and the divine, and perhaps the notion that culture is ultimately a form of humanism. It is possible to see a pattern of human-centered expression and intention at the heart of such an aesthetic. An ongoing, lively debate about aesthetics with Harrison, a mentor and friend, has led me to note the anthropocentricity of many African cultures and their creative expressions. Yet that emphasis often is inseparable from reflections of the Divine.

Individuality is considered and honored within a larger reality of family, community, and cosmological existence. To illustrate this for the Yoruba, there is a saying: "There are 401 orishas." This means, as many as you can think of plus one; thus numberless:

> Some of these deities were worshipped throughout Yorubaland, but others were of only local significance. . . . An individual might worship his deity or deities in his or her own compound but more generally all the worshippers of a deity or group of related deities would join together into a cult group or worship community for ceremonies and festivals. . . . Although there were community cults, particularly those associated with the ruler and his family, each individual's worship was his or hers alone and no one was persecuted because he or she did or did not worship a particular Orisha.[8]

Accordingly, the idea is that within the whole there is room for innumerable variations of individuality. In the arts this system of belief does not produce abstract, existential contemplations, though abstractions support creative expression. The human body is a living symbol of humanity and social being, not a political thing that can be racialized. In a spiritual universe or ontological frame, corporeal issues tend to give way to ideas—to expression and expressive ideas—so that the physical world also marks conceptual relationships and unseen perspectives.

Jazz, or black classical music, analogously, is played in ensembles of various sizes, and individuals often are celebrated for their creative dialogues with each other in performance. Collaborations, for example, between Miles Davis and John Coltrane, or with Dizzy Gillespie and Cuban percussionist Chano Pozo, have become legendary. There is a balance of individual creativity, virtuosity, and context at play. And always there is an implication of freedom and being: sassy, contemplative, hot, cool, raucous, adept, sexual, religious, angry, seductive, rhythmic, esoteric, personal, percussive, orchestral, minimalist, brassy, Saturday night, Sunday morning, ancestral, or space-is-the-place futuristic.

Writing about saxophonist Charlie Parker, Arthur C. Brooks argues that the freedom of jazz flourishes because of its disciplined "adherence to boundaries and rules. And therein it achieves the nature of true freedom, in both art and life."[9] Brooks says that "the chord structure is spelled out over the melody with zero ambiguity. When improvising after the melody, the jazz player must stay within these chords. This is devilishly hard, once again requiring years of work and study."[10] Brooks echoes the notions of pedagogy discussed earlier regarding Henry Ossawa Tanner's *The Banjo Lesson*, indicating that Africana musical traditions are born and borne of study, discipline, and virtuosity behind any sense of improvisation—and implying that similar painting histories are likewise. To return to Jeff Donaldson's statement from the 1970 CONFABA (the Conference on the Functional Aspects of Black Art) meeting described in the introductory chapter: "It was explicit that the function of art is to liberate man in the spiritual sense of the word, to provide more INTERNAL space."[11]

Mutu also spoke about rooting her creativity in her history and experience and not in contemplation of oppression: "I remember at that time [in the late 1990s] thinking how much I wanted to claim my presence without necessarily confirming the terror and racism and colonialism thrust upon us. There was a people before colonization. There was a history before the missionaries. In fact, there were thousands of years of original languages and culture that eventually migrated to all of these other continents before any of these brutalities and atrocities were placed upon us. There still is a language separate from all of these atrocities within us."[12]

The late work of John Coltrane in many ways echoes the earlier contentions made here about artwork having, at its best, layers of signification to larger and larger connections beyond individuality, perhaps beyond culture. On his signature 1965 composition, *A Love Supreme*, Coltrane wrote on the bottom of the music sheet, "All paths lead to God" (figure C.3). He wrote on

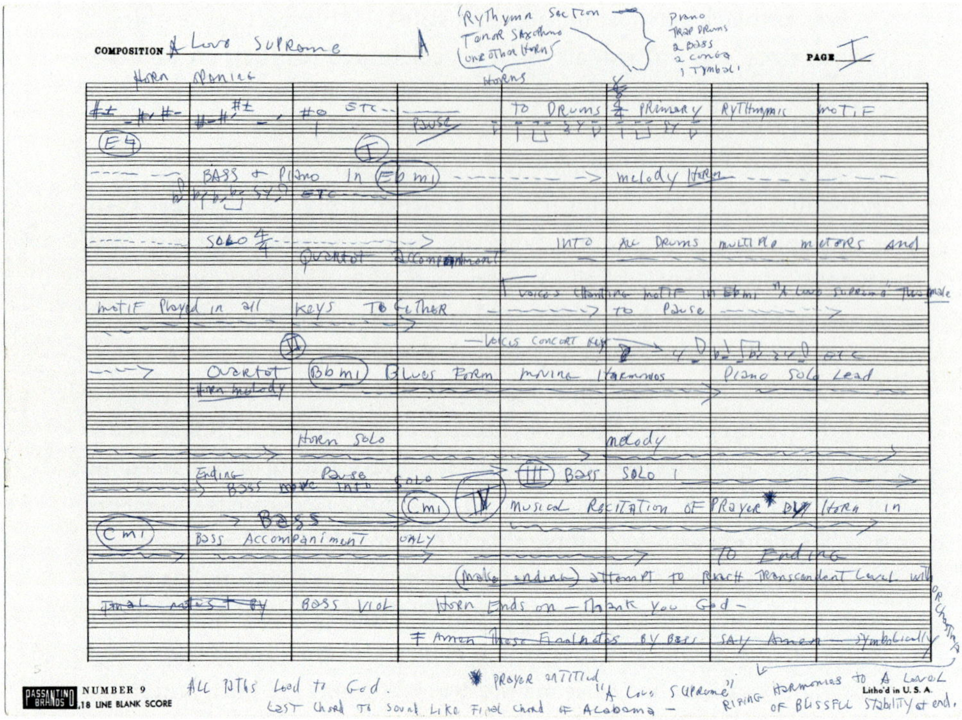

C.3 John Coltrane, handwritten outline for *A Love Supreme*, 1964. John Coltrane Music Manuscript, Archives Center, National Museum of American History, Smithsonian Institution, Washington, DC. Used by permission.

the liner notes to the album, "No road is an easy one, but they all go back to God."[13] Coltrane also wrote that the fourth movement of the album composition, "Psalm," was a "musical recitation of prayer by horn."[14] Perhaps it is within these larger realms where the specific can find universality.

Late Coltrane works evoke the sounds of prayer meetings, speaking in tongues, and higher states of consciousness. There is a visual and aural nexus not unlike old ideas found in Yoruba culture and the signs and signifiers that evoke spiritual ideas and beliefs. We can return to Dianne Stewart's idea of humans vivifying the earth and creating all manner of possibilities with divine breath as embodied in the ideas of *òrò* and Ẹmí from the Yoruba. Jazz can be more than jazz, and visual abstraction can contain or imply more than the history of art.

The point is that abstraction in African American painting often is similar to jazz, and jazz can be individuality within cultural speech.

Representational visual elements are stripped away as artists explore both technical and virtuosic mastery, as well as challenging artistic conventions, but the work often is layered with metaphysical, aesthetic, and spiritual meditations and references. Or it can be filled with creative play and signifying. Clyde Taylor's idea of "mythophones as highly charged symbolizations, in music and language, of entire cultural outlooks" seems appropriate as a description.[15]

Horn player Yusef Lateef came to live with a spiritual commitment to his Islamic faith and to the seriousness of his music. In a 2012 interview, he said, "I stopped playing in clubs where alcohol was served. I get calls but I've turned them down, that's why you haven't seen me. Plus the money they were paying me back in the '50s is the same money they offered me in the 80's. There's a lack of appreciation. A lack of observation. A lack of development."[16]

In an approach to evoke spiritual consciousness, photographer and artist Adger Cowans has done a series of works abstracted from the surface imagery of water and another series with the reflections of metal (see figure C.4). He says that a part of his effort is to move past recognizable elements to affect the part of the brain that might engage in spiritual thought and encounters.[17] Dòwòti Désir writes about this series of photographs, saying, "[These works] are a reflection of who he is and what is divine within him. . . . Close to nature, Cowans is the silent warrior on our path, the mabuya or the chameleon whose most powerful attribute is its ability to emulate or recreate the environment around them in every meticulous detail, while remaining true to its core. His digital techniques succeed to awakening our chakras, and our primal memories."[18]

Ben Jones, employing symbols and signifiers, has made direct references to African spiritual systems in his work while linking Yoruba and Cuban orisha with jazz singers and others. He has reinterpreted the traditional church fan into a heart shape with the kind of appendaged energy forms displayed atop Renée Stout's *Headstone for Marie Laveau* (figure 6.14). With photo imagery and painted marks evoking Haitian *veve*, West African Nsibidi signs, and the kind of marks often used ritually atop the heads of Yoruba ceremonial participants, jazz singer Billie Holiday (figure C.5) has been linked to the Yoruba and Cuban orisha Yemoja or Yemanja. The blue and white color emphasis and a cowrie shell in a third-eye position make this implication. Cowrie shells evoke ideas of fecundity and the abundance from the sea. Yemoja, in Yoruba, translates to "mother of the fishes," and her ceremonial affiliate beads are blue and

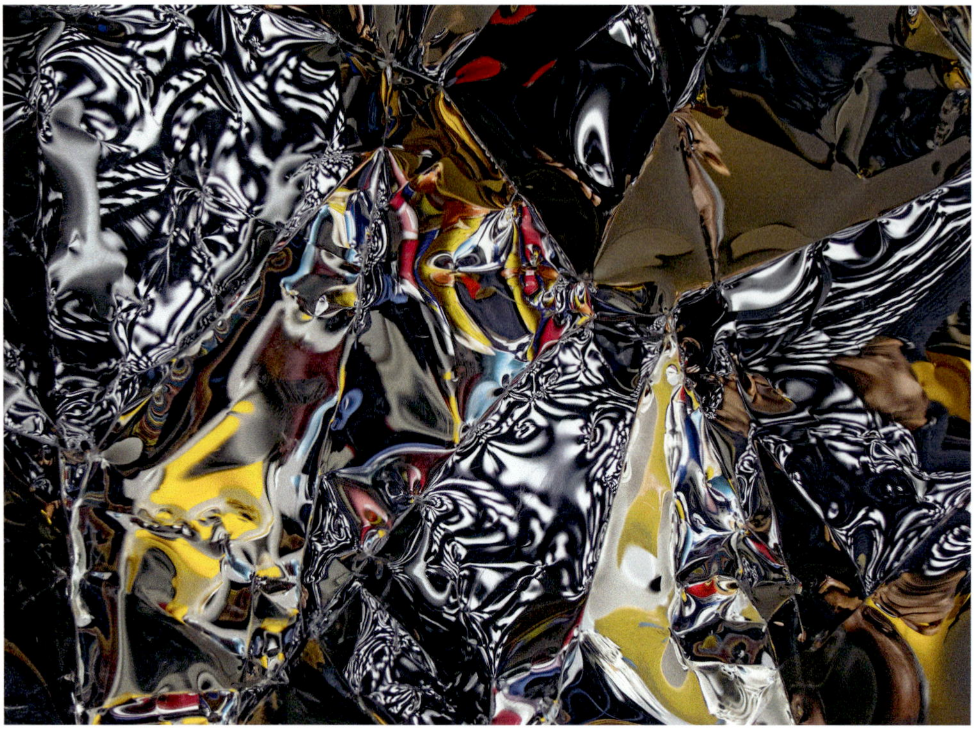

C.4 Adger Cowans, *Reflect*, 2014. Photograph. Used by permission of the artist.

white. Ben Jones used symbolic elements around and atop a familiar face to bridge the representational to abstraction. He employs devices that embody Clyde Taylor's ideas about the mythogram; evocative triggers calling up a matrix of practices and meanings, such as his use of the church fan as a point of departure. This fan is charged with spiritual energy.

Many African American artists dissociate their ethnicity from their work in an effort to elude the effects and outcomes of racial designations. In a possible explanation of this denial, José Esteban Muñoz, in queer theory, developed the idea of disidentification as a means of reconfiguring one's status and relationship to a dominant and hostile culture that has encoded the outsider's existence as a trope for marginality and powerlessness. It is a strategy to "situate oneself both within and against the various discourses through which one is called to identify."[19] Therefore, Kara Walker's work has this seemingly complicated tactic as a possible interpretation because her imagery clearly does not represent the majority view and establishes her as standing outside of it when making satirical

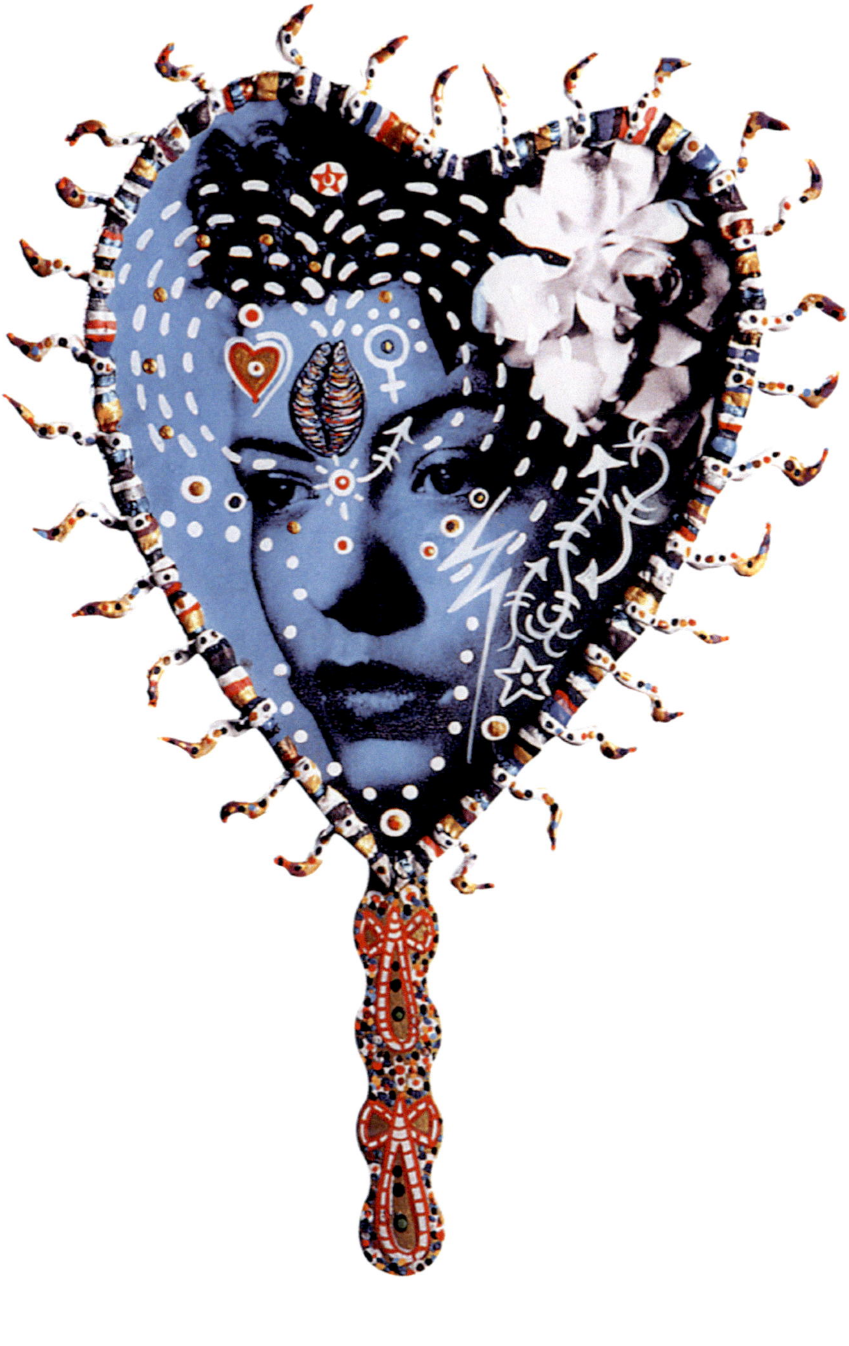

C.5 Ben Jones, *Billie Holiday #1*, 1998. Mixed media, 15 × 10 in. From the collection of Sydne Tarry. Used by permission of the artist.

and signifying social critiques. She has taken imagery and the silhouette form from the center of eighteenth- and nineteenth-century "exclusionary machinations" and twisted and placed them in a contemporary context to reveal the absurdities of racial representations and practices still in play today. However, Walker's work addresses the art world, the white gaze, while she disrupts its assumptions and narratives.

Jack Whitten often built paintings with abstracted imagery, an emphasis on technique and materials, but his titles can coagulate these efforts into suggestive forms that evoke the implied subject matter or personalities. Similar to proverbs, Whitten's works do not lead directly to meaning but point toward relationships, connections, interior realities and characteristics. His 1994 work *Black Monolith II (Homage to Ralph W. Ellison)* (figure C.6) riffs on Ellison, *Invisible Man*, and ancestral stelae and takes the approach of many abstractionists in using a title to open symbolic and metaphorical, and therefore cultural, implications to audiences. The work has the material suggestions of a Byzantine mosaic in its formalities and fragmental organization. As a monolith, it implies steles, commemorative markers of something, or someone, sacred or profound. It marks Whitten as a citizen of his time and a possessor of Africana history, global histories, and artistic virtuosity. Similar interpretations might be pulled from the work of Leonardo Drew, Norman Lewis, Martin Puryear, and many others whose work evokes rather than purports.

Jazz did not form to appeal to a white audience but was tied to voicings and cultural references found in the raucous life of Storyville in New Orleans. It is tied to pain and creative persistence and ecstatic suggestion. The phrasing of jazz horn players, scat singing, train sounds, bent notes, instrumental vocalizations, so many abstract sonic elements drawn from the black experience populate the history of jazz and its interplay with Africana life. Toni Morrison, who has stated publicly that she does not write for the white gaze, wrote about the sonic element in her novels in her 1984 essay "Rootedness: The Ancestor as Foundation":

> There are things that I try to incorporate into my fiction that are directly and deliberately related to what I regard as the major characteristics of Black art, whatever it is. One of which is the ability to be both print and oral literature: to combine those two aspects so that the stories can be read in silence, of course, but one should be able to hear them as well. It should try deliberately to make you stand up and make

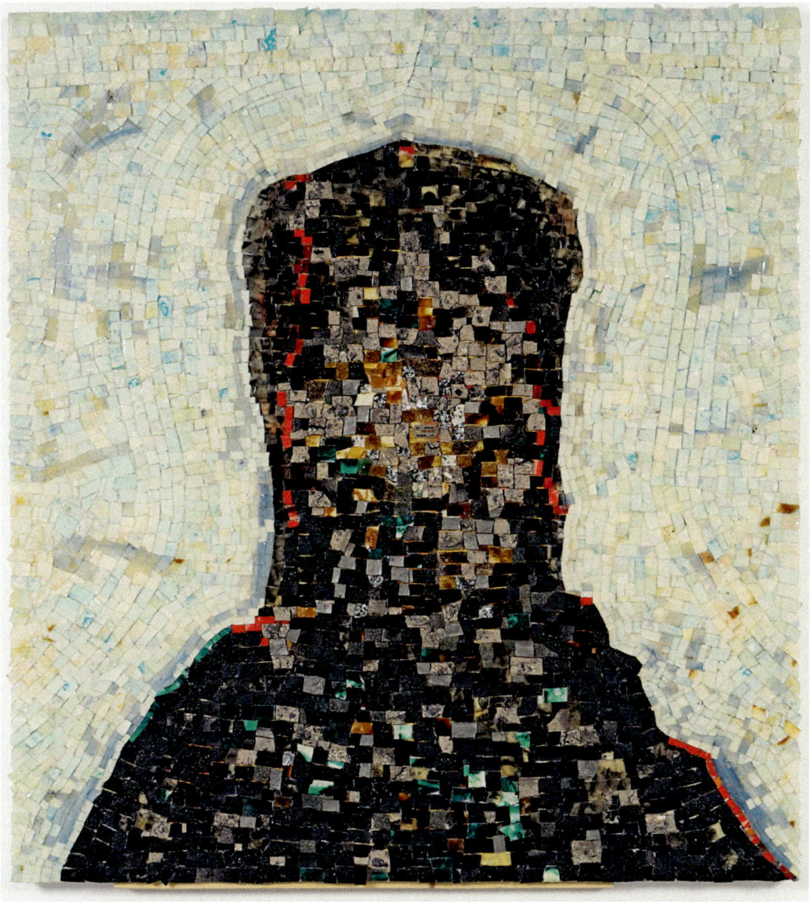

C.6 Jack Whitten, *Black Monolith II (Homage to Ralph W. Ellison)*, 1994. Acrylic, molasses, copper, salt, coal, ash, chocolate, onion, herbs, rust, eggshell, and razor blade on canvas, 58½ × 52½ × 1¾ in. Brooklyn Museum, NY, William K. Jacobs, Jr. Fund, 2014.65. © Jack Whitten Estate. Courtesy of Jack Whitten Estate and Hauser and Wirth. Photo: John Berens.

you feel something profoundly in the same way that a Black preacher requires his congregation to speak, to join him in the sermon, to behave in a certain way, to stand up and to weep and to cry and to accede or to change and to modify—to expand on the sermon that is being delivered. In the same way that a musician's music is enhanced when there is a response from the audience.[20]

Morrison's intent articulates what had been visualized by Archibald Motley Jr. in the 1929 painting *Tongues (Holy Rollers)*, mentioned in chapter 5 (figure 5.3); a work filled with sound. She mentions that her novel *Song of Solomon* allowed her to blend "the acceptance of the supernatural and a profound rootedness in the real world at the same time with neither taking precedence over the other. It is indicative of the cosmology, the way in which Black people looked at the world."[21] The supernatural might involve speaking in tongues or shouting, as can almost be heard in Motley's painting. It might involve incantations and intonations from a conjure woman, or the preacher turning the Bible into an incantatory text.

Considering the inspiration of jazz music in the abstract expressionist art movement, Ann Gibson suggests the difference between artists within African American culture and others. She says that a number of abstract expressionist artists, such as Jackson Pollock, "adapted the formal structures of jazz but left its explicit references to its African American roots behind," but Norman Lewis "meshed analyses of the structure of jazz with visual references to its production."[22]

Creating for the Africana gaze (or ear) might involve signifying and misdirection and the verbal play often heard in communal spaces, even in the blanketing reality of contemporary capitalist globalism and its monetizing of all human activity. Morrison refers to "anather way of knowing things" and uses the idea of the ancestor to suggest the deeper links and broader connections available in a communal gaze.[23] With the elevation of individuality and personality in artistic expression, the culturally rooted extra-mainstream point of view with an implied "we" in either the written narrative or visual imagery can be problematized. Morrison argues:

> This is disturbing to people and critics who view the artist as the supreme individual. It is disturbing because there is a notion that that's what the artist is—always in confrontation with his own society. . . .
>
> When you kill the ancestor you kill yourself. I want to point out the dangers, to show that nice things don't always happen to the totally self-reliant if there is no conscious historical connection.[24]

Africana cultural and ancestral connections, even when visual, imply or play with tongues and speech. When colliding against race, this creative free play is suppressed or subjugated in the silencing of the utterances and gestures of black life. This takes on a million small and large forms. Writing about James Baldwin, David Leeming described Baldwin's 1962 visit to Senegal, where he encountered students reciting from a history book:

> When he entered the room, the children were reciting in unison from a history textbook. The words seemed to have little to do with the lives of those in the room, and upon reading the opening passage of the book (published and written in France)—"Our ancestors, who came from Gaul . . ."—he was enraged by the irony. These children were being denied their own heritage; the object was to turn them into absurd replicas of their colonizers. He thought of the analogous situation of millions of black children in American classrooms reading about "our ancestors," the Europeans, the pilgrims, the writers of the Constitution, and the pioneers.[25]

What kind of self-slaughter happens when one, in killing the ancestor, is grafted to an ancestor whose presence is effacing? An ancestor whose language manufactures a reality antithetical to your cultural history? Moans, significations, dual audience conversations, sanctuaries (and even their excesses), idiomatic speech, and transformations of lived experience into art become set adrift with false ancestors as well as loss of real ones. Cataracts appear to blur the Africana gaze.

> Much-missed gentle one
> blooming in the moonlight of yesteryears
> calls to me
> calls to me. . . .
>
> OBIORA UDECHUKUWU, "Affirmations" (1990)

§

Two strategies Muñoz describes for marginalized peoples are to identify or counteridentify with what the dominant ideology declares one to be. Both tactics, however, are to define oneself around or against what the designation of the dominant group is declared to be. None of these strategies self-identifies or self-defines; therefore, they link the subjects to a relationship with the oppressive group and ideas.

Black as an identity has been ground into the epistemological frame for so long that it has naturalized a racialized reality (and ontology) that is a fundamental assumption. African cultural identity is not separable from racialized experiences and structures; they are linked but not equally exchangeable. The escape from racialization many artists have attempted in seeking to be "just artists" is potentially realized through culture.

Seeking individuality and freedom divorced from one's cultural rootedness in this context, for the Africana artist, can seem to be the task of Sisyphus, who in Greek mythology as punishment for his self-aggrandizing deceitfulness was tasked to roll a large boulder up a hill only to have it eternally roll back to the bottom before he reached the top. An interpretation of this myth is that the task itself, the goal, is an empty aspiration, a meaningless objective. The task often, for many, is the acceptance of black people into the dominant, exclusionary society. As Morrison wrote about the aspirational narratives of writings by the enslaved (and echoed in artistic efforts perhaps), "We were seldom invited to participate in the discourse even when we were its topic."[26] Must we strip ourselves of culture and personality to be accepted in American society?

Language, speech, and the performance of culture become foundational in the identification of an Africana aesthetic. Historian Ras Michael Brown says that the range of what Kongo people did anywhere is the potential of what they could have done everywhere. He also suggests that culture must be multigenerational.[27] This leads back to the ancestor, and as mentioned in an earlier chapter, Africans displaced from Kongo attempted to relocate their ancestors, spirits, and relationship to the earth in the Carolina Lowcountry during their enslavement, even translating the Central African BaKongo *simbi* spirit into *cymbee*.[28]

As we consider our forebears and ancestors, they are, as Toni Morrison has written, "my access to me; they are my entrance into my own interior life."[29] They are sanctuary. Morrison points out that most early African American narratives "were written to say principally two things. One: 'This is my historical life—my singular, special example that is personal, but that also represents the race.' Two: 'I write this text to persuade other people—you, the reader, who is probably not black—that we are human beings worthy of God's grace and the immediate abandonment of slavery.'"[30]

This is not to say that there is an "African" culture, but we might locate in evidence Yoruba and Kongo language or practice in Haiti, Cuba, Trinidad, and Brazil manifesting in their African-derived religions in similar ways and terminologies, for example. Africana cultural expression in today's world often finds sanctuarial spaces within which to grow and evolve. Verbal expression (human voicings) often animates it and links old spiritual etymologies to contemporary creative practices.

Rowland Abiodun has written several times about the social aspects of Yoruba aesthetics organized through human and cultural qualities such as *ìlutí* (good hearing), *ìwàpẹlẹ* (existence, gentle character), *imọjú-mọra* (a sense of what is appropriate for the moment or circumstance), *ẹwà* (beauty, embellishment, adornment), and *ashé* (the power to make things happen, released unseen energy, divine essence). Here we also join with Paul Carter Harrison to harness African spiritual dynamics such as *ashé* as integral to his long-standing legacy projects—projects that "interrogate the meaning of Black art and investigate the African cultural continuities that filter into the expressive practices of the African Diaspora as a by-product of humanistic impulses."[31]

To read Africana (and/or African American) art expression through artistic, cultural, and individual voicings and intonations connected to a sense of spiritual practices found in vernacular and communal histories has been the point of this journey. Integrating the work of Africana artists into various mainstream canons on its own terms will enrich our understanding of the art. The rich biographies from which the art comes will add untold layers of wealth to our appreciation and understanding of the works.

> I run chords
> *needing the space*
> that only the horn provides
> riffin Seventh Avenue blues, the Kansas City
> four/four, the women, striding, digging the cool murmur
> of morning
> a sledgehammer of meaning
> balled in sound
> slams against the back of my head.
>
> LARRY NEAL, "Riffin in the Chili House (in Memory of Bird)" (1974)

Notes

Foreword

1 Donaldson, *CONFABA*. Appendix 3, "Task Force 5 Philosophy Recommendations," 103.

2 Ted Gioia, "How Wayne Shorter Transformed Jazz Composition in the 1960s," *Honest Broker*, March 3, 2023, https://www.honest-broker.com/p/how-wayne-shorter-transformed-jazz.

Editors' Introduction

1 James Baldwin uses the term *racial nightmare* in his essay "The Fire Next Time" (379).

Introduction: Sanctuary and the Black Interior

Epigraphs: Ta-Nehisi Coates, "My President Was Black: A History of the First African American White House—and of What Came Next," *Atlantic*, January/February 2017, https://www.theatlantic.com/magazine/archive/2017/01/my-president-was-black/508793/. Muhammad Ali, "'The Rumble in the Jungle': Muhammad Ali vs George Foreman 30.10.1974 (October 30, 1974)." Classic Boxing Matches, September 30, 2016, accessed July 17, 2025, https://youtu.be/ElWMImS6K78?si=CUhpBwI8dG7dMjGP.

1 Morrison, *Origin of Others*, 15.

2 Robinson, "Sense of Self," 332.

3 Ta-Nehisi Coates, "My President Was Black: A History of the First African American White House—and of What Came Next," *Atlantic*, January/February 2017.

4 Jennifer Baker, "Art Must Engage with Black Vitality, Not Just Black Pain," *Electric Literature*, September 21, 2017, https://electricliterature.com/art-must-engage-with-black-vitality-not-just-black-pain-d39b7cd690c1.

5 R. Thompson, "Communiqué from Afro-Atlantis," 68.

6 Paul Carter Harrison, taped interview with the author, Atlanta, Georgia, April 17, 2018.

7 Coates, *Between the World and Me*, 62.

8 Postal worker Victor Green published the *Green Book* guide beginning in 1936 to help African American travelers find restaurants, auto shops, and accommodations as they traveled. Green said that he was inspired by the Jewish press, "which had long published information on restricted places." Ana Swanson, "The Forgotten Way African Americans Stayed Safe in a Racist America," *Wonkblog*, *Washington Post*, January 8, 2016.

9 Alexander, *Black Interior*, x.

10 Romare Bearden to Mary Schmidt Campbell, postmarked September 22, 1973, quoted in Fine, "Spaces Between," 33.

11 R. Thompson, "Communiqué from Afro-Atlantis," 70.

12 Stewart, *Three Eyes*, x.

13 Stewart, *Three Eyes*, 6.

14 Mveng, "Third World Theology," 220, quoted in Stewart, *Three Eyes*, 5–6.

15 "One ever feels his twoness,—an American, a Negro; two souls, two thoughts, two unreconciled strivings; two warring ideals in one dark body, whose dogged strength alone keeps it from being torn asunder." Du Bois, *Souls of Black Folk*, 44.

16 Coates, "My President Was Black."

17 Compare the surveillance and separation of black people undergoing legalized segregation to Foucault's description of leprosy as an alleged threat to the social order:

> If it is true that the leper gave rise to rituals of exclusion, which to a certain extent provided the model for and general form of the great Confinement, then the plague gave rise to disciplinary projects. Rather than the massive, binary division between one set of people and another, it called for multiple separations, individualizing distributions, an organization in depth of surveillance and control, an intensification and a ramification of power. The leper was caught up in a practice of rejection, of exile-enclosure; he was left to his doom in a mass among which it was useless to differentiate; those sick of the plague were caught up in a meticulous tactical partitioning in which individual differentiations were the constricting effects of a power that multiplied, articulated and subdivided itself; the great confinement on the one hand; the correct training on the other. The leper and his separation; the plague and its segmentations. . . . The exile of the leper and the arrest of the plague do not bring with them the same political dream. The first is that of a pure community, the second that of a disciplined society. Foucault, *Discipline and Punish*, 198.

18 Foucault, *Discipline and Punish*, 196.

19 Martha Schwendener, "At the Studio Museum in Harlem, 4 Shows Engage a Cultural Conversation," *New York Times*, January 7, 2016.

20 Morrison, *Origin of Others*, 29.

21 Christine Acham, "Shifting Shonda: The Evolving Politics of Shonda-Land." Public presentation, Emory University, January 28, 2016.

22 Ta-Nehisi Coates, "Fear of a Black President," *Atlantic*, September 2012, http://theatlantic.com/magazine/archive/2012/09/fear-of-a-black-president/309064/.

23 For a repudiation of this idea *before* the murder of Trayvon Martin and the almost weekly police shootings of unarmed black males in the two years after that, see Wise, *Colorblind*.

24 Du Bois, in his text *The Souls of Black Folk* (1903), suggests a Hegelian argument of hybridity in a thesis-antithesis dialectic leading to synthesis, or something new. Also see, for example, Gilroy, *Black Atlantic*.

25 Woodbine, *Black Gods*.

26 Powell, *Blues Aesthetic*.

27 K. Thompson, *Shine*, 2.

28 Hall, "What Is This 'Black.'"

29 K. Thompson, *Shine*, 5–6.

30 K. Thompson, *Shine*, 221.

31 See Andrew Rosenthal, "Beyoncé's Halftime Show Inspires Ridiculous Criticism," *Taking Note* (blog), *New York Times*, February 8, 2016.

32 Jon Caramanica, "Jay Z and Beyoncé: Activism Gone Vocal," *New York Times*, July 8, 2016.

33 Interestingly, Brown's song paraphrased the lyrics of the spiritual "I've Been 'Buked," as follows:

> I've been 'buked an' I've been scorned, children
> I've been 'buked an' I've been scorned
> I've been talked about, sho's you're born.

Those lyrics became in Brown's song,

> We've been 'buked and we've been scorned
> We've been treated bad, talked about as sure as you're born.

This double voicing must have resonated powerfully with those familiar with the gospel song.

34 The recent music video by Beyoncé and Jay-Z, "Apeshit," filmed in the Louvre in Paris, caused attendance at the museum to rise 25 percent since its release, according to the museum's December 27 press release. (Nate Freeman, "Beyoncé and Jay-Z helped the Louvre break the all-time attendance record for a museum," *Artsy*, January 3, 2019.) The video had over 147 million views. [*Ed. note*: by the time of this book's publication, the number of views had topped 287.5 million. "THE CARTERS—*APESHIT* (Official Video)," YouTube, accessed July 15, 2025, https://www.youtube.com/watch?v=kbMqWXnpXcA.]

35 Okri, *Famished Road*, 244–45.

36 See, for example, Gayle, *Black Aesthetic*. During CONFABA fifty historians, educators, scholars, and visual artists met to "organize the study of African American Art."

37 Program for CONFABA, Northwestern University, Evanston, Illinois, May 1970, published in Gaither, "Heritage Reclaimed," 25.

38 Nelson Stevens, personal conversation, and confirmed in a telephone conversation, May 11, 2019.

39 Locke, "Legacy."

40 Andrews, "From Black to Blues," 37.

41 T. J. Anderson, taped interview with the author, Atlanta, Georgia, November 11, 2012.

42 Dianne Stewart, personal conversation with the author, June 22, 2016.

43 Schwendener, "4 Shows."

44 Baraka, *Blues People*.

45 Janson and Janson's *Short History of Art* has been the canonical text in many schools and colleges for decades and often is a site for debates about inclusion because the book is more precisely a history of Western art. Originally coauthored in 1962 by H. W. Janson and his son, Anthony F. Janson (until the sixth edition in 2001), the seventh (2006) and eighth (2010) editions are newly authored by Penelope J. E. Davies with five other art historians and billed as a history of "the Western tradition."

46 Sartre, *Black Orpheus*, 23.

47 Richard Powell has published a recent book exploring the way Colescott and other African American artists have used satire in their work to make commentary. Powell, *Going There*.

48 Sanders, "Spirited Pattern and Decoration," 70–71.

49 Sanders, "Spirited Pattern and Decoration," 36.

50 Sanders writes that the Dutch encountered "wax-resist dyed textiles in the seventeenth century on the Indonesian island of Java, and by the nineteenth century, Dutch textile manufacturers had found a way to imitate Javanese hand-drawn batik by roller printing a resin resist on the cloth prior to dyeing." West Africans appreciated "the slightly off-register effects and asymmetry of pattern that made the images seem to dance and sparkle." Sanders, "Spirited Pattern and Decoration," 73.

51 Thompson indicates that African narrow-strip textiles are "enlivened by rich and vivid suspensions of the expected placement of the weft-blocks . . . thus characterized by designs virtually to be scanned metrically, in visual resonance with the famed off-beat phrasing of melodic accents in African and Afro-American music." These textiles "[introduce] to the history of art an extraordinary idiom, unique to the black world." He also suggests that the asymmetrical, complicated uses of patterning work are for spiritual protection. R. Thompson, *Flash of the Spirit*, 207–22 (quotation from p. 207).

52 Ellis, "New Black Aesthetic," 235.

53 Vinson Cunningham, "Can Black Art Ever Escape the Politics of Race?," *New York Times*, August 20, 2015.

54 Aldin, liner notes to *Muddy Waters*.

55 Cunningham, "Can Black Art Ever Escape."

Chapter 1. The Moan: Calling Forth Culture

Epigraph: Amiri Baraka, "Why's/Wise," and Rob Brown (saxophone), February 21, 2009, Media Sanctuary, December 9, 2009, https://youtu.be/mKfQNO66GPk?si=8tuypeFk-MIchijq.

1 Moyo Okediji, personal communication with the author, May 2014.

2 Clarke, Introduction, n.p.

3 Ethnic rivalries and economic incentives, family or clan lineages, and the complicity of Africans in the slave trade, capturing people from other groups for various goods bartered by Europeans, would have worked against a sense of commonality before the Atlantic voyages despite the captives having embarked from the same port. See Eltis and Richardson, *Atlas*.

4 Phillips, *Slavery from Roman Times*, 174, quoted in Eltis and Richardson, *Atlas*, 24.

5 Hartman, *Lose Your Mother*, 6.

6 Ed Spriggs, taped conversation, Atlanta, Georgia, May 17, 2012. Spriggs, the second director of the Studio Museum in Harlem, was one of the instigators at San Francisco State University in the late 1960s of what is now the academic field of black or African American studies.

7 Glissant, *Poetics of Relation*, 5.

8 Glissant, *Poetics of Relation*, 6–7.

9 Glissant, *Poetics of Relation*, 7.

10 Taylor, "'Salt Peanuts,'" 2.

11 Taylor, "'Salt Peanuts,'" 3.

12 The Yoruba began to be captured and taken into the slave trade in great numbers during and after their civil wars in the first decades of the nineteenth century, a period after US law prohibited the direct importation of slaves from Africa. See, for example, Ajayi, "Aftermath of the Fall"; and Ajayi and Smith, *Yoruba Warfare*.

13 Eltis and Richardson, *Atlas*, 21.

14 Abiodun asserts that *ọ̀rọ̀* is more than just speech. "Rather, it means 'a matter, that is, something that is the subject of discussion, concern, or action.'" Abiodun, "Verbal and Visual Metaphors," 252–55.

15 Abiodun, "Verbal and Visual Metaphors," 255.

16 Abiodun, "Verbal and Visual Metaphors," 253. I am grateful to Rowland Abiodun for referring me back to this passage. Telephone conversation, January 31, 2014.

17 Abiodun thinks Ẹmí may be the result of para-literate feedback and, therefore, a direct lift from Christian theology. Telephone conversation, June 22, 2016.

18 Stewart, "I Had a Family," 6. See also Stewart, *Obeah, Orisa, and Religious Identity*, 59.

19 Stewart, "I Had a Family," 9. See also Stewart, *Obeah, Orisa, and Religious Identity*, 61–62.

20 Stewart, "I Had a Family," 5–6. See also Stewart, *Obeah, Orisa, and Religious Identity*, 59.

21 Abiodun, *Yoruba Art and Language*, 61.

22 Abiodun, *Yoruba Art and Language*, 62.

23 Stewart, "I Had a Family," 3. See also Stewart, *Obeah, Orisa, and Religious Identity*, 58.

24 See Griaule and Dieterlen, *Pale Fox*, 98.

25 Griaule, *Conversations with Ogotemmêli*, 20.

26 Calame-Griaule, *Words and the Dogon World*, xvi.

27 Griaule and Dieterlen, *Pale Fox*, 68, quoted in Harris, "Visual Tropes," 57–58.

28 Double consciousness: "It is a peculiar sensation, this double consciousness. . . . One ever feels his twoness,—an American, a Negro; two souls, two thoughts, two unreconciled strivings; two warring ideals in one dark body, whose dogged strength alone keeps it from being torn asunder." DuBois, *Souls*, 7.

29 Enwezor, "Diasporic Imagination," 67.

30 Enwezor, "Diasporic Imagination," 69.

31 Glissant, *Poetics of Relation*, xiv.

32 Glissant, *Poetics of Relation*, 7. Glissant, in some ways, continued the ideas of Aimé Césaire and was continued himself in the writing of Patrick Chamoiseau, especially in the novel *Slave Old Man* in 2018 (originally *L'esclave vieil homme et le molosse*, 1997).

33 Gomez, *Exchanging Our Country Marks*, 2–3.

34 Gomez, *Exchanging Our Country Marks*, 6.

35 Hartman, *Lose Your Mother*, 6.

36 Gomez, *Exchanging Our Country Marks*, 13.

37 Gomez, *Exchanging Our Country Marks*, 11.

38 Gomez, *Exchanging Our Country Marks*, 20. Gomez documents that in Louisiana at the end of the eighteenth century, "Bambara males were approximately 93 percent of the Bambara population, Wolof males 60 percent of the Wolof population, and Igbo males 55 percent of the Igbo population. One of the consequences of these importation patterns is that Bambara men necessarily married Wolof, Igbo, and American-born women, whereas Wolof men tended to marry Wolof women." This indicates the continued ethnic presences in the United States of Africans that allowed the persistence of certain cultural elements and linguistic patterns for a time. Gomez, *Exchanging Our Country Marks*, 43.

39 María Magdalena Campos-Pons, taped interview with the author, Jamaica Plain, Massachusetts, August 7, 1999, quoted in Harris, "Meanwhile the Girls Were Playing," 17.

40 Jon Lockard, telephone conversation with the author, July 17, 2012.

41 Toll, *Blacking Up*, 260.

42 Toll, *Blacking Up*, 246.

43 Africans resisted slavery at every point in the process from capture, to transfer, to captivity on the coast, through the Middle Passage, to existence in the slavery system. Various slave and black codes in the American South suppressing the use of African instruments caused black people to embrace new instrumentations of their music in the nineteenth century.

44 Ong, *Orality and Literacy*, 34.

45 Taylor, "'Salt Peanuts,'" 2.

46 Taylor, "'Salt Peanuts,'" 3.

47 Ong says, "The more sophisticated orally patterned thought is, the more it is likely to be marked by set expressions skillfully used. . . . The law itself in oral cultures is enshrined in formulaic sayings, proverbs, which are not mere jurisprudential decorations, but themselves constitute the law." Ong, *Orality and Literacy*, 35.

48 Denise Grady, "Stark Reminders of How Uncivil a War It Was," *New York Times*, January 20, 2014.

49 The lyrics are:

> Southern trees bear a strange fruit
> Blood on the leaves and blood at the root
> Black bodies swingin' in the Southern breeze
> Strange fruit hangin' from the poplar trees
> Pastoral scene of the gallant South
> The bulgin' eyes and the twisted mouth
> Scent of magnolias sweet and fresh
> Then the sudden smell of burnin' flesh
> Here is a fruit for the crows to pluck
> For the rain to gather, for the wind to suck
> For the sun to rot, for the tree to drop
> Here is a strange and bitter crop

Lyrics, Warner/Chappell Music, Inc., Universal Music Publishing Group.

50 Quoted in J. Allen, *Without Sanctuary*, 179.

51 Litwack, "Hellhounds," 8–9.

52 Dunbar, *Lyrics of Lowly Life*, 167.

53 Chireau, *Black Magic*, 126.

54 "James Sparkman, a slaveowner in South Carolina, was 'astounded' that former slaves, many of whom had been indoctrinated with Christian teachings by white plantation ministers, quickly backslid 'into Fetishism and voodooism' when freedom came." Chireau, *Black Magic*, 126–27.

55 Quoted in Mellon, *Bullwhip Days*, 186–87.

56 Enwezor, "Diasporic Imagination," 69.

57 Enwezor, "Diasporic Imagination," 69.

58 R. Thompson, "Royalty, Heroism," 263, 265.

59 Glissant, *Poetics of Relation*, 11.

60 Glissant, *Poetics of Relation*, 7–8.

Chapter 2. Etymologies and Black Love

1 Fine, "Spaces Between," 33–36.

2 Fine, "Spaces Between," 10. On correlating Bearden's art and jazz, see the contrary perspective in Völz, "'Blues and the Abstract Truth': Or, Did Romare Bearden Really Paint Jazz?" in Lock and Murray, eds., *The Hearing Eye*.

3 R. Thompson, *Flash of the Spirit*, xiii.

4 R. Thompson, *Flash of the Spirit*, xiii.

5 R. Thompson, "Communiqué from Afro-Atlantis," 69.

6 Muddy Waters changed some of the original lyrics to the song written by Preston Foster, which he first heard performed by Ann Cole in 1956 while she was on tour with him. The Foster lyrics were:

> Got my Mojo working but it just won't work on you
> Got my Mojo working but it just won't work on you
> I want to love you so that I don't know what to do
> I got my black cat bones all pure and dry
> I got my 4 leaf clover all hanging high
> I got my Mojo working but it just won't work on you
> I want to love you so 'til I don't know what to do
>
> [repeat, with varied spells: hoodoo ashes,
> black snake boots, red hot tips, etc.]
> —Preston "Red" Foster, "Got My Mojo Working" (1956)

For comparison of lyrics, see "Got My Mojo Working," White Gum (blog), accessed July 17, 2025, https://www.whitegum.com/introjs.htm?/songfile/GOTMYMOJ.HTM, and Gary Martin, Phrase Finder, accessed July 17, 2025, https://www.phrases.org.uk/meanings/got-my-mojo-working.html. See also Ilona Bray and Richard Stim, "How Copyright Law Found Its Mojo," in *The Judge Who Hated Red Nail Polish* (Berkeley, CA: Nolo 2010), 173–75.

7 R. Thompson, *Flash of the Spirit*, chap. 2 ("The Sign of the Four Moments of the Sun: Kongo Art and Religion in the Americas").

8 R. Thompson, "Communiqué from Afro-Atlantis," 69.

9 During a recent visit to Phillips's studio, we listened to *Song for Biko*, by Don Cherry with South African horn player Dudu Pukwana. He pointed out *Ethiopique 14: Negus of Ethiopian Sax,* by Ethiopian saxophonist Gétatchèw Mèkurya; *Four Now*, by the World Saxophone Quartet with

African Drums; and various other CDs by John Coltrane, Thelonious Monk, and Miles Davis (including the Miles Davis and John Coltrane recordings from Konserthuset, Stockholm, from March 22, 1960). Baltimore, Maryland, April 25, 2015.

10 R. Thompson, "Communiqué from Afro-Atlantis," 70.

11 Blassingame, *Slave Testimony*, 458–59.

12 Ramsey, *Race Music*, 33.

13 "Ethnic identity operates much the same way that musical practice does. . . . Musical gestures, genres, and styles are performed; likewise, ethnicity and nearly every other aspect of identity should be considered performances. Blackness doesn't really exist until it is done, or 'practiced,' in the world. Musical styles and ethnicities are loaded signifiers, each doing important cultural work in the social world." Ramsey, *Race Music*, 39.

14 Levine, *Black Culture*, 5.

15 Snead, "Repetition," 63.

16 Snead, "Repetition," 68.

17 Ong, *Orality and Literacy*, 34.

18 O'Meally, *Jazz Cadence*, 4.

19 Maultsby, "Africanisms," 334, 328.

20 Tate and Jafa, "Sound She Saw," 223.

21 Tate and Jafa, "Sound She Saw," 223.

22 Gomez, *Exchanging Our Country Marks*, 28.

23 David Lubin in his chapter "Reconstructing Duncanson" argues that Robert Duncanson's selection and use of water in his Hudson River–style landscapes of the mid-nineteenth century symbolically articulated a black perspective, a desire for respite and peace from the pain of slavery and racial oppression. He argues, "In terms of the slave spirituals of the era, they are painterly depictions of the shores of Canaan, the land of milk and honey. Duncanson's work portrays the home that lies over Jordan, the campground where all is Peace. . . . In the case of *Blue Hole*, that serene body of water is not an obstacle to be crossed in order to achieve freedom but rather the trope of freedom itself, a place where one can go fishing all day long, unhurried and unafraid." Lubin, *Picturing a Nation*, 119.

24 Andrews, "From Black to Blues," 37.

25 Andrews, "From Black to Blues," 38.

26 Andrews, "From Black to Blues," 39.

27 Powell, *Homecoming*, 170.

28 Tate and Jafa, "Sound She Saw," 224.

29 Tate and Jafa, "Sound She Saw," 224.

30 For an extended expression of this notion, see R. Thompson, *African Art in Motion*.

31 [*Ed. Note*: Compare this insightful song review: "As the hope and optimism of the '60s gave way to the fear and loathing of the '70s, few records evoked the creeping paranoia of the post-Altamont/pre-Watergate period quite so vividly as the O'Jays' 1972 smash 'Back Stabbers.'

Although the betrayals Eddie Levert's anguished vocals relate are specific to the two-timing and lies lurking behind friendship and romance, it's not difficult to read the song as an allegory for the insidious hypocrisies sweeping across the sociopolitical landscape as a whole. As records like Marvin Gaye's 'What's Going On,' Curtis Mayfield's 'Freddie's Dead,' and the Undisputed Truth's 'Smiling Faces Sometimes' (the title of which 'Back Stabbers' directly quotes) attest, it was a paranoia particularly acute throughout the African-American community." Jason Ankeny, "Back Stabbers: The O'Jays," AllMusic song review, n.d. Accessed June 26, 2025. https://www.allmusic.com/song/back-stabbers-mt0002028094.]

32 Perkinson, "Gift/Curse," 19.

33 Perkinson, "Gift/Curse," 20–35.

34 If we accept Michel Foucault's description of the panopticon, discussed in the introduction, rehabilitation was only a rhetorical possibility as the depravity of internal blackness in a racialized context has been treated as a permanent condition worthy of persistent suspicion and quarantine. Foucault, *Discipline and Punish*, 196, 198.

35 Perkinson, "Gift/Curse," 29.

36 Perkinson, "Gift/Curse," 37–39 (italics mine). The author is paraphrasing and analyzing Gilroy's important text *Black Atlantic*.

37 Moyo Okediji addresses dismemberment and the re-memberment of the social body in terms of Yoruba culture through the diaspora and the social, political, and emotional reconnections in recent decades between Africans and African descendants in the Americas through nostalgia and memory in his book *The Shattered Gourd*.

38 Ramsey, *Race Music*, 4.

39 "We younger Negro artists who create now intend to express our individual dark-skinned selves without fear or shame. If white people are pleased we are glad. If they are not, it doesn't matter. We know we are beautiful. And ugly too. The tom-tom cries and the tom-tom laughs. If colored people are pleased we are glad. If they are not, their displeasure doesn't matter either. We build our temples for tomorrow, strong as we know how, and we stand on top of the mountain, free within ourselves." Hughes, "Negro Artist," 181.

40 Murry DePillars, telephone conversation with the author, July 2, 2006.

41 For example, Senegambians, especially the Bambara (or Bamana), were an important Mande-speaking group with a large presence in Louisiana, though Wolof and Igbo peoples also had a documented presence. Wolof males were 60 percent of the Wolof population in Louisiana, and Igbo males were 55 percent of the Igbo population. Wolof and Igbo males tended to marry women of their own ethnic group (and they had higher ratios of children than other ethnicities). However, Bambara males were 93 percent of their population, so they married Wolof, Igbo, and American-born women. Gomez, *Exchanging Our Country Marks*, 43–47.

42 Hughes, "Negro Artist," 177.

Chapter 3. From *The Banjo Lesson* to *The Piano Lesson*: Reclaiming the Song

1 Baraka, *Blues People*, ix.
2 Baraka, *Blues People*, xii.
3 Pereira, *August Wilson*, 88.
4 Pereira, *August Wilson*, 88–89.
5 Gura and Bollman, *America's Instrument*.
6 Alexander, *Black Interior*, x.
7 Abrahams, *Singing the Master*, xviii.
8 Abrahams, *Singing the Master*, 47.
9 Abrahams, *Singing the Master*, xxii.
10 Abrahams, *Singing the Master*, 86–95.
11 As W. T. Lhamon elaborates, "Abstracting themselves as blacks allowed the heterogeneous parts of the newly moiling young workers all access to the same identity tags. Irish, German, French, Welsh, and English recent immigrants, as well as American rustics, could all together identify in the 1830s with Jim Crow, Bone Squash, and Jumbo Jim, then in the forties with Tambo and Bones. . . . Precisely because middle-class aspirants disdained the black jitterbug in every region, the black figure appealed all across the Atlantic as an organizational emblem for workers and the unemployed. Hated everywhere, he could be championed everywhere alike." Lhamon, *Raising Cain*, 44, 118–26.
12 The blacked-up performers played against Mr. Interlocutor, whom Mark Twain described as a figure "clothed in the faultless evening costume of the white society gentleman [who] used a stilted, courtly, artificial and painfully grammatical form of speech." Twain, *Autobiography*, 64–65, quoted in Abrahams, *Singing the Master*, 135. The hypercorrect upper-class white trying to keep order was laughed at as much as were the speech and wild dances of the end men in blackface.
13 Lieberfeld, "Million-Dollar Juke Joint," 218.
14 Lieberfeld, "Million-Dollar Juke Joint," 220.
15 For a wonderful discussion of this document and its implications and impact, see Aptheker, "*One Continual Cry*."
16 Hills, "Painting Race," 133, 136.
17 Hills, "Painting Race," 128.
18 Davis, "Eastman Johnson's *Negro Life*," 67–73.
19 J. Wilson, "Lifting the 'Veil,'" 44.
20 J. Wilson, "Lifting the 'Veil,'" 36.
21 J. Wilson, "Lifting the 'Veil,'" 43.
22 J. Wilson, "Lifting the 'Veil,'" 44.
23 J. Wilson, "Lifting the 'Veil,'" 38.
24 Brooks, *Bodies in Dissent*, 3.
25 O'Meally, *Jazz Cadence*, 3.

26 Richard Long, telephone interview with the author, tape recording, December 4, 2004.

27 Long, telephone interview.

28 See Todd Smith, *Celebration and Vision*, 21.

29 Bearden, interviewed in Schwartzman, *Romare Bearden*, 34.

30 Bearden, interviewed in Schwartzman, *Romare Bearden*, 34.

31 Bearden, interviewed in Schwartzman, *Romare Bearden*, 34.

32 A. Wilson, foreword, 8.

33 A. Wilson, foreword, 8.

34 Wilson quoted in Shannon, *Dramatic Vision*, 146.

35 Wilson quoted in Shannon, *Dramatic Vision*, 146.

36 Kim Pereira writes, "This play depicts a growing realization by blacks that they can call the South their home, because several generations of their families grew up there and paid a great price on the plantations that built the South. Besides, they have discovered that the North is not as rosy as it once looked." Pereira, *August Wilson*, 94.

37 Shannon, *Dramatic Vision*, 147.

38 Shannon, *Dramatic Vision*, 144.

39 Pereira, *August Wilson*, 87–88.

40 Wahlman, *Signs and Symbols*, 86. See also Tobin and Dobard, *Hidden in Plain View*.

41 Wahlman, *Signs and Symbols,* 86.

Chapter 4. Fish Fry Music: A Blues Aesthetic

Epigraph: Son House, performer. "Ain't But One Kind of Blues" soliloquy in *Black Snake Moan*, film directed by Craig Brewer (Paramount Vantage, 2006). Nelson Stevens, personal conversation, Atlanta, Georgia, March 11, 2016.

1 Dave Tell and Davis Houck, "Mound Bayou." Emmett Till Memory Project. Accessed June 27, 2025. https://tillapp.emmett-till.org/items/show/10.

2 Isaiah Montgomery's story is emblematic of the constant threat of white violence and corruption that led to various strategies of accommodation by conservatives like Montgomery and Booker T. Washington, and to aggressive approaches by W. E. B. Du Bois and African Methodist Episcopal (AME) bishop Benjamin Tucker Tanner, father to Henry Ossawa Tanner. Five years before Washington's infamous 1895 Atlanta Compromise Address, Montgomery made a conciliatory speech at the 1890 Mississippi Constitutional Convention ceding black disenfranchisement as a means to protect Mound Bayou from the type of terrorist violence common to Mississippi from the end of Reconstruction through the mid-1960s.

According to historian Neil McMillen, "Blacks outnumbered whites in every decade from 1840 to 1940. Clearly, in this black majority state of Mississippi, the first requirement of unchallenged white rule was black disfranchisement." Neil R. McMillen, "Isaiah T. Montgomery, 1847–1924 (Part II)," *Mississippi History Now*, February 2007, https://www.mshistorynow.mdah.ms.gov/issue/isaiah-t-montgomery-1847–1924-part-ii.

3 Cone, *Spirituals and the Blues*, 98.

4 Baraka, "'Blues Aesthetic,'" 105–7.

5 Andrews, "From Black to Blues," 37.

6 King, interviewed in Scorsese, *The Blues: Feel Like Going Home*.

7 King, interviewed in Scorsese, *The Blues*.

8 Waters, "Long Distance."

9 "The 'Delta' isn't really the Mississippi's delta, which lies several hundred miles farther south at the river's mouth. It's a flat, fertile, leaf-shaped plain that stretches from just south of Memphis down to Vicksburg, a distance of around two hundred miles, with the river on the west and the state's central hills some eighty-five miles to the east at the widest point." Palmer, *Deep Blues*, 8.

10 Palmer, *Deep Blues*, 2.

11 Palmer, *Deep Blues*, 3.

12 Palmer, *Deep Blues*, 3–4.

13 Palmer writes about how the system, full of abuses, also worked to set black people and poor "white trash" white people against one another. "When there were outbreaks of night riding or lynchings, poor whites were the perpetrators; planters often stepped in to protect 'their' blacks." Palmer, *Deep Blues*, 9–10.

14 Wadsworth Jarrell, personal email correspondence, August 30, 2015.

15 Jarrell, correspondence.

16 Jarrell, correspondence.

17 Kai, "AfriCOBRA Universal Aesthetics," 9.

18 Powell, *Blues Aesthetic*, 19.

19 Powell, *Blues Aesthetic*, 20.

20 Powell, *Blues Aesthetic*, 21.

21 Andrews, "From Black to Blues," 38.

22 Andrews, "From Black to Blues," 39.

23 Bill Ferris, "From the Diddy Bow to Bo Diddley," interview on *The Story with Dick Gordon*, November 4, 2011, WUNC, North Carolina Public Radio, accessed June 27, 2025, https://dayhoffwestminster.blogspot.com/2011/11/from-diddy-bow-to-bo-diddley.html.

24 Rowland Abiodun has written that Eshu's praise name (*oríkì*) celebrates him for being the lord of *orita* or road meetings. This implies that he represents "the meeting point of roads, and not the crossroads as it has always been erroneously translated." Abiodun, *Yoruba Art and Language*, 73.

25 An ice course is a cool drink of poisoned whiskey. Palmer, *Deep Blues*, 3.

26 R. Thompson, "Kongo Influences," 153.

27 R. Thompson, "Kongo Influences," 154.

28 Scorsese, "Foreword," xiii.

29 Abiodun, *Yoruba Art and Language*, 74.

30 Litwack, "Hellhounds," 8.

31 Robert Johnson, "Hellhound on My Trail," song quoted in Litwack, "Hellhounds," 8.

32 See Berns, *Dear Robert*.

33 Kongo ideas and practices have been identified in Brazilian capoeira, organized into Angola and Regional styles; South Carolina grave decoration; linguistic markers like jukebox and mojo; Haitian Vodou use of *veve* (ground emblazoning); and the use of *tobys* or charms in black vernacular practices. Robert Farris Thompson has done a great deal of work in this area. See, for example, his classic book *Flash of the Spirit*.

34 Consider Luc de Heusch's related description of *minkisi* as "spirits of the dead metonymically caught in a metaphorical trap." Heusch, *Why Marry Her?*, 182.

35 Renée Stout, taped conversation with the author, Buffalo, New York, March 26, 2015.

36 A *New York Times* review of Gerhard Richter's work *Six Gray Mirrors* (2003), in the Dia Beacon in New York, points out that the work is dependent on the viewer's interaction with it as well as the environment where it is installed. The work is purposely devoid of meaning, and the reviewer links the artist to John Cage's declaration "I have nothing to say and I am saying it." The work engages the emotional and psychological and the interpersonal experiences of vexation, emptiness, frustration; "the true substance of nothing." It is about introspection rather than communal evocations. Jason Farago, "Gerhard Richter's 'Six Gray Mirrors,' a Study in Reflections," *New York Times*, August 20, 2015.

37 Stout, conversation with the author.

38 Stout, conversation with the author.

39 Lyrics by Willie Dixon, "I'm Your Hoochie Coochie Man," performed by Muddy Waters. The song features a final section involving a gypsy prophecy of good fortune. The number seven is repeated: on the seventh hour, on the seventh day, etc. That cascade of sevens evokes a folklore theme ("the seventh son of a seventh son"), as Dixon later highlighted in his 1955 song, "The Seventh Son":

> On the seventh hours
> On the seventh day
> On the seventh month
> The seven doctors say
> He was born for good luck
> And that you'll see
> I got seven hundred dollars
> Don't you mess with me

In addition, the final stanza makes reference to beliefs regarding good fortune or providential divine favor that may also be found in African cultures. Twins Seven Seven, the famous Yoruba artist from the Mbari Mbayo workshop of the early 1960s in Osogbo, Nigeria, perhaps called himself this literally in order to mythologize his stature as the only surviving child of seven sets of twins born to his mother. Wikipedia, "The Seventh Son," accessed July 18, 2025, https://en.wikipedia.org/wiki/The_Seventh_Son.

40 Abiodun, *Yoruba Art and Language*, 74.

41 Bearden, "Rectangular Structure," 12, quoted in Gelburd and Golden, *Romare Bearden*, 33.

42 Abiodun indicates that with Eshu, for example, the sculpture "does not depict *Èṣù* but his or her devotee, and it is an integral part of the visual oriki to exhibit the attributes of *Èṣù's ìwà* [essential character and nature]." Abiodun, *Yoruba Art and Language*, 260.

43 Nelson Stevens, personal conversation, Atlanta, Georgia, March 11, 2016, and telephone conversation, June 22, 2017. Ed Spriggs, who served as the first permanent director of the Studio Museum in Harlem from 1968 to 1975, said that black artists made a "pilgrimage" to MoMA to see the work. Ed Spriggs, personal conversation, Atlanta, September 26, 2017.

44 Linsley, "Wifredo Lam," 294.

45 Linsley, "Wifredo Lam," 294.

46 Quoted in Yau, "Please Wait," 136.

47 Linsley, "Wifredo Lam," 296.

48 Yau, "Please Wait," 135.

49 Chireau, *Black Magic*, 123.

50 Chireau, *Black Magic*, 123.

51 Quoted in Mellon, *Bullwhip Days*, 96.

52 Quoted in Mellon, *Bullwhip Days*, 97.

53 Beverly Buchanan, "Sassafras and Yellow Root," 48.

54 See, for example, MacGaffey, "Eyes of Understanding."

55 Theophus Smith, *Conjuring Culture*, 3–4, 5.

56 Theophus Smith, *Conjuring Culture*, 4.

57 Theophus Smith, *Conjuring Culture*, 6.

58 Rachael DeLue, "Conjure and Collapse in the Art of Romare Bearden," *nonsite.org*, no. 7, October 11, 2012.

59 DeLue, "Conjure and Collapse." In her note for this idea, DeLue cites previous writing about Bearden, including Powell, "Conjuring Reality"; O'Meally et al., *Romare Bearden*; and Fine and Francis, *Romare Bearden, American Modernist*.

60 DeLue, "Conjure and Collapse."

61 Cone, *Spirituals and the Blues*, 99.

Chapter 5. Gospel, *Tongues*, and Bearing Witness

1 The Legends Ball, held on a three-day weekend in 2005, honored twenty-five women: Maya Angelou, Shirley Caesar, Diahann Carroll, Elizabeth Catlett, Ruby Dee, Katherine Dunham, Roberta Flack, Aretha

Franklin, Nikki Giovanni, Dorothy Height, Lena Horne, Coretta Scott King, Gladys Knight, Patti LaBelle, Toni Morrison, Rosa Parks, Leontyne Price, Della Reese, Diana Ross, Naomi Sims, Tina Turner, Cicely Tyson, Alice Walker, Dionne Warwick, and Nancy Wilson. In attendance were Halle Berry, Tyler Perry, Alicia Keys, Janet Jackson, Sidney Poitier, and John and Kelly Travolta, among many others. It was subsequently broadcast as a one-hour special on ABC television on May 22, 2006. *Oprah Winfrey's Legends Ball, 2005*, ABC TV Special, May 22, 2006, transcription accessed June 29, 2025, https://www.youtube.com/watch?v=2zlFL-A1rrI.

2 Geraldyn Dismond, "In New York Town," *Chicago Bee*, March 17, 1928, quoted in Mooney, *Archibald Motley Jr.*, 50.

3 Locke, "Enter the New Negro."

4 Locke, "Enter the New Negro."

5 Mooney, *Archibald J. Motley Jr.*, 50.

6 Richard Powell has indicated that Archibald Motley revealed an interest in genre scenes with a lost 1921 painting, *Black and Tan Cabaret*, described in the *Arts* a year later as an open-air social gathering with a diversity of people "smoking, drinking, whispering" as the musicians played. This was followed by *Syncopation* in 1924 and *Stomp* in 1927. Powell, "Becoming Motley, Becoming Modern," 113–14.

7 Mooney, *Archibald J. Motley Jr.*, 53.

8 Johnson, *God's Trombones*, 4.

9 Johnson, *God's Trombones*, 5.

10 Hurston, "Shouting," 34.

11 Hurston, "Shouting," 34.

12 Hurston, "Shouting," 34.

13 Parrish, *Slave Songs*, 55, quoted in Rosenbaum, *Shout Because You're Free*, 2.

14 Rosenbaum, *Shout Because You're Free*, 2.

15 "Like their slave ancestors, today's shouters apply the term 'shout' specifically to the movements rather than to the vocal or accompanying percussive components of the shout tradition." Rosenbaum, *Shout Because You're Free*, 2–3.

16 Quoted in Rosenbaum, *Shout Because You're Free*, 3. Rosenbaum continues, "It is understandable that outside commentators should confuse shout as movement with the English word for a loud vocalization." Nonetheless, he adds, "In inland areas where the ring shout has been forgotten, the term 'shout' is still commonly used to describe the violent movements rather than the vocalization of a worshiper seized by the Spirit."

17 Cook quoted in Rosenbaum, *Shout Because You're Free*, 4.

18 Parrish, *Slave Songs*, 57.

19 "According to Lawrence McKiver, 'every bit of it is an African act. The old people, that's what they tell me. Nobody does it but our kind of people. The shout . . . it's just an African act. You can tell by the singing, tell by the song, tell by the beat, it's actually an African beat. I think they

come in 1722 when the blacks came over here. It came down through the generations.'" Rosenbaum, *Shout Because You're Free*, 18.

20 Parrish, *Slave Songs*, 80.

21 Parrish, *Slave Songs*, 81.

22 Griaule's most famous works are a diary of religious instructions by the high priest of the Dogon people of Mali in West Africa titled *Conversations with Ogotemmêli* (1965; originally published in 1948 as *Dieu d'Eau* [God of water]) and a finished anthropological report on the Dogon religion titled *Le Renard Pale* or *The Pale Fox* (1965). However, "A number of anthropologists are highly critical of his work and argue that Griaule's claims about Sirius and his elaborate accounts of cosmic eggs and mystic vibrations do not accurately reflect Dogon belief." Wikipedia, "Marcel Griaule," accessed June 28, 2025, https://en.wikipedia.org/wiki/Marcel_Griaule.

23 Theophus Smith, *Conjuring Culture*, 6.

24 Robinson, "Sense of Self," 339–40.

25 Theophus Smith, *Conjuring Culture*, 10.

26 Richard Powell, conversation with the author, December 28, 2014, and on several other occasions. The black population of Chicago more than doubled from 1910 to 1920, going from 44,000 to more than 109,000, and doubled again from 1920 to 1930. Spear, *Black Chicago*.

27 Powell, "Becoming Motley, Becoming Modern," 117.

28 Powell, "Becoming Motley, Becoming Modern," 117.

29 Powell argues that Motley's distance from black Chicago should be reevaluated "as Bronzeville's open invitations to partake in its many cultural offerings . . . were almost always accepted and invariably acted upon by the artist." Powell, "Becoming Motley, Becoming Modern," 117.

30 Cone, *Spirituals and the Blues*, 16.

31 Cone, *Spirituals and the Blues*, 29.

32 Cone, *Spirituals and the Blues*, 28–29.

33 The word *Obeah*, a term for a kind of folk magic or sorcery practiced primarily in the Caribbean, may come from term *bayi* (sorcery) in the Akan Twi language (of Ghana). Obeah also has been attributed to the Igbo of present-day Nigeria. They were skilled herbalists and feared. In a 1787 letter to an English newspaper, practitioners were called *Obiu-women* and explained as "wise women." Our Special Correspondent, "The Outbreak in Jamaica," *Times* (London), April 2, 1866, the Times Digital Archive.

Chapter 6. *Undone*: Bottle Trees, Charms, and Flashing Spirits

1 Robert Farris Thompson indicates that after having been documented on the coast of northern Kongo at Loango in 1776, bottle trees were "detected on the island of Dominica in the West Indies." *Flash of the Spirit*, 142.

2 R. Thompson, "Kongo Influences," 175.

3 R. Thompson, "Kongo Influences," 175.
4 Alison Saar, taped telephone conversation, August 22, 2016.
5 Saar, conversation.
6 Saar, email correspondence with the author, August 17, 2016.
7 Saar, conversation.
8 Christopher Knight, "Saar's Spare Forms Resonate with Richness," *Los Angeles Times*, January 15, 1999.
9 Numbers 6:2: "When either man or woman shall make a special vow, the vow of a Nazirite, to separate himself unto Jehovah, 3. he shall separate himself from wine and strong drink. . . . 5. All the days of his vow of separation there shall no razor come upon his head: until the days be fulfilled, in which he separateth himself unto Jehovah, he shall be holy; he shall let the locks of the hair of his head grow long (American Standard Version).
10 Saar, taped telephone conversation, August 22, 2016.
11 I have written previously about this iconic work in Harris, "Ritual Bodies—Sexual Bodies"; and MacGaffey and Harris, *Astonishment and Power*.
12 R. Thompson, "Kongo Influences," 174.
13 Rueff and Koelbing, *Ein schön lustig Trostbüchle*. This book was essentially copied from Eucharius Rösslin's *Der Swangern Frauwen und Hebammen Rosegarten*. (The rose garden for pregnant women and midwives), 1513.
14 *Ère-ìbejì* figures are used to represent twins who have returned to the spirit world. Rowland Abiodun writes, "*Ère-ìbejì* represents departed twins and is a part of the ritual sacrifice to prevent future twins in the family from departing too soon." Abiodun, *Yoruba Art and Language*, 269. Among the ideas surrounding twins is the idea that they are associated with the orisha Shango, who is "reputed to have fathered twins, according to Yoruba oral traditions." Abiodun, *Yoruba Art and Language*, 59.
15 Richard B. Woodward, "Things Man Made: Allison Saar's Untitled (from the Crossroads installation)," accessed July 18, 2025, https://blackbird-archive.vcu.edu/v11n1/gallery/woodward_r/saar.shtml.
16 Shani Harris, personal conversations with the author, September 3, 2013, and April 5, 2015.
17 Indigo-dyed cloth has histories in Mali and Senegal and goes back to early Dogon practices in the eleventh century.
18 First published in W. Allen et al., *Slave Songs*, 23.
19 R. Thompson, "Kongo Influences," 153.
20 R. Thompson, "Kongo Influences," 154.
21 Wikipedia, "Kongo Cosmogram," last edited May 26, 2025, 5:49, https://en.wikipedia.org/wiki/Kongo_cosmogram.
22 R. Thompson and Cornet, *Four Moments*.
23 R. Thompson and Cornet, *Four Moments*.
24 MacGaffey, "Personhood of Ritual Objects," 49.
25 R. Thompson, "Kongo Influences," 171.
26 R. Thompson, *Face of the Gods*, 48–49.

27 Musée royal de l'Afrique central (MRAC).

28 MacGaffey, "African Objects and the Idea of Fetish," 125.

29 R. Brown, *African-Atlantic Cultures*, 2. Brown documents through data and analysis the powerful presence of Central African peoples in South Carolina as well as the demographics of the growth of the African population to the point of reaching a numerical majority by 1710, and how "the period between 1670 and 1740 marked an exceptionally intense era of Africanization of the Lowcountry population." R. Brown, *African-Atlantic Cultures*, 1–42.

30 He writes, "Shrine and pilgrim are blurred into a mutual idiom. It is the *nganga*'s trembling shoulders, like a shrine flag fluttering in the wind, that identify the working altar." R. Thompson, *Face of the Gods*, 48.

31 R. Brown, *African-Atlantic Cultures*, 82–83.

32 R. Brown, *African-Atlantic Cultures*, 66–67.

33 R. Brown, *African-Atlantic Cultures*, 68.

34 R. Brown, *African-Atlantic Cultures*, 3.

35 R. Brown, *African-Atlantic Cultures*, 2–4.

36 Morrison, "Rootedness," 343.

37 Locke, "Legacy," 254–67.

38 Enwezor, "Diasporic Imagination."

39 Enwezor, "Diasporic Imagination," 67–68.

40 [*Ed. note*: There are various versions of the lyrics. Here is a common version: "Little Sally Walker, sitting in the saucer, rise, Sally, rise, wipe your weeping eyes, put your hands on your hips and let your backbone slip, shake it to the east, shake it to the west, shake it to the one that you love best." Singing Bell: The Best Hub for Music & Songs for Kids, accessed July 2, 2025, https://www.singing-bell.com/little-sally-walker-lyrics-printable-pdf/.]

41 "Alison Saar: *Lost/Found* Exhibition," Phyllis Kind Gallery, 2003, accessed July 2, 2025, https://phylliskindgallery.com/exhibits/2003/index_110603.html.

42 Saar, interviewed in Hadley Roach, "Thread to the Word: Alison Saar," *BOMB Magazine*, November 17, 2011, accessed July 2, 2025, https://bombmagazine.org/articles/2011/11/17/thread-to-the-word-alison-saar/.

43 Saar, interviewed in Roach, "Thread to the Word."

44 Brown is citing Frank Hagenbucher-Sacripanti's *Les fondements spirituels du pouvoir au royaume de Loango* (31, 22, 52, 66). R. Brown, *African-Atlantic Cultures*, 108–9.

Chapter 7. Talking in Tongues: Revisiting/Reflecting Kara Walker

1 [*Ed. note*: Often cited in relation to African American vernacular and artistic expression is the explication of the term *signifying* in Gates, *The Signifying Monkey*.]

2 [*Ed. note*: See the virtual tour of selected works by Walker with excellent commentary provided by Cate Clother in "Sugar: The Work of Kara Walker."]

3 Glossolalia "consists of strings of syllables, made up of sounds taken from all those that the speaker knows, put together more or less haphazardly but emerging nevertheless as word-like and sentence-like units because of realistic, language-like rhythm and melody." Samarin, "Sociolinguistic vs. Neurophysiological Explanations for Glossolalia," 293.

4 Clother, "Sugar: The Work of Kara Walker."

5 John Hope Franklin wrote, "The actual statutory recognition of slavery in Virginia came in 1661. . . . In 1662, Virginia took another step toward slavery by indicating in its laws that children born in the colony would be held in bond or free according to the condition of the mother." Franklin, *From Slavery to Freedom*, 56–58.

6 Franklin, *From Slavery to Freedom*, 57.

7 Peale painted George Washington's portrait, was a friend and correspondent of Thomas Jefferson and other notables of the day, and maintained a museum featuring taxidermy animals, ethnographic artifacts, and art. He fathered seventeen children with three different wives, and many of his children became artists as well.

8 Shaw, "'Moses Williams,'" 24–25.

9 Rembrandt Peale, "The Physiognotrace," *The Crayon* 4 (1857): 307–8, quoted in Shaw, "'Moses Williams,'" 26.

10 Shaw, "'Moses Williams,'" 37.

11 Shaw, "'Moses Williams,'" 38.

12 Shaw, "'Moses Williams,'" 25.

13 Shaw, "'Moses Williams,'" 37.

14 In 1774 Edward Long responded to early antislavery arguments with his virulently racist publication *History of Jamaica* (London, 1774), which tried to prove that black people were a distinct species naturally inferior to *Homo sapiens*. His ideas are explored in greater depth in my 2003 book, *Colored Pictures*, 128.

15 Frazier, *Black Bourgeoisie*, 13–14. Census figures show that in 1850 the South had a free black population of 235,569, and 101,308 of them were considered mulattoes. For the entire nation, there were 434,495 free black people (12 percent of the total), 159,095 of whom were classified as mulattoes. Of 3,204,313 enslaved people, only 246,656 were classified as mulattoes. J. Smith and Horton, *Historical Statistics*, 1819–20.

16 Morrison, *Playing in the Dark*, xii, 17.

17 Holland Cotter, "Black and White, but Never Simple," *New York Times*, October 12, 2007.

18 A *carte de visite* was a small albumen print photograph mounted on a paper card and was traded among visitors and friends. It was patented in France by André Adolphe Eugène Disdéri in 1854 and became popular

around the world after he published Napoleon III's photos in this format in 1859.

19 See, for example, Shaw, *Seeing the Unspeakable.*

20 Ramsey, *Race Music*, 33.

21 See chapter 2, note 13.

22 For a wonderful analysis of the conflict between the rhetoric of a post-black, postracial society and the way things actually work on the ground, see Wise, *Colorblind*, especially section 2.

23 Moyo Okediji, personal communication, August 31, 2010.

24 Blake Gopnik, "Kara Walker, 'Tired of Standing Up,' Promises Art, Not Answers," *New York Times*, August 16, 2017. Also, Sarah Cascone, "Personal and Politically Charged, the Press Release for Kara Walker's New Show Is a Work of Art All by Itself," *ARTNET News*, August 15, 2017, https://news.artnet.com/exhibitions/kara-walker-sikkema-jenkins-press-release-1051934.

Conclusion. Bebop Ghosts and Freedom Songs

1 Wise's full quotation reads: "We can't all 'just be individuals' because no one is just that, nor has anyone ever lived as such, anywhere, at any time, on the face of the Earth. Indeed, there is no such thing as an individual human being abstracted from their social context. Human beings have never lived in isolation. Humans have always been social, and have experienced life as members of certain groups, be they tribes, communities, families and in more modern times nationalities, races, economic classes and religions." Wise, *Colorblind,* 156. On Western civilization, see Kwame Anthony Appiah, "There Is No Such Thing as Western Civilization," *Guardian*, November 9, 2016, https://www.theguardian.com/world/2016/nov/09/western-civilisation-appiah-reith-lecture. This is an edited version of Appiah's BBC Reith lecture "Culture," the fourth part of the series "Mistaken Identities," which is available on the Radio 4 website.

2 Personal notes, Washington, DC, fall 2003.

3 Oliver Lee Jackson, taped interview with the author, Oakland, California, August 18, 2019.

4 Adger Cowans, taped interview with the author, Atlanta, Georgia, July 29, 2019.

5 Jackson, interview with the author.

6 Paul Carter Harrison, taped interview with the author, Atlanta, Georgia, April 17, 2018.

7 Carrie Mae Weems, "Wangechi Mutu and Carrie Mae Weems on the Profound Impulse to Make Art," *Interview*, December 7, 2020, https://www.interviewmagazine.com/art/wangechi-mutu-and-carrie-mae-weems-discuss-the-power-of-creation.

8 Clark, Mary Ann, *Then We'll Sing a New Song,* 93–94.

9 Arthur C. Brooks, "Charlie Parker and the Meaning of Freedom," *New York Times*, August 29, 2017.

10 Brooks, "Charlie Parker."

11 Program for CONFABA, Northwestern University, Evanston, Illinois, May 1970, published in Gaither, "Heritage Reclaimed," 25.

12 Weems, "Wangechi Mutu."

13 Mike Springer, "John Coltrane's Handwritten Outline for His Masterpiece *A Love Supreme*," Open Culture, September 23, 2013. [*Ed. note*: Springer's September 23, 2013 online website document has been updated, with its visual artifact of Coltrane's handiwork, and posted at a different Open Culture website now dated April 6, 2023. Accessed July 3, 2025, https://www.openculture.com/2023/04/behold-john-coltranes-handwritten-outline-for-his-masterpiece-a-love-supreme.html. Also: the music of the "Love Supreme" fourth movement accompanying its unpronounced "Psalm" text, is now visually scrolling on video and was posted July 4. 2014. Accessed July 3, 2025. https://www.openculture.com/2014/07/john-coltrane-turn-handwritten-poem-into-musical-passage-on-a-love-supreme.html.]

14 Springer, "John Coltrane's Handwritten Outline."

15 Taylor, "'Salt Peanuts,'" 3.

16 Yusef Lateef, interview by Ken Weiss, *Jazz Inside Magazine* 3, no. 8 (March 2012), 38.

17 Adger Cowans, telephone conversation with the author, July 17, 2017.

18 Désir, "Master Cowans," 277.

19 Muñoz, *Disidentifications*, 31.

20 Morrison, "Rootedness," 341.

21 Morrison, "Rootedness," 342.

22 Gibson, *Abstract Expressionism*, 32, quoted in Wood, "'Pure Eye Music,'" 107–8.

23 Morrison, "Rootedness," 342.

24 Morrison, "Rootedness," 343–44.

25 Leeming, *James Baldwin*, 182. Thanks to Professor Dagmawi Woubshet for this reference.

26 Morrison, "Site of Memory," 111.

27 Ras Michael Brown, lecture, Emory University, Atlanta, November 29, 2016.

28 See R. Brown, *African-Atlantic Cultures*.

29 Morrison, "Site of Memory," 115.

30 Morrison, "Site of Memory," 104.

31 Harrison, *ASHÉ*, xii.

Bibliography

Abiodun, Rowland. "Verbal and Visual Metaphors: Mythical Allusions in Yoruba Ritualistic Art of *Orí*." *Word and Image* 3, no. 3 (1987): 252–70.

Abiodun, Rowland. *Yoruba Art and Language: Seeking the African in African Art.* New York: Cambridge University Press, 2014.

Abrahams, Roger. *Singing the Master: The Emergence of African American Culture in the Plantation South.* New York: Pantheon Books, 1992.

Ajayi, J. F. A. "The Aftermath of the Fall of Old Ọyọ." In *History of West Africa*, vol. 2, edited by J. F. A. Ajayi and Michael Crowder. New York: Columbia University Press, 1973.

Ajayi, J. F. Ade, and Robert Smith. *Yoruba Warfare in the Nineteenth Century.* London: Cambridge University Press in association with Ibadan University, 1964.

Aldin, Mary Katherine. Liner notes for *Muddy Waters: Folk Singer.* Recorded 1963–64. MCA Records CHD-12027, 1999, compact disc.

Alexander, Elizabeth. *The Black Interior.* Saint Paul, MN: Graywolf, 2004.

Allen, James. *Without Sanctuary: Lynching Photography in America.* Santa Fe, NM: Twin Palms, 2000.

Allen, William Francis, Charles Pickard Ware, Lucy McKim Garrison, and Irving Schlein. *Slave Songs of the United States: The Complete Original Collection.* 1867. New York: Oak, 1965.

Andrews, Dwight D. "From Black to Blues." In *The Blues Aesthetic: Black Culture and Modernism*, by Richard J. Powell. Washington, DC: Washington Project for the Arts, 1989.

Aptheker, Herbert. *"One Continual Cry": David Walker's Appeal to the Colored Citizens of the World (1829–1830), Its Setting and Its Meaning.* 1965. New York: Humanities Press, 1971.

Baldwin, James. "The Fire Next Time." In *The Price of the Ticket: Collected Nonfiction, 1948–1985.* New York: St. Martin's/Marek, 1985.

Baraka, Amiri. "The 'Blues Aesthetic' and the 'Black Aesthetic': Aesthetics as the Continuing Political History of a Culture." *Black Music Research Journal* 11, no. 2 (1991): 101–9.

Baraka, Amiri (LeRoi Jones). *Blues People: The Negro Experience in White America and the Music That Developed from It.* New York: Quill/William Morrow, 1963.

Bearden, Romare. "Rectangular Structure in My Montage Paintings." *Leonardo* 2, no. 1 (1969): 11–19.

Bechet, Sidney. *Treat It Gentle*. New York: Hill and Wang, 1960.

Berns, Marla C. *Dear Robert, I'll See You at the Crossroads: A Project by Renée Stout*. Santa Barbara: University of California at Santa Barbara, 1995.

Beyoncé, performer. "Formation," song. By Beyoncé with Mike Will Made It, Swae Lee, and Pluss. On *Lemonade.*

Beyoncé (Beyoncé Giselle Knowles). *Lemonade*. Parkwood Entertainment and Columbia Records, 2016, video and film.

Blassingame, John W., ed. *Slave Testimony: Two Centuries of Letters, Speeches, Interviews, and Autobiographies*. Baton Rouge: Louisiana State University Press, 1977.

Brewer, Craig, dir. *Black Snake Moan*. Paramount Vantage, 2006.

Brooks, Daphne A. *Bodies in Dissent: Spectacular Performances of Race and Freedom, 1850–1910*. Durham, NC: Duke University Press, 2006.

Brown, James, performer. "Say It Loud—I'm Black and I'm Proud." By James Brown and Pee Wee Ellis. On *Say It Loud—I'm Black and I'm Proud*. King Records SKAO-91987, 1969, vinyl.

Brown, Ras Michael. *African-Atlantic Cultures and the South Carolina Lowcountry*. New York: Cambridge University Press, 2012.

Buchanan, Beverly. "Sassafras and Yellow Root." Smithsonian: Celebrating 175: Artist Statements and Writings by Beverly Buchanan, ca. 1972, 1981–2008. Page 48 of 78. Accessed August 18, 2025. https://transcription.si.edu/view/41782/AAA-AAA_buchbeve_3248236.

Calame-Griaule, Geneviève. *Words and the Dogon World*. Philadelphia: Institute for the Study of Human Issues, 1986.

Césaire, Aimé. *Notebook of a Return to the Native Land*. Translated and edited by Clayton Eshleman and Annette Smith. Middletown, CT: Wesleyan University Press, 2001.

Chamoiseau, Patrick. *Slave Old Man: A Novel.* Translated by Linda Coverdale. New York: New Press, 2018. Published in French, 1997.

Chireau, Yvonne P. *Black Magic: Religion and the African American Conjuring Tradition*. 2003. Berkeley: University of California Press, 2006.

Clark, Mary Ann. *Then We'll Sing a New Song: African Influences on America's Religious Landscape*. Lanham, MD: Rowman and Littlefield, 2012.

Clarke, John Henrik. Introduction to *The Middle Passage: White Ships/Black Cargo*, by Tom Feelings. New York: Dial Books, 1995.

Clother, Cate. "Sugar: The Work of Kara Walker." Cordella Magazine online. Cordella Press. Accessed July 2, 2025, https://www.cordella.org/sugar.

Coates, Ta-Nehisi. *Between the World and Me*. New York: Random House, 2015.

Cone, James H. *The Spirituals and the Blues*. 1972. New York: Orbis Books, 2022.

Cooke, Sam, performer. "Chain Gang." By Charles Cooke and Sam Cooke. On *Chain Gang*. RCA Victor 47–7783, 1960, vinyl.

Crouch, Stanley, writer. "Premature Autopsies." Performed by Rev. Jeremiah Wright Jr. On *The Majesty of the Blues*, by Wynton Marsalis. Columbia CK 45091, 1989, compact disc.

Davies, Penelope J. E., et al. *Janson's History of Art: The Western Tradition*. 7th ed. Upper Saddle River, NJ: Pearson Education 2007.

Davis, John. "Eastman Johnson's *Negro Life at the South* and Urban Slavery in Washington, D.C." *Art Bulletin* 80, no. 1 (1998): 67–92.

Davis, Miles, performer. *Sanctuary*. Composed by Wayne Shorter. On *Bitches' Brew*. Columbia Records, 1970, vinyl.

Désir, Dòwòti. "Master Cowans: All Things Earthly." Afterword to *Personal Vision: Photographs*, by Adger Cowans. New York: Glitterati, 2017.

Donaldson, Jeff. *CONFABA—Conference on the Functional Aspects of Black Art*. In "It's a Black Thing—You Wouldn't Understand: The Wall of Respect, Africobra, and the Birth of a New Aesthetic," by James Wellington Phillips, Appendix III. Master's thesis, University of British Columbia, 2000.

Du Bois, W. E. B. *The Souls of Black Folk: Essays and Sketches*. Chicago: A. C. McClurg, 1903.

Dunbar, Paul Laurence. *Lyrics of Lowly Life*. New York: Dodd, Mead, 1896.

Ellis, Trey. "The New Black Aesthetic." *Callaloo*, no. 38 (Winter 1989): 233–43.

Eltis, David, and David Richardson. *Atlas of the Transatlantic Slave Trade*. New Haven, CT: Yale University Press, 2010.

Enwezor, Okwui. "The Diasporic Imagination: The Memory Works of María Magdalena Campos-Pons." In *Maria Magdalena Campos-Pons: Everything Is Separated by Water*, edited by Lisa D. Freiman. New Haven, CT: Yale University Press, 2007.

Feelings, Tom. *The Middle Passage: White Ships/Black Cargo*. New York: Dial, 1995.

Fine, Ruth. "Romare Bearden: The Spaces Between." In *The Art of Romare Bearden*. Washington, DC: National Gallery of Art, 2003. Exhibition catalog.

Fine, Ruth, and Jacqueline Francis, eds. *Romare Bearden, American Modernist*. Studies in the History of Art 71. Washington, DC: National Gallery of Art, Center for Advanced Study in the Visual Arts, 2011. Distributed by Yale University Press.

Foster, Preston "Red," lyricist. "Got My Mojo Working." Dare Music, 1956. Recorded by Ann Cole and the Suburbans, Baton (1957), Sonic Hits, accessed July 17, 2025, https://sonichits.com/video/Ann_Cole/Got_My_Mojo_Working_%28But_I_Just_Wont_Work_On_You%29. Adapted by Muddy Waters (aka McKinley Morganfield), Chess Records 1652 (1957), Discogs, accessed July 17, 2025, https://www.discogs.com/release/7232785-Muddy-Waters-Rock-Me-Got-My-Mojo-Working.

Foucault, Michel. *Discipline and Punish: The Birth of the Prison*. New York: Vintage Books, 1995.

Franklin, John Hope. *From Slavery to Freedom: A History of African Americans*. 7th ed. New York: Alfred A. Knopf, 1994.

Frazier, E. Franklin. *Black Bourgeoisie*. 1957. New York: Simon and Schuster, 1997.

Gaither, Edmund Barry. "Heritage Reclaimed: An Historical Perspective and Chronology." In *Black Art—Ancestral Legacy: The African Impulse in African-American Art*. Dallas: Dallas Museum of Art, 1989. Distributed by Harry N. Abrams. Exhibition catalog.

Gates, Henry Lewis, Jr. *The Signifying Monkey: A Theory of African-American Literary Criticism*. New York: Oxford University Press, 1988.

Gayle, Addison, Jr., ed. *The Black Aesthetic*. New York: Doubleday, 1972.

Gelburd, Gail, and Thelma Golden. *Romare Bearden in Black and White: Photomontage Projections, 1964*. New York: Whitney Museum of American Art, 1992. Distributed by Harry N. Abrams. Exhibition catalog.

Gibson, Ann Eden. *Abstract Expressionism: Other Politics*. New Haven, CT: Yale University Press, 1997.

Gilroy, Paul. *The Black Atlantic: Modernity and Double Consciousness*. Cambridge, MA: Harvard University Press, 1993.

Glissant, Édouard. *Poetics of Relation*. Translated by Betsy Wing. Ann Arbor: University of Michigan Press, 1997.

Gomez, Michael A. *Exchanging Our Country Marks: The Transformation of African Identities in the Colonial and Antebellum South*. Chapel Hill: University of North Carolina Press, 1998.

Greenberg, Alan. *Love in Vain: A Vision of Robert Johnson*. New York: Da Capo, 1994. Screenplay originally published in 1983 by Doubleday. Reprint, University of Minnesota, 2012.

Griaule, Marcel. *Conversations with Ogotemmêli: An Introduction to Dogon Religious Ideas*. London: Oxford University Press, 1965.

Griaule, Marcel, and Germaine Dieterlen. *The Pale Fox*. Translated by Stephen C. Infantino. Chino Valley, AZ: Continuum Foundation, 1986.

Gura, Philip F., and James F. Bollman. *America's Instrument: The Banjo in the Nineteenth Century*. Chapel Hill: University of North Carolina Press, 1999.

Hagenbucher-Sacripanti, Frank. *Les fondements spirituels du pouvoir au royaume de Loango*. Paris: O.R.S.T.O.M., 1973.

Hall, Stuart. "What Is This 'Black' in Black Popular Culture?" In *Black Popular Culture*, edited by Michele Wallace and Gina Dent. Seattle: Bay, 1992.

Harris, Michael D. "Alison Saar: The Nature of Us." Essay accompanying the exhibition of the same title (curated by Harris), at the Gantt Center for African American Arts and Culture, Charlotte, NC, January 28–July 8, 2017. https://ganttcenter.org/public/assets/AlisonSaarEssay.pdf.

Harris, Michael D. *Colored Pictures: Race and Visual Representation*. Chapel Hill: University of North Carolina Press, 2003.

Harris, Michael D. "Meanwhile the Girls Were Playing: Maria Magdalena Campos-Pons." *Nka: Journal of Contemporary African Art*, no. 13/14 (Spring/Summer 2001): 48–55.

Harris, Michael D. "Ritual Bodies—Sexual Bodies: The Role and Presentation of the Body in African-American Art." *Third Text* 4, no. 12 (1990): 81–95.

Harris, Michael D. "Visual Tropes: The Kanaga Mask of the Dogon Peoples of West Africa." Master's thesis, Yale University, 1989.

Harrison, Paul Carter, Michael D. Harris, and Pellom McDaniels III, eds. *ASHÉ: Ritual Poetics in African Diasporic Expression*. New York: Routledge, 2022.

Hartman, Saidiya. *Lose Your Mother: A Journey Along the Atlantic Slave Route*. New York: Farrar, Straus and Giroux, 2008.

Heusch, Luc de. *Why Marry Her?: Society and Symbolic Structures*. New York: Cambridge University Press, 1981.

Hills, Patricia. "Painting Race: Eastman Johnson's Pictures of Slaves, Ex-Slaves, and Freedmen." In *Eastman Johnson: Painting America*, edited by Teresa Carbone and Patricia Hills. New York: Brooklyn Museum of Art, in association with Rizzoli International Publications, 1999. Exhibition catalog.

Holiday, Billie, vocalist. "Strange Fruit." By Abel Meeropol. On *Strange Fruit/Fine and Mellow*. Commodore 526, 1939, 78 rpm.

Holloway, Joseph. *Africanisms in American Culture.* Bloomington: Indiana University Press, 1990.

Honour, Hugh. *The Image of the Black in Western Art.* Vol. 4, *From the American Revolution to World War I.* Cambridge, MA: Harvard University Press, 1989.

Hughes, Langston. "The Negro Artist and the Racial Mountain." In *The Black Aesthetic*, edited by Addison Gayle Jr. Garden City, NY: Doubleday, 1971. Previously published in *Nation*, June 23, 1926, 694.

Hurston, Zora Neale. "Shouting." In *Negro: An Anthology*, edited by Nancy Cunard and Hugh D. Ford. New York: Continuum, 1996. Originally published in London: Wishart, 1934.

Janson, Anthony F., and H. W. Janson. *A Short History of Art.* 7th ed. Upper Saddle River, NJ: Prentice Hall, 2006.

Johnson, James Weldon. *God's Trombones: Seven Negro Sermons in Verse.* New York: Viking Press, 1927.

Jones, LeRoi. See Baraka, Amiri.

Kai, Nubia. "AfriCOBRA Universal Aesthetics." In *AfriCOBRA: The First Twenty Years.* Atlanta: Nexus Contemporary Art Center, 1990. Exhibition catalog.

Larson, Nella. *Passing.* 1927. New York: Macmillan Collector's Library, 2020.

Leeming, David Adams. *James Baldwin: A Biography.* New York: Knopf, 1994.

Lester, George. "The Fisk University and the Jubilee Singers," *The Wesleyan-Methodist Magazine* 121 (January 1898): 39–42.

Levine, Lawrence W. *Black Culture and Black Consciousness: Afro-American Folk Thought from Slavery to Freedom.* New York: Oxford University Press, 1977.

Lhamon, W. T., Jr. *Raising Cain: Blackface Performance from Jim Crow to Hip Hop.* Cambridge, MA: Harvard University Press, 1998.

Lieberfeld, Daniel. "Million-Dollar Juke Joint: Commodifying Blues Culture." *African American Review* 29, no. 2 (1995): 217–21.

Linsley, Robert. "Wifredo Lam: Painter of Negritude." In *Race-ing Art History: Critical Readings in Race and Art History*, edited by Kymberly N. Pinder. New York: Routledge, 2002. Originally published in *Art History* 11, no. 4 (1988): 526–44.

Litwack, Leon F. "Hellhounds." In *Without Sanctuary: Lynching Photography in America.* Santa Fe, NM: Twin Palms, 2000.

Lock, Graham, and David Murray, eds. *The Hearing Eye: Jazz and Blues Influences in African American Visual Art.* New York: Oxford University Press, 2009.

Locke, Alain. "Enter the New Negro." *Survey Graphic*, March 1925.

Locke, Alain. "The Legacy of the Ancestral Arts." In *The New Negro*, edited by Alain Locke. 1925. New York: Atheneum, 1992.

Long, Edward. *The History of Jamaica or, General Survey of the Antient and Modern State of the Island: With Reflections on Its Situation, Settlements, Inhabitants,*

Climate, Products, Commerce, Laws, and Government. London: T. Lowndes, 1774.
Lubin, David. *Picturing a Nation: Art and Social Change in Nineteenth-Century America.* New Haven, CT: Yale University Press, 1994.
MacGaffey, Wyatt. "African Objects and the Idea of Fetish." *RES: Anthropology and Aesthetics*, no. 25 (Spring 1994): 123–31. https://www.jstor.org/stable/20166895.
MacGaffey, Wyatt. "The Eyes of Understanding: Kongo Minkisi." In *Astonishment and Power: The Eyes of Understanding: Kongo Minkisi/The Art of Renée Stout*, by Wyatt MacGaffey and Michael D. Harris. Washington, DC: Smithsonian Institution Press, 1993.
MacGaffey, Wyatt. "The Personhood of Ritual Objects: Kongo *Minkisi*." *Etnofoor* 3, no. 1 (1990): 45–61.
MacGaffey, Wyatt, and Michael D. Harris. *Astonishment and Power: The Eyes of Understanding: Kongo Minkisi/The Art of Renée Stout.* Washington, DC: Smithsonian Institution Press, 1993.
Maultsby, Portia K. "Africanisms in African American Music." In *Africanisms in American Culture*, edited by Joseph E. Holloway. Bloomington: Indiana University Press, 1990.
Mellon, James, ed. *Bullwhip Days: The Slaves Remember, an Oral History.* New York: Avon Books, 1988.
Mooney, Amy M. *Archibald J. Motley Jr.* Petaluma, CA: Pomegranate, 2004.
Morrison, Toni. *The Origin of Others.* Cambridge, MA: Harvard University Press, 2017.
Morrison, Toni. *Playing in the Dark: Whiteness and the Literary Imagination.* New York: Vintage Books, 1993.
Morrison, Toni. "Rootedness: The Ancestor as Foundation." In *Black Women Writers (1950–1980): A Critical Evaluation*, edited by Mari Evans. Garden City, NY: Anchor Press/Doubleday, 1984.
Morrison, Toni. "The Site of Memory." In *Inventing the Truth: The Art and Craft of Memoir*, edited by William Zinsser. 2nd ed. Boston: Houghton Mifflin, 1995.
Muñoz, José Esteban. *Disidentifications: Queers of Color and the Performance of Politics.* Minneapolis: University of Minnesota Press, 1999.
Mveng, Engelbert. "Third World Theology—What Theology? What Third World? Evaluation by an African Delegate." In *Irruption of the Third World: Challenge to Theology*, edited by Virginia Fabella and Sergio Torres. Maryknoll, NY: Orbis Books, 1983.
Neal, Larry. "Riffin in the Chili House (in Memory of Bird)." In *Hoodoo Hollerin' Bebop Ghosts.* Washington, DC: Howard University Press, 1974.
O'Jays, The, performers. "Back Stabbers." Philadelphia International, 1972, vinyl.
Okediji, Moyo. *The Shattered Gourd: Yoruba Forms in Twentieth-Century American Art.* Seattle: University of Washington Press, 2003.
Okri, Ben. *The Famished Road.* New York: Nan A. Talese/Doubleday, 1991.
O'Meally, Robert, ed. *The Jazz Cadence of American Culture.* New York: Columbia University Press, 1998.
O'Meally, Robert, Kobena Mercer, Romare Bearden, Pamela Ford, and Amy M. Mooney. *Romare Bearden in the Modernist Tradition.* New York: Romare Bearden Foundation, 2010.

Ong, Walter. *Orality and Literacy: The Technologizing of the Word*. 1982. London: Routledge, 1988.

Palmer, Robert. *Deep Blues: A Musical and Cultural History from the Mississippi Delta to Chicago's South Side to the World*. New York: Penguin Books, 1982.

Parrish, Lydia. *Slave Songs of the Georgia Sea Islands*. Athens: University of Georgia Press, 1992.

Pereira, Kim. *August Wilson and the African-American Odyssey*. Urbana: University of Illinois Press, 1995.

Perkinson, Jim. "The Gift/Curse of 'Second Sight': Is 'Blackness' a Shamanic Category in the Myth of America?" *History of Religions* 42, no. 1 (2002): 19–58.

Phillips, William D., Jr. *Slavery from Roman Times to the Early Transatlantic Trade*. Minneapolis: University of Minnesota Press, 1985.

Powell, Richard J. "Becoming Motley, Becoming Modern." In *Archibald Motley: Jazz Age Modernist*, edited by Richard J. Powell. Durham, NC: Nasher Museum of Art at Duke University, 2014. Exhibition catalog.

Powell, Richard J. *The Blues Aesthetic: Black Culture and Modernism*. Washington, DC: Washington Project for the Arts, 1989. Exhibition catalog.

Powell, Richard J. "Conjuring Reality." In *Conjuring Bearden*, edited by Richard J. Powell, Margaret Ellen Di Giulio, Alicia Garcia, Victoria Trout, and Christine Wang. Durham, NC: Nasher Museum of Art at Duke University, 2006. Distributed by Duke University Press. Exhibition catalog.

Powell, Richard J. *Going There: Black Visual Satire*. New Haven, CT: Yale University Press, 2020.

Powell, Richard J. *Homecoming: The Art and Life of William H. Johnson*. Washington, DC: National Museum of American Art, Smithsonian Institution, 1991.

Ramsey, Guthrie P., Jr. *Race Music: Black Cultures from Bebop to Hip-Hop*. Berkeley: University of California Press, 2003.

Roach, Max, and Oscar Brown, Jr., performers. "We Insist!: Freedom Now Suite." Libretto by Abbey Lincoln, Michael Olatunji, and Coleman Hawkins. Candid Records, 1960, vinyl.

Robinson, Beverly J. "The Sense of Self in Ritualizing New Performance Spaces for Survival." In *Black Theatre: Ritual Performance in the African Diaspora*, edited by Paul Carter Harrison, Victor Leo Walker II, and Gus Edwards. Philadelphia: Temple University Press, 2002.

Rosenbaum, Art. *Shout Because You're Free: The African American Ring Shout Tradition in Coastal Georgia*. Athens: University of Georgia Press, 1998.

Rösslin, Eucharius. *Der Swangern Frauwen und Hebammen Rosegarten* (The rose garden for pregnant women and midwives). Germany: 1513.

Rubin, William S. *Dada, Surrealism, and Their Heritage*. 1968. New York: Museum of Modern Art, 1977. Exhibition catalog.

Rueff, Jacob, and Huldrych M. Koelbing. *Ein schön lustig Trostbüchle von den Empfengknussen und Geburten der Menschen*. Zürich: Christoffel Forschoeur, 1554.

Samarin, William J. "Sociolinguistic vs. Neurophysiological Explanations for Glossolalia: Comment on Goodman's Paper." *Journal for the Scientific Study of Religion* 11, no. 3 (1972): 293–96.

Sanders, Sophie. "Spirited Pattern and Decoration in Contemporary Black Atlantic Art." PhD diss., Temple University, 2013.

Sartre, Jean-Paul. *Black Orpheus*. Translated by S. W. Allen. Paris: Présence africaine, 1963.

Schwartzman, Myron. *Romare Bearden: His Life and Art*. New York: Harry N. Abrams, 1990.

Scorsese, Martin, dir. *The Blues*. PBS film series, 2003.

Scorsese, Martin. "Foreword." In Alan Greenberg, *Love in Vain*.

Shannon, Sandra G. *The Dramatic Vision of August Wilson*. Washington, DC: Howard University Press, 1996.

Shaw, Gwendolyn DuBois. "'Moses Williams, Cutter of Profiles': Silhouettes and African American Identity in the Early Republic." *Proceedings of the American Philosophical Society* 149, no. 1 (2005): 22–39.

Shaw, Gwendolyn DuBois. *Seeing the Unspeakable: The Art of Kara Walker*. Durham, NC: Duke University Press, 2004.

Shorter, Wayne, performer. "Sanctuary." On Davis, *Bitch's Brew*.

Smallwood, Richard, performer. "I Love the Lord." On *The Richard Smallwood Singers*. Onyx International Records R3803, 1982, vinyl.

Smith, Jessie Carney, and Carrell Peterson Horton, eds. *Historical Statistics of Black America*. New York: Gale Research, 1995.

Smith, Theophus H. *Conjuring Culture: Biblical Formations of Black America*. New York: Oxford University Press, 1994.

Smith, Todd D. *Celebration and Vision: The Hewitt Collection of African-American Art*. Charlotte, NC: Bank of America, 1999.

Snead, James A. "Repetition as a Figure of Black Culture." In *The Jazz Cadence of American Culture*, edited by Robert O'Meally. New York: Columbia University Press, 1998.

Spear, Allan H. *Black Chicago: The Making of a Negro Ghetto, 1890–1920*. Chicago: University of Chicago Press, 1967.

Stewart, Dianne. "I Had a Family That Belonged to All Kinds of Things: Yoruba-Orisa Kinship Principles and the Poetics of Social Prestige." Unpublished manuscript. Last modified May 10, 2020.

Stewart, Dianne M. *Obeah, Orisa,* and *Religious Identity in Trinidad*. Vol. 2, *Orisa: Africana Nations and the Power of Black Sacred Imagination*. Durham, NC: Duke University Press, 2022.

Stewart, Dianne M. *Three Eyes for the Journey: African Dimensions of the Jamaican Religious Experience*. New York: Oxford University Press, 2005.

Tate, Greg, and Arthur Jafa. "The Sound She Saw: Arthur Jafa in Conversation with Greg Tate." In *Ming Smith: An Aperture Monograph*, edited by Brendan Embse. New York: Aperture Foundation, 2020.

Taylor, Clyde. "'Salt Peanuts': Sound and Sense in African/American Oral/Musical Creativity." *Callaloo*, no. 16 (October 1982): 1–11.

Thompson, Krista. *Shine: The Visual Economy of Light in African Diasporic Aesthetic Practice*. Durham, NC: Duke University Press, 2015.

Thompson, Robert Farris. *African Art in Motion: Icon and Act in the Collection of Katherine Coryton White.* Los Angeles: University of California Press, 1979. Exhibition catalog.

Thompson, Robert Farris. "Communiqué from Afro-Atlantis." In *NeoHooDoo: Art for a Forgotten Faith*, edited by Franklin Sirmans. Houston: Menil Foundation, 2009. Distributed by Yale University Press. Exhibition catalog.

Thompson, Robert Farris. *Face of the Gods: Art and Altars of Africa and the African Americas.* New York: Museum for African Art, 1993.

Thompson, Robert Farris. *Flash of the Spirit: African and Afro-American Art and Philosophy.* New York: Vintage Books, 1983.

Thompson, Robert Farris. "Kongo Influences on African-American Artistic Culture." In *Africanisms in American Culture*, edited by Joseph E. Holloway. Bloomington: Indiana University Press, 1990.

Thompson, Robert Farris. "Royalty, Heroism, and the Streets: The Art of Jean-Michel Basquiat." In Lock and Murray, *The Hearing Eye.*

Thompson, Robert Farris, and Joseph Cornet. *The Four Moments of the Sun: Kongo Art in Two Worlds.* Washington, DC: National Gallery of Art, 1981. Exhibition catalog.

Tobin, Jacqueline, and Raymond G. Dobard. *Hidden in Plain View: A Secret Story of Quilts and the Underground Railroad.* New York: Anchor Books, 2000.

Toll, Robert C. *Blacking Up: The Minstrel Show in Nineteenth-Century America.* New York: Oxford University Press, 1974.

Twain, Mark. *The Autobiography of Mark Twain.* Edited by Charles Neider. New York: Harper and Row, 1966.

Udechukwu, Obiora. "Affirmations." In *What the Madman Said.* Bayreuth, Germany: Boomerang, 1990.

Völz, Johannes. "'Blues and the Abstract Truth': Or, Did Romare Bearden Really Paint Jazz?" In Lock and Murray, *The Hearing Eye.*

Wahlman, Maude Southwell. *Signs and Symbols: African Images in African-American Quilts.* Atlanta, GA: Tinwood Books, 2001.

Walker, David. *Appeal to the Colored Citizens of the World* (1829–30). University Park, PA: Penn State University Press, 2000.

Wardlaw, Alvia J. *Black Art Ancestral Legacy: The African Impulse in African American Art.* New York: Harry N. Abrams, 1990.

Waters, Muddy, performer. *Folk Singer.* MCA Records reissue, 1999, CD; Chess 12027, 1964, Vinyl.

Waters, Muddy, performer. "Got My Mojo Working." Lyrics adapted from Preston "Red" Foster. *Rock Me/Got My Mojo Working.* Chess Records 1652, 1957, vinyl.

Waters, Muddy, performer. "I'm Your Hoochie Coochie Man." By Willie Dixon. On *I'm Your Hoochie Coochie Man/She's So Pretty.* Chess 1560, 1954, vinyl.

Waters, Muddy, performer. "Long Distance." By McKinley Morganfield. On *Folk Singer.* Chess 1483, 1964, vinyl.

Waters, Muddy, performer. "Louisiana Blues." On *The Best of Muddy Waters.* Chess 1427, 1958, vinyl.

Waters, Muddy, performer. "My Captain." By Willie Dixon. On *Folk Singer*. Chess 1483, 1964, vinyl.

Waters, Muddy, performer. "She Moves Me." On *The Best of Muddy Waters*. Chess 1427, 1958, vinyl.

Welty, Eudora. *One Time, One Place: Mississippi in the Depression; A Snapshot Album*. Jackson: University Press of Mississippi, 1996.

Wilson, August. Foreword to *Romare Bearden: His Life and Art*, by Myron Schwartzman. New York: Harry N. Abrams, 1990.

Wilson, August. *Joe Turner's Come and Gone*. London: Samuel French, 1988.

Wilson, August. *Ma Rainey's Black Bottom*. New York: New American Library, 1985.

Wilson, Judith. "Lifting the 'Veil': Henry O. Tanner's *The Banjo Lesson* and *The Thankful Poor*." *Contributions in Black Studies*, 9/10 (1990–1992): 31–54.

Wise, Tim. *Colorblind: The Rise of Post-Racial Politics and the Retreat from Racial Equity*. San Francisco: City Lights Books, 2010.

Wood, Sara. "'Pure Eye Music': Norman Lewis, Abstract Expressionism, and Bebop." In *The Hearing Eye: Jazz and Blues Influences in African American Visual Art*, edited by Graham Lock and David Murray. New York: Oxford University Press, 2009.

Woodbine, Onaje X. O. *Black Gods of the Asphalt: Religion, Hip-Hop, and Street Basketball*. New York: Columbia University Press, 2016.

Yau, John. "Please Wait by the Coatroom." In *Out There: Marginalization and Contemporary Cultures*, edited by Russell Ferguson, Martha Gever, Trinh T. Minh-ha, and Cornel West. New York: New Museum of Contemporary Art, 1990.

Index

Note: Page numbers in *italics* refer to figures.